Bugs

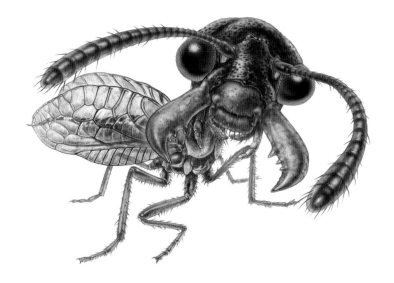

Bugs

Nature's Tiniest and Terrifying Creatures

Paula Hammond

amber
BOOKS

This edition published in 2018

Published by
Amber Books Ltd
United House
North Road
London
N7 9DP
United Kingdom
www.amberbooks.co.uk
Appstore: itunes.com/apps/amberbooksltd
Facebook: www.facebook.com/amberbooks
Twitter: @amberbooks

ISBN: 978-1-78274-690-4

Project Editor: Sarah Uttridge
Design: Hawes Design

Printed in China

Artwork Credits:
All © International Masters Publishing Ltd AB

CONTENTS

Introduction

Planet Earth is an amazing place. A small, misshapen ball, it travels through space at a speed of 107,200km/h (66,610mph), taking 365 days, six hours, nine minutes and 9.54 seconds to revolve around our sun. And it is a world rich in life. From the dark, ice-cold ocean depths to the arid, sun-scorched deserts, there are few places where animals do not thrive. No matter how harsh the environment, there is a creature ready to turn a hostile habitat into a home.

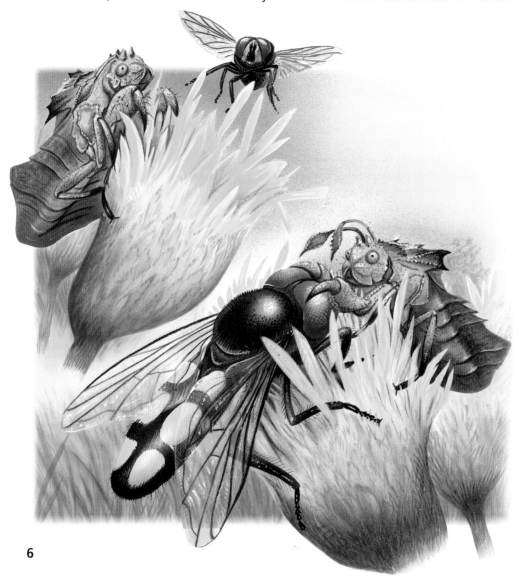

Humans can, quite rightly, boast about their ingenuity and creativity. It has, after all, allowed us to spread across the globe. Yet, for all our achievements, we have played only a small part in our planet's history. In 1999, this was graphically demonstrated by geologist and mineralogist John Mason. In *Elementals,* an exhibition at the Museum of Modern Art in Wales, he showed how the history of our planet would look if it was condensed into just one year. On this scale, it is only at about 11.37 p.m. on New Year's Eve that humans finally make an appearance. In the time that it takes for party revellers to begin their countdown to the New Year, Rome would have conquered Britain, Columbus discovered America, and Neil Armstrong walked on the Moon. The earliest and simplest forms of life – bacteria – evolved in the oceans around three and a half billion years ago. That is around mid-March on John Mason's scale – a full eight months earlier than any human.

OUR AMAZING PLANET

Even today there are still parts our planet – rainforest, desert, mountain and ice-flow – on which no human foot has ever set foot; and these are just the parts of our globe which lie above ground. We have yet to fully explore the world beneath our feet. We know as little about the microscopic life that can be found just below the soil, as we do about whatever weird and wonderful creatures may exist in the caverns and sub-terrain caves many kilometres down. This surface world, which we have only partially explored, accounts for just 29 per cent of our planet. A further 71 per cent is made up of the oceans, which are almost entirely uncharted. However, one thing is certain. When we do finally reach these dangerous and inhospitable regions, we will definately not be alone.

Whether they fly, swim or crawl beneath the ground, animals are everywhere. Worldwide, it is estimated that there may be 13–15 million individual species, and thousands more are discovered each year. This might be a world that we dominate, but it really belongs to the other animals.

A NAME SAYS IT ALL

Life on Earth is so widespread and diverse that we struggle to fully understand it. Our earliest attempts to impose some system and order on this mass of life date back to Ancient Greece and the work of Aristotle (384–322 BCE), who began to divide animals and plants in to groups depending on their size and shape. Aristotle's theories were to form the template for our understanding

An Ambush bug sits motionless on a flower as a hoverfly hovers. The fly lands to feed and the bug pounces, seizing its prey with its pincer-like front legs, the fly tries desperately to escape but the bug's grip is simply too strong.

of the animal world for the next 2000 years. It was not until the 1600s that the English biologist John Ray began to challenge these ideas. Then, in the 1700s, a Swedish naturalist, Carolus Linnaeus (1707–1778), suggested a system that has come to be known as taxonomy.

Taxonomy is a method of scientific classification which attempts to sort all known living things into groups, based on their biological similarities. It was first proposed by Linnaeus in his books *Species Plantarum* (1753) and *System Naturae* (1758). Today, many of his classifications are still accepted, although modern knowledge and techniques have refined the process of species identification. In modern taxonomy, living things are divided into five main groups, known as Kingdoms. These include Animals, Fungi, Monerans (such as algae), Plants and Protists (one-celled organisms like bacteria). Each of these Kingdoms is divided further into a Phylum, Class, Order, Family, Genus and Species. So far, using this system, zoologists have named and described around one and a half million species. This includes around 2800 species of snake, 3400 types of lizard, 23 'crocodilians' (a group that includes crocodiles, alligators and gharials) and 4100 species of frogs and toads. At least half of all known animals are believed to be insects, and of these, around one in three is a type of beetle or weevil. In fact, 99 per cent of all known animals are no bigger than a bee.

Unfortunately, this is not a fool-proof system. Millions of animals are still to be identified and some experts disagree about the current classification of specific species. The task of refining and clarifying this huge 'catalogue of nature' is ongoing. We still have much to learn, and new discoveries are made every year. What we do know, though, is that all animals (whether classified or not!) form part of a tangled web of life which involves every living thing on the planet. This heterogeneous community is interdependent. Herbivores eat plants, carnivores eat herbivores, and the bodies of both provide the nutrients that plants need to grow. Within this elaborate system, each animal has its own way of surviving and thriving.

THE FIGHT TO SURVIVE

Despite their differences, the prime drive of every species is to be successful: to grow, to reproduce, and to have offspring which do the same. Fortunately, nature has provided solutions to all of these problems.

To grow, all animals need to feed. Some, are omnivores, which means that they eat both plants and animals. Some are herbivores and survive on a diet of rich vegetation. Some are carnivores, who must hunt and kill other animals for their food. Some are opportunists, who will eat whatever nature puts their way, including manmade materials like paper. Others are parasites. They may not kill animals to feed, but they live off – and sometimes in – the bodies of

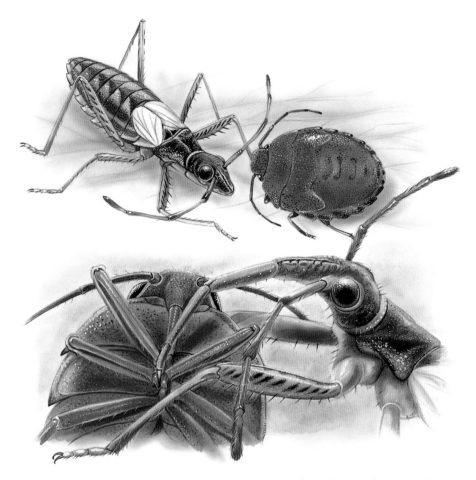

Damsel bugs in the family Nabidae are found in the Americas and across Europe and Asia, wherever there is vegetation to hide in and other invertebrates to feed on. Here a damsel bug is attacking a shield bug nymph whilst it is innocently feeding.

others, and this is usually harmful to their less than willing 'hosts'.

Ultimately, what an animal eats depends on just what specialized tools Mother Nature has devised for them. Sharp, slicing canines and flat grinding molar teeth do the same jobs of tearing up food, but the first are intended to rip flesh, and the second to pulp vegetable matter. A long, pointed proboscis is just as good at sucking up plant sap as body fluids, but bugs cannot hunt meat if they do not have the equipment to subdue their prey – in other words, powerful forelegs and paralyzing toxins. Some animals, of course, simply grow to vast sizes, and dominate their environment: they sit at the top of the food chain and have the pick of available resources. Some have evolved claws, stingers, lures or electric charges, which enable them both to attract and to subdue prey (as well as to avoid ending up on something else's menu). Some have developed into strange and curious shapes and colours – a form of ingenious natural camouflage, which gives them the edge when hunting. Some have taken a more dramatic approach. They have adapted to live in the harshest and most unforgiving environments, where the competition for food

The male Mole cricket must advertise his charms more loudly than his rivals to win a mate. To do this, he digs himself a special burrow – one that is designed to amplify his 'song' so that a female can hear it clearly from some distance.

Some Net-casting spiders prefer to target crawling prey. Others attack airborne insects, often throwing their nets up into the air. Most specialize in only one technique, but a few snatch any opportunity that comes their way.

is scarce. Others have even seemingly defied the very laws of nature in order to win themselves a tasty meal. If this sounds unlikely, then read on. Contained in this volume are fish that crawl and hop on land, snakes and lizards that fly, and spiders that spend their entire lives in underwater 'diving bells'.

LOOKING FOR MR. RIGHT

Reproducing is every animal's aim, and like all parents, animals face the same important questions. How do they find a mate? How do they make sure that

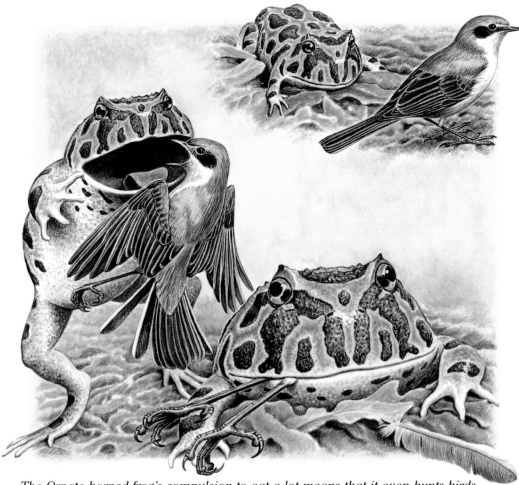

The Ornate horned frog's compulsion to eat a lot means that it even hunts birds which is a surprise considering the bulk of the frog. Patience is the key here. The patient predator waits for ages until an unwary victim flutter within range.

they make the right choice from the available candidates? And, assuming that all goes well with the nuptials, how can they give any offspring the best possible start in life? Again, nature has provided some ingenious solutions.

In the depths of the ocean, 3000m (9842ft) down, the Deep Sea Gulper Eel uses a bio-luminescent 'lure', at the end of its tapered tail, to attract a mate. Cicada males, on the other hand, serenade the females using a pair of specially evolved plates in their abdomen, called tymbals. The resulting 'song' is so loud that a male Cicada can advertise his availability to a female over 500m (1640ft) away. Dancing Flies on the look out for a mate are equally impressive, performing incredible aerial acrobatics and handing out gift-wrapped presents to persuade their would-be dates that they are Mr. Right. Others do without gifts or fancy displays and simply fight for the right to breed. In a world where everyday is a struggle for survival, it makes sense for the female to choose the biggest and strongest males. After all, they will be passing on their genetic characteristics to the young. So, even the lowly Stag Beetle comes equipped with a pair of diminutive antlers, which it uses to challenge other males for dominance and to win the right to mate and breed.

However, this is just half the battle. Once a female has mated, she must ensure that the young make it to adulthood. The Alligator Gar, for example, lays large toxic, green eggs, which predators sensibly avoid. The stick insect, or Macleay's Spectre, lays hundreds of tiny eggs containing a nodule of nutrients that ants find irresistible. These ants take the snack-filled 'seeds' back to their nests, where the young stick insects hatch, protected by a whole colony of ants. The Cuckoo Wasp seals her young up in the burrows of other insects, where they munch their way through the food that other doting mothers have provided for their offspring. Some animals even lay their eggs in the still living bodies of insects and grubs. This ensures that, when the eggs hatch, the young have access to a ready supply of fresh food.

CREATURES GREAT AND SMALL

In this book, we will be looking, up close, at some of these fascinating animals, providing information on their habitats, their life cycles and some of the techniques that they use to thrive and reproduce.

This selection includes a cross-section of 300 species — from Aphids to Violet Beetles, from Anacondas to Thorny Devils, from Anglerfish to Spider Crabs. This guide is intended to act as an introduction to the world of the animal kingdom and, hopefully, to inspire further, more detailed, reading on topics of interest. To human eyes, many of the creatures included here may seem monstrous. Even the smallest of them could be described as 'ugly' and 'cruel'. However, unlike us, the lifestyles of most animals are not dictated by whims and fancies. They cannot choose where and how to live. They are simply the product of trial and error. Every animal on our planet has adapted and changed, over millennia, so that they can best exploit their environment. Poisonous snakes, lizards, spiders and jellyfish may fill us with dread, but they are simply survivalists. Big teeth and big claws do not make an animal beastly, just a good hunter. When reading this volume, it is worth remembering that adjectives such as 'vicious' or 'victim' are human words. An animal that feeds on the young of another species is not cruel. It may seem so to us, but Nature is not partial, just highly practical. If the animals contained in this volume are monsters, then surely they are only miniature ones.

Harlequin Beetle

The harlequin beetle makes its home in Latin America's tropical forests. Members of this species are also found on islands in the Caribbean, where they are known as jak-tree borers, as their larvae are found mainly in jackfruit trees. After breeding, the female harlequin drills a hole in a tree trunk, where she lays her eggs. It takes around 10 days for these to hatch into grubs. These caterpillar-like larvae spend around eight months feeding on wood pulp until they are ready to pupate. They then seal themselves up in a wooden cocoon and remain there for four months until they change into fully grown adults. The startling-looking adult beetle that emerges has legs which are almost as long as its entire body. When threatened, an adult harlequin will stand bolt upright. This sudden increase in size is enough to startle any potential predator.

Acrocinus longimanus

Where in the world:	Southern and Central Latin America; Caribbean
Habitat:	Tropical forests
Size:	Body up to 10cm (4in) long; forelegs up to 12cm (4.7in)
Reproduction:	Lays 15–20 eggs in trees
Life span:	Unknown
Typical diet:	Adults drink tree sap

Asian Long-Horn Beetle

The life cycle of this voracious eater begins when the female lays her eggs in a purpose-dug hollow in a tree. Once hatched, the white, caterpillar-like grubs burrow their way into the trunk. These deep tunnels do irreparable damage to the tree, cutting through the tiny pipelines that carry water and nutrients from the roots to the leaves. Inside the tree, the grubs pupate from their larval stage into a pupa. It is in this state that the beetle's body undergoes all the changes needed to turn it into a fully formed adult. Pupas do not feed and are generally immobile. Most species of long-horn beetle live in old or dying trees; however, the Asian variety is an especially unwelcome guest because it feasts on young, healthy trees. Unfortunately, by the time the adult burrows its way out of its home in search of a mate, the tree is already critically ill.

Anolophora glabripennis

Where in the world:	Japan; Korea; China; introduced to USA
Habitat:	Primarily trees
Size:	1.5–2.5cm (0.6–1in) long
Reproduction:	Sexually mature at 3 years; up to 30 eggs laid in trees
Life span:	Up to 5 years
Typical diet:	Living tree tissue

Sabre-Tooth Ground Beetle

Ground beetles belong to the family Carabidae, which includes around 29,000 individual species. Although they vary in appearance, these insects typically have long, flat bodies, which enable them to crawl easily into cracks and crevices. Members of the genus *Anthia* are distinguished from other ground beetles by two prominent characteristics. First are their oversized, curved mandible jaws – their 'sabre-teeth'. Second is their ability to spray attackers with a cocktail of noxious chemicals. This is ejected from special glands in the beetle's rear with such force that it can hit a target over 30cm (12in) away. This toxic fluid contains formic acid, which not only smells and tastes foul, but can also burn skin and blind if it comes into contact with eyes. So effective is this deterrent that one species of desert lizard (*Eremia lugubris*) has adopted the beetle's markings to scare predators.

Anthia species

Where in the world:	Southern Africa
Habitat:	Adaptable. Found in tropical forest and desert
Size:	2.5–5cm (1–2in) long, depending on species
Reproduction:	Eggs laid on ground, under vegetation or stones
Life span:	Averages 5 months
Typical diet:	Opportunistic feeders, which will eat virtually anything

Common Aphid

There are around 2250 species of common aphid, varying in colour from green to black. These soft-bodied bugs use their tube-shaped mouth parts to suck up plant juices. Most aphids produce a sweet liquid, known as 'honeydew', which is excreted from a pair of tubes on their abdomen, called 'cornicles'. This is meant to deter predators, but some species of ant like it so much that they actively 'farm' aphids. The secret to the common aphid's success is that they breed very quickly. Males and females mate in early winter. Fertilized eggs are laid, from which the young hatch. This second generation then gives birth to live young, which are born from unfertilized eggs within the female's body. This process of asexual reproduction (known as 'parthenogenesis') produces vast numbers of aphids, which occasionally reach epidemic proportions and can seriously damage food crops.

Family Aphididae

Where in the world:	All over the world, excluding the coldest and warmest regions
Habitat:	On vegetation
Size:	1–8mm (0.04–0.3in) long, depending on species
Reproduction:	Asexual reproduction; up to 9 eggs laid
Life span:	Up to 2 weeks
Typical diet:	Plant sap

Spittle Bug

There are 850 species of spittle bug. These tiny insects are typically yellow when they first hatch. They then rapidly progress through five stages of development, which are known as 'instars'. During the earliest stages, these young nymphs have no distinct colourings or wings. It takes around two months for them to finally emerge as pale to dark, fully formed adults. Spittle bugs are difficult to spot on vegetation thanks to the thick bubbles of opaque liquid which they produce. This liquid – the spittle – is secreted from the bug's anus. As it emerges, the insect bobs up and down to fill the spittle with air. It then uses its hind legs to wrap the bubble-filled mass around its body. This not only shields the bug from predators, but also helps to protect it from extreme temperatures and prevent its body from drying out, which would be fatal.

Family Aphrophoridae

Where in the world:	All over the world, excluding Arctic and Antarctic
Habitat:	Woodlands, gardens and meadows
Size:	5–20mm (0.2–0.8in) long, depending on species
Reproduction:	Eggs laid in late summer on plants
Life span:	Up to 6 months
Typical diet:	Plant sap

Bee Assassin Bug

Assassin bugs are fierce predators. While many species of bugs live on a diet of plant juices, assassins make a meal of the liquefied bodies of other insects. They do this by injecting their victim with a powerful cocktail of chemicals, which paralyses their prey and breaks down its flesh into a 'protein soup'. This is then sucked up via the bug's elongated snout. Bee assassins, as their name implies, are specialists in hunting bees and other nectar-loving insects. Even for such a proficient predator as the assassin, bees make a dangerous opponent. To reduce the risk of being injured or stung, the assassin injects its venom directly into its prey's head, which rapidly disables the bee. Bee assassin bugs are often extremely colourful, which allows them to blend in with the bright colours of the flower heads, where they lie in wait for passing bees.

Apiomerus species

Where in the world:	Southern USA to Central Latin America
Habitat:	Wherever there are bees and flowers
Size:	2.5–3cm (1–1.2in) long, depending on species
Reproduction:	Eggs laid on foliage
Life span:	Unknown
Typical diet:	Bees and nectar-loving insects

Fungus Bug

Fungus-feeding bugs can be found in a few insect families, but they are most prevalent in the family Aradidae. Aradids are true bugs. This means that they have a long, piercing, syringe-like mouth part, which sucks up food in a liquid form. Beetles, in contrast, have mandibles, which are designed to cut and shred their meals into small, digestible chunks. Fungus bugs are easily recognized by their flat, almost barklike bodies, which allow the bug to squeeze itself into narrow cracks and crevices in wood and remain there, perfectly camouflaged from any predators. Their diet, as their common name suggests, consists of the fungal hyphae (or filaments) that grow on decaying wood. Some species may also feed on the fungus that can be found in bird or rodent nests. In their immature, 'nymph' stage, fungus bugs are wingless and may be easily mistaken for beetles.

Family Aradidae

Where in the world:	All over the world, excluding Arctic and Antarctic
Habitat:	In dead and decaying wood
Size:	9–14mm (0.4–0.6in) long, depending on species
Reproduction:	Eggs laid under bark or in leaf litter
Life span:	Unknown
Typical diet:	Fungi sap

Toe-biter

There are approximately 150 known species of toe-biters, which are a type of giant water bug of the family Belostomatidae. These huge bugs are accomplished swimmers, with streamlined, oval bodies and two pairs of flattened legs, which they use like paddles. At their rear are a pair of retractable appendages and these, when they are put together, form a 'breathing tube' that enables the bug to stay submerged in water while hunting. Their front legs are designed for grasping prey, and they will readily seize anything which enters the water – hence their name. Toe-biters have an extremely elaborate mating ritual, which begins with the male and female 'sparring'. After mating, the female lays a few eggs on the male's back. This continues until around 150 have been deposited. The male toe-biter takes responsibility for caring for the eggs until they hatch, in around three weeks.

Family Belostomatidae

Where in the world:	USA; Latin America; Sub-Saharan Africa; Southeast Asia
Habitat:	Freshwater environments
Size:	Up to 15cm (6in) long, depending on species
Reproduction:	Up to 150 eggs laid on male's back; a few are laid after each mating
Life span:	Averages 1 year
Typical diet:	Small insects, invertebrates, salamanders and fish

Bombardier Beetle

Bombardier beetles have developed a unique method of defending themselves from predators. In the beetle's abdomen are two separate sacs. In one is a chemical called 'hydroquinone'. In the other is hydrogen peroxide. When the beetle is threatened, it releases jets of these liquids at its attacker. As the two chemicals meet, they combine to create a highly volatile liquid, which explodes from the beetle's rear with an audible pop. This corrosive mixture is so potent that it can burn and blister skin, and even cause temporary blindness if it hits the eye. This assault is usually enough to persuade any predator to keep well away. However, if the bombardier is faced with an especially tenacious attacker, it can fire short blasts of toxic spray until the predator gets the message. The beetle is also capable of rotating the end of its abdomen to direct its attack.

Brachinus crepitans

Where in the world:	Throughout Europe
Habitat:	Grasslands
Size:	7–10mm (0.3–0.4in) long
Reproduction:	Lays eggs on ground or rotting vegetation
Life span:	Averages 2 weeks as an adult
Typical diet:	Invertebrates

Violet Ground Beetle

Ground beetles belong to the family Carabidae, which includes around 29,000 individual species. Although they vary greatly in appearance, these widespread insects typically have long, flat bodies, which enable them to crawl into cracks and crevices with ease. At first glance, the violet ground beetle, in common with many ground beetles, appears to be dark brownish-black in colour. Its true glory is revealed only in direct sunlight, when light is refracted off the ridges on the beetle's back to give a vibrant violet glow. Its large, powerful mandibles tell us that it is a hunter and a carnivore. Small insects and invertebrates are all on the menu, but, if food is scarce, then it will also scavenge for carrion. As a nocturnal feeder, the beetle has poor eyesight, but its large, bulbous eyes work well enough up close, when the beetle is ready for the kill.

Carabus violaceus

Where in the world:	Through Central Europe into Southern Russia, Siberia and Japan
Habitat:	Adaptable. Prefers woodland, but found in urban areas
Size:	2–3cm (1–1.2in) long
Reproduction:	Lays eggs in spoil
Life span:	Averages 2 years
Typical diet:	Small insects and invertebrates

Common Green Tiger Beetle

Despite their common name, tiger beetles do not have tiger stripes. Rather, the name refers to their skill as hunters. However, many members of this widespread genus are distinguished by their iridescent coloration. The green tiger beetle is perhaps the most beautiful of all. This small, emerald green insect has long legs, large eyes and a broad head. After mating, females lay their eggs, one by one, in holes in soil, sand or rock faces. Once hatched, the larvae, which are eruciform (caterpillar-like), use their flat heads to turn these egg chambers into underground burrows. It is here that the larvae hunt and feed, until they have stored enough energy in their bodies to fuel the transformation from juvenile to adult. As is common with many species of beetles and bugs, the green tiger spends the majority of its life in its larval form, and just a few short months as an adult.

Cicindela campestris

Where in the world:	From Europe to North Africa
Habitat:	Warm, dry heath lands and sandy regions
Size:	Up to 1.5cm (0.6in) long, depending on species
Reproduction:	Lays eggs in soil
Life span:	Averages 2 years
Typical diet:	Insects, carrion or plant sap, depending on species

Bed Bug

There are around 90 species of bed bugs, which can be found wherever there are host animals for them to feed on. Only three known species are believed to feast on humans, the most widespread of which is *Cimex lectularius*. This is found in temperate regions, from Europe to Northern America and into Central Asia. In warmer regions, *Cimex lectularius* is replaced by *Cimex hemipterus*. Bed bugs feed on the fresh blood of their host, using an elongated mouth, called a 'proboscis', which contains sharp needle-like stylets. As the bug feeds, its soft body swells and turns purple with the intake of blood. The larval bed bug goes through five distinct stages until it reaches its adult form. To fuel each stage, it must feed and moult. Bed bugs used be found in epidemic numbers in Europe, but modern detection and management have reduced their numbers.

Family Cimicidae

Where in the world:	All over the world
Habitat:	On human hosts
Size:	45mm (1.8in) long, depending on species
Reproduction:	Females lay 200–500 eggs on rough surfaces
Life span:	6–10 months
Typical diet:	Fresh blood

Nut Weevil

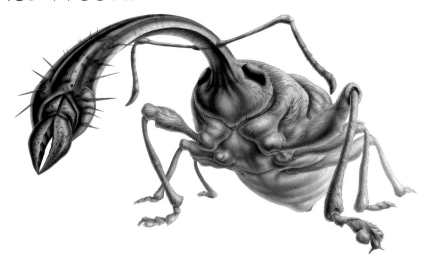

Hazelnuts, chestnuts and pecans all regularly play host to the nut weevil. In the spring, female nut weevils use the mandibles at the tip of their elongated snout to drill through the outer shell of the nut. Hazelnuts are preferred, and the meticulous mother always selects the greenest nuts, which still have relatively soft shells. Once a hole is made, the nut weevil deposits her eggs using a long tube (the ovipositor) on her abdomen. She then seals the hole. It takes around 10 days for larvae to hatch and begin to feed. Once they are ready to change into their adult form, they chew a perfectly round hole in the side of the nut and drop to the ground, where they cocoon themselves in the soil. It may take three years for cocooned larvae to pupate into adults but, once mature, they are ready to recommence their nut feast.

Curculio species

Where in the world:	Europe; Asia and Eastern USA
Habitat:	Gardens and orchards
Size:	Up to 9mm (0.4in) long, depending on species
Reproduction:	Lays 25–40 eggs in nuts
Life span:	Averages 3 years
Typical diet:	Larvae: nuts. Adults: nuts and fruit pulp

Hercules Beetle

The Hercules beetle is one of the world's largest insects – a title shared with the elephant and Goliath beetles. The males of the species are a shiny olive-green in colour, with large black spots. On the top and bottom of the thorax are huge curved horns, which meet to form a pair of formidable-looking pincers. These horns, which can be up to 9cm (3.5in) long, are used in combats with rivals for a mate. These fights rarely result in severe injuries. The curved shape of the horn is designed to flip an opponent over on his back, rather than kill. The females of the species are a reddish brown, with a small bump on the head, in place of the horns. In fact, male and females look so different that for many years it was assumed they were each members of a different species.

Dynastes hercules

Where in the world:	Central and South Latin America
Habitat:	Tropical rainforest
Size:	Up to 18cm (7in) long; 15–35g (0.5–1.2oz) in weight
Reproduction:	Lays eggs on rotting wood
Life span:	Averages 3 years
Typical diet:	Larvae: wood pulp. Adult: plant sap

European Giant Diving Beetle

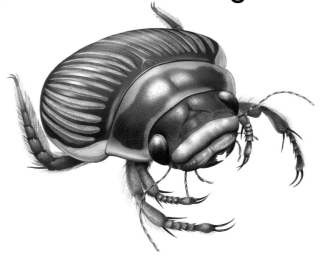

This large and impressive water beetle can be found throughout Western Europe, as far as Asia. This fierce predator makes its home in any still, stagnant or slow-running water sources where food such as aquatic insects, small fish and frogs are common. As a water-dwelling species, its body is designed in a convex streamlined shape that enables it to move through the water with ease. This distinctive insect is dark brown to blackish in colour, with yellow legs and a broad yellow-orange boarder, which runs around the edge of its head and body. Unusually in the insect world, males are smaller than females and can be distinguished by their smooth wing cases (called 'elytra'). These are generally ridged in females. Both males and females have large, broad, flattish heads, strong forelegs and sharp, powerful mandibles for tearing and slashing prey.

Dytiscus marginalis

Where in the world:	From Western Europe into Central Asia
Habitat:	Primarily still, stagnant water sources
Size:	Up to 4cm (1.6in) long
Reproduction:	Lays up to 1000 eggs on underwater plants
Life span:	Averages 3 years
Typical diet:	Aquatic insects, small fish, frogs and carrion

Click Beetle

There are around 9000 known species of click beetle, and there may be many more still to be discovered. These adaptable beetles vary in appearance from species to species, although most are brown-yellow in colour, with an elongated body. Their defining characteristic is their ability to catapult themselves up to 30cm (12 in) in the air to escape predators. They are capable of doing this thanks to a unique in-built 'catapult'. The front part of the beetle's body (the thorax) is hinged. As the beetle flexes its muscles against this hinge, tension is built up until the 'hinge' snaps shut. The release in tension throws the beetle into the air with an audible 'click'. Adult beetles feed on any decaying matter, but their larvae (called 'wireworms') bore into the roots and seeds of garden plants, maize and wheat, and are considered to be a pest by farmers.

Family Elateridae

Where in the world:	All over the world, excluding Arctic and Antarctic
Habitat:	Wherever there is abundant vegetation
Size:	1–7cm (0.4–2.8in), depending on species
Reproduction:	Eggs laid in soil
Life span:	Averages 2 years
Typical diet:	Larvae: roots. Adults: any decaying matter

Skunk Beetle

Skunk beetles belong to a huge group of insects known as darkling beetles, which form the family Tenebrionidae. Fog-basking beetles also belong to this family. In common with their desert-dwelling cousins, skunk beetles have the habit of performing mini handstands. However, in the case of skunk beetles, these acrobatics have nothing to do with water collecting. When in danger, skunk beetles spray their enemies with a potent mix of chemicals, which they squeeze out of a narrow nozzle in their rear. So, a raised abdomen means a toxic attack is on the way. This does not always work. The grasshopper mouse has developed a clever trick to avoid being attacked. It quickly pushes the beetle's rear end into the soil. Like many beetles, the skunk is a nocturnal feeder, using the cooler evenings to scavenge for rotting vegetation and carrion.

Eleodes longicollis

Where in the world:	Southern USA
Habitat:	Arid, desert environments
Size:	2–3.5cm (0.8–1.4in) long
Reproduction:	Eggs laid close to food sources
Life span:	Averages 3 years
Typical diet:	Decaying animal and vegetable matter

Butterfly Bug

Butterfly bugs belong to the family Flatidae. Members of this group are often called flatid plant-hoppers, due to their skill at jumping. When still in its juvenile nymph form, the butterfly bug is wingless, but it is able to protect itself from attackers by using cunning and camouflage. At the rear of the nymph's body is a tuft of long streamers. This odd, waxy tail serves three purposes. It helps to keep the young insect warm, it enables it to blend in with the moss and lichen that are found on tree branches and rock crevices, and it can be used to startle attackers. In common with the tree hoppers of the family Membracidae, butterfly bugs gather together on branches when feeding, all facing the same way, to give the impression that they are part of the plant. When predators approach, they flare out their tails, which is usually enough to alarm the attacker.

Family Flatidae

Where in the world:	All over the world, except the coolest regions
Habitat:	Adaptable
Size:	2.5cm (1in) long
Reproduction:	Eggs laid in late September; remain dormant until spring
Life span:	Up to 4 months
Typical diet:	Plant sap

31

Lantern Bug

The lantern bug is also known as the peanut-head or alligator bug, because of the elongated, bulbous appendage on its head. According to some observers, this bulbous 'snout' has been seen to glow, although its main purpose seems to be not illumination, but defence. At first glance, this brightly coloured head could easily belong to a small reptile – although local tribespeople think that it looks more like an unshelled peanut. This is an example of Batesian mimicry, where one harmless animal imitates a more dangerous species for protection. Nor is this the lantern bug's only means of defence. It has large, brightly coloured eyespots on its wings, which are intended to startle attackers. It also produces a spray similar to the spray of a skunk. It is possible that this spray is produced as a direct result of the lantern bug feeding on the toxic sap found in numerous species of Peruvian trees.

Fulgoridae laternaria

Where in the world:	China; imported to Peru
Habitat:	Tropical rainforests
Size:	1–16cm (0.4–6.3in), depending on species
Reproduction:	Lays eggs in rotting bark and underside of leaves
Life span:	1–2 years
Typical diet:	Plant sap

Toad Bug

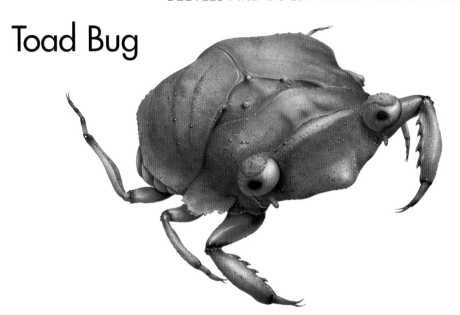

It would be easy to mistake a toad bug for the genuine article. These flat, squat-bodied bugs have a broad head and large, bulging eyes on either side of their head. Add the apparent lack of insect mouth parts (which are tucked away beneath the head) and antenna that are so small they are barely visible, and this small insect achieves a very fine impression of a small toad. They even hop in preference to flying. In common with many real amphibians, the toad bug makes its home anywhere there's water, especially mud flats or the rocky edges of freshwater lakes and rivers. Here they feed on aquatic insects, using their long hind legs to make impressive leaps that pin prey to the ground. They then insert their sharp proboscis and pump their victim with a mix of toxins and digestive juices, which paralyse and dissolve flesh.

Family Gelastocoridae

Where in the world:	USA; Latin America; Southern Asia; Australia; Southern Africa
Habitat:	Moist environments, around freshwater pools or streams
Size:	6mm–1cm (0.2–0.4in) long, depending on species
Reproduction:	Lays tiny oval eggs
Life span:	Unknown
Typical diet:	Insects

33

Goliath Beetle

There are five known species of Goliath beetle. The majority of these huge armoured insects can be found in the tropical rainforests of Central Africa, although one – *Goliathus albosignatus* – prefers the more temperate environment in the eastern part of the continent. Like all true beetles, a Goliath's life cycle is one of metamorphosis (change). Once hatched, the larvae begins to feast on rotting wood and detritus on the rainforest floor. It may take many months, even years, for the larvae to reach maximum size. Once fully grown, it builds a cocoon around itself and spends several months in a pupal stage, during which it neither eats nor moves. Once it has shed its cocoon, it emerges as a six-legged flying beetle, the primary focus of which is to find a mate. Adult Goliaths are one of the world's largest insects – a title shared with the Hercules and elephant beetles.

Goliathus species

Where in the world:	Central and Eastern Africa
Habitat:	Primarily in tropical rainforest
Size:	11cm (4.3in) long, 100g (3.5oz) in weight, varying with the species
Reproduction:	Eggs laid in decaying plant matter
Life span:	Averages 3 years
Typical diet:	Larvae: rotting vegetation. Adults: plant sap

Great Silver Beetle

G reat silver beetles can be found throughout Central Europe, although loss of habitat is now threatening many species. *Hydrophilus piceus*, which is the largest of the great silver beetles, is rare, and has vanished almost entirely from the UK, excepting a few refuges on the Somerset Moors and Levels. In their larval stage, silver beetles are voracious eaters. They have huge mandibles (powerful jaws) and are able to use these to hunt and kill within a few days of being born. Their preferred foods are tadpoles, water snails and other aquatic invertebrates, but they will feast on carrion and detritus if fresh prey is scarce. Despite spending their entire lives in water, great silver beetles are poor swimmers and lack the gills necessary to breathe underwater. Instead, they are able to trap air in the thin hairs which cover their body.

Hydrophilus species

Where in the world:	Throughout Europe
Habitat:	Primarily still, stagnant water sources
Size:	Up to 5cm (2in) long, depending on species
Reproduction:	50–100 eggs laid in cocoon attached to the underside of a floating leaf
Life span:	Averages 3 years
Typical diet:	Larvae: water snails and aquatic invertebrates. Adults: plants

Colorado Beetle

Also known as the potato beetle, this stout yellow insect is one of the most destructive crop pests. Naturally, Colorado beetles eat a weed called buffalo bur (*Solanum rostratum*); however, when farmers arrived in Colorado in the 1850s, this adaptable little beetle switched its attention to the potato plant. By 1875, the beetle had eaten its way – from farm to farm – to the Atlantic coast. It arrived in Europe in 1921, and is now found on farms from Asia to Africa. Part of its success lies in its rapid lifecycle. Colorado beetles lay their eggs, in clusters, on the underside of potato leaves in spring. Once hatched, the orange-red larvae spend around three weeks eating. They then drop to the ground and build a burrow, where they change into fully formed adults in around two weeks. These adults then return to feeding. This pattern may be repeated three times a season.

Leptinotarsa decemlineata

Where in the world:	USA; Europe; Asia; Africa
Habitat:	Potato crops
Size:	10mm (0.4in) long
Reproduction:	Lays up to 30 eggs on underside leaves; up to 3 broods per season
Life span:	Up to 2 years
Typical diet:	Leaves of potatoes and other food crops

European Stag Beetle

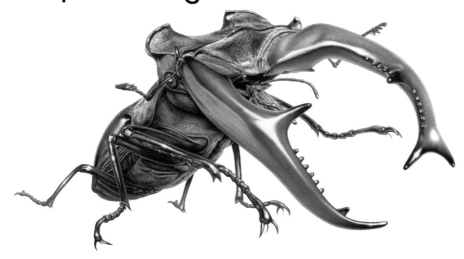

Europen stag beetles are members of the family Lucanidae, which includes around 1300 species. Adults are strikingly attractive, with purple wing cases (elytra) and huge reddish mandibles that jut out like a pair of antlers. In fact, these mandibles are used in very much the same way as a male deer uses his antlers – in combats for a mate. Despite their huge size, such combats are rarely fatal, as these curved horns are designed to intimidate or tip an opponent over, rather than actually injure him. Stag beetles used to be a common sight throughout Europe; however, they are now becoming rare in many regions, due to loss of habitat, especially oak woodlands, which are the favoured egg-laying sites of female stags. Larvae eat decaying wood, but some believe that an adult stag's life is so short that it has no need to feed at all.

Lucanus cervus

Where in the world:	Southern and Central Europe.
Habitat:	Deciduous woodlands, parks and gardens, especially in oak trees
Size:	Males up to 10cm (4in) long, including jaws. Females half the size
Reproduction:	Lays eggs in rotting wood
Life span:	Averages 5 years
Typical diet:	Larvae: rotting wood. Adult: tree sap or nothing at all

Sawyer Beetle

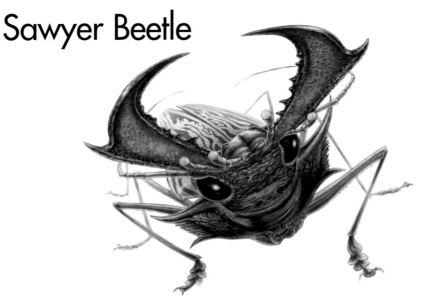

In common with many other beetles, the sawyer beetle spends much of its short, seven-year life span in its larval stage. After breeding, females lay their eggs in a specially dug hole in the bark of a tree. Once hatched, the larva grub, which looks like a white caterpillar, begins to eat. By the time that it is ready to pupate, it may be up to 25cm (10in) long. In some species of sawyer beetle, these huge babies live off decaying plant matter, but others feed on living trees. These voracious feeders burrow deep tunnels into the tree's trunk. They do irreparable damage to the tree by cutting the tiny pipelines that carry water and nutrients from the roots to the leaves. *Macrodontia cervicornis* is considered a pest by loggers, but is highly sought-after by insect collectors. For both of these reasons, rainforest sawyer beetles are increasingly rare in their natural habitat.

Macrodontia cervicornis

Where in the world:	Southwestern Latin America
Habitat:	Tropical rainforests
Size:	Up to 16cm (6.3in) long
Reproduction:	Eggs laid on bark
Life span:	Up to 7 years
Typical die:	Larvae: wood pulp. Adults: tree sap and fruit pulp

Elephant Beetle

The elephant beetle has the distinction of being one of the world's largest insects – a title it shares with the Hercules and Goliath beetles. This mini monster of the rainforest spends much of its life in its larval stage. Feeding almost exclusively on a diet of decaying wood, it can take the elephant beetle up to four years to fully mature. Then, it may live for only a few months as an adult; however, that is more than long enough to find a mate. While the adult male is competing for a female, his huge, spiked horn plays a vital role in tests of strength with rivals. Despite this, these fights rarely result in severe injuries. The curved shape of the single horn is designed to flip an opponent over on his back, rather than kill. So highly regarded are elephant beetles that local tribespeople often wear these horns as a symbol of strength.

Megasoma elephas

Where in the world:	Latin American isthmus
Habitat:	Warm, moist lowlands
Size:	Up to 13cm (5.1in) long
Reproduction:	Lays eggs in decaying bark
Life span:	Up to 5 years
Typical diet:	Larvae: wood pulp. Adults: tree sap and nectar

Blister Beetle

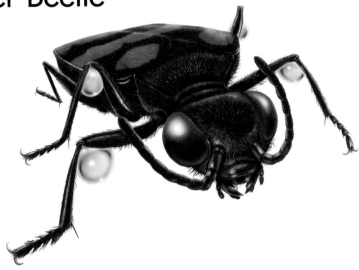

There are 3000 known species of blister beetle. This widespread family makes its home in any warm, dry region, excluding the Arctic, Antarctic and New Zealand. These beetles are an adaptable family, which varies in appearance and habits from region to region. Their colour may be anything from dun brown to vibrant red or vivid metallic blue, as found in members of the *Mylabris* species. Blister beetles get their common name from the oily fluid produced by the adults to deter predators. This is called 'cantharidin' and can cause human skin to blister or burn. In common with many beetles, blisters begin life in a larval, grublike form, which is very different in appearance and habits from the adult. This immature beetle feeds on small insects and insect eggs; however, the adults are herbivores and live exclusively on plants.

Family Meloidae

Where in the world:	Excluding the Arctic, Antarctic and New Zealand
Habitat:	Warm, dry regions with abundant vegetation
Size:	5–35mm (0.2–1.4 in) long, depending on species
Reproduction:	Eggs laid in soil
Life span:	Averages 1 year
Typical diet:	Larvae: insects. Adults: plants

Tree Hopper

There are 2500 known species of tree hoppers but, as this widespread family makes its home in tropical forests, there may be many more still to be discovered. These curious-looking bugs have a large thorn-shaped spine on their backs, called a 'pronotum'. This comes in a wide variety of colours and provides the bug with excellent natural camouflage. For example, one species, the Guatemalan *Antianthe expansa*, has a mottled green pronotum. When feeding, groups of tree hoppers gather together on a branch, all facing the same way, to give the impression that they are the spines on the plant. Some species of tree hoppers are 'farmed' by ants for the sweet liquid that they excrete from their bodies, which is called 'honeydew'. Ants also farm aphids in the same way. Tree hoppers are often considered to be pests because they feed on fruit trees.

Family Membracidae

Where in the world:	All over the world, excluding the coldest regions
Habitat:	Trees and shrubs
Size:	Up to 1.5cm (0.6in) long, depending on species
Reproduction:	Eggs laid in vegetation
Life span:	Up to 2 years
Typical diet:	Plant sap

Water Scorpion

Despite their common name, water scorpions are bugs, not arachnids (as true scorpions are). As with all insects, they have only six legs, wings and a pair of antennae. In water scorpions, these antennae are very small and concealed at the base of the eyes. They do, however, resemble scorpions, with their large pincer-style front legs and their long 'tail', which is actually a breathing tube. Water scorpions spend much of their time hanging upside-down on pond vegetation, and this tube acts like a snorkel to enable them to breathe while submerged. These flat-bodied bugs are divided into two main species: the Nepidae and the Ranatra. In general, the Nepidae are more widespread, although rare in Australia and the cooler regions of the world. Ranatra are easily distinguished from their cousins, as they are typically long-bodied and look more like praying mantises than scorpions.

Nepidae species

Where in the world:	All over the world, excluding Arctic and Antarctic
Habitat:	Primarily freshwater
Size:	Up to 23mm (0.9in) long, depending on species
Reproduction:	Eggs laid in vegetation April–May
Life span:	Unknown
Typical diet:	Small fish, tadpoles, fish larvae and aquatic invertebrates

Sexton Beetle

S exton is the name given to someone who digs graves, which is why the sexton beetle is sometimes called the burying beetle. *Nicrophorus vespillo* makes its home throughout Europe, North Asia and the USA. However, species of sexton can be found all over the world – in fact, wherever there is an abundance of dead animals. Sextons feed on carrion, but, rather than share their food with others, they drag animal corpses to safe spots, where they bury them. A big feast is the key for a male to release pheromones to attract a female. Between them, the pair bury the corpse. The female then lays her eggs in tunnels beside the carcass. After five days, the young grubs hatch. Initially, the mother regurgitates food for them, but they are soon able to feed for themselves. They mature so quickly that they are ready to pupate before the body rots.

Nicrophorus vespillo

Where in the world:	Europe; Northern Asia; North America
Habitat:	Anywhere corpses are abundant
Size:	Up to 16cm (6.3in) long
Reproduction:	Up to 24 eggs laid
Life span:	Averages 1 year
Typical diet:	Dead animals

Stink Bug

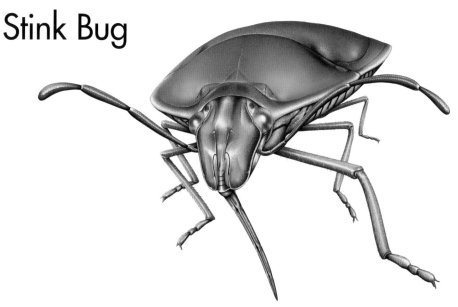

There are around 5500 stink bugs in the family Pentatomidae. These attractive insects are also known as shield bugs, due to the characteristic shield shape of their bodies. Many species are brightly coloured, with patternations that mimic vegetation, as in the case of the green stink bug (*Nezara viridula*), which has a body that looks like layers of overlapping leaves. Most species are herbivores, but some hunt live prey and use this camouflage to great effect. They do not set cunning traps, but simply creep up on slow-moving insects, inject their proboscis, flood their victim with paralysing toxins and begin to feed. As might be expected, stink bugs give off a foul smell to deter predators. Unlike skunk beetles or lantern bugs, who spray their noxious gasses and liquids directly at attackers, stink bugs exude foul odours from special glands in the side of their thorax.

Family Pentatomidae

Where in the world:	All over the world, excluding the coldest regions
Habitat:	Plants, trees and shrubs
Size:	0.5–2.5cm (0.2–1in) long, depending on species
Reproduction:	20–30 barrel-shaped eggs laid
Life span:	Up to 1 year
Typical diet:	Plant sap or insects, depending on species

Ambush Bug

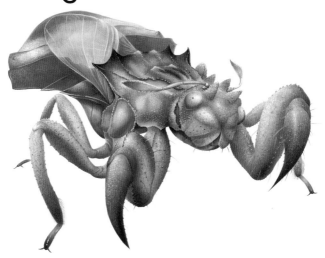

A dult ambush bugs have two pairs of wings, yet when they are born they are wingless. Instead, young ambush bugs ('nymphs') have miniature bumps on their backs, called 'buds'. As the bug grows, and moults its tough, outer shell, these buds finally develop into fully formed wings. However, ambush bugs are poor fliers and take to the air only in search of food or if danger threatens. Many bugs feed on plants, but ambush bugs are carnivores, and they use their natural camouflage to hide on flower heads or among vegetation, until prey approaches. Once a victim is in sight, the ambush bug pounces, grasping its prey in its large front legs, with a vicelike grip. It then extends its piercing mouth parts and injects its captive with digestive enzymes that dissolve its flesh, enabling the bug to suck up a liquid meal.

Family Phymatidae

Where in the world:	Tropical regions, excluding Australia and New Zealand
Habitat:	Primarily flowering plants
Size:	Up to 1.2cm (0.5in) long, depending on species
Reproduction:	Egg laying
Life span:	Averages 1 year
Typical diet:	Small insects

Dung Beetle

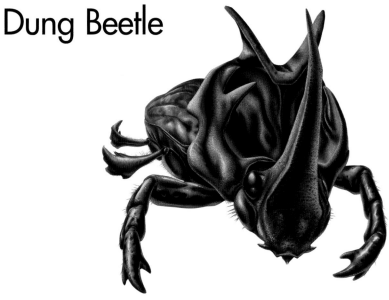

Dung beetles are also commonly called scarabs; their name is a bit of a misnomer, as only a small proportion of the 20,000 or so known species feed on manure. Perhaps the most well-known dung beetle is the sacred scarab (*Scarabaeus sacer*), which the Ancient Egyptians regarded as an emblem of resurrection and immortality. These enterprising scavengers can be found wherever there is a fresh supply of animal dung, which forms the beetle's primary food source. Using their broad, spadelike front feet and flat heads, dung beetles will either bury their share of the manure, so that they can enjoy their faecal feast in private, or form it into a ball and roll it away. During the breeding season, the female will create dung 'brood balls'. She lays one egg into each of these, then seals up the nest, for around four weeks, until the young hatch.

Scarabaeus sacer, Gymnopleurus virens & others

Where in the world:	All over the world, excluding desert and polar regions
Habitat:	Wherever there is a supply of animal dung
Size:	Up to 6cm (2.4in), depending on species
Reproduction:	Lays up to 10 eggs in dung 'brood balls'
Life span:	Averages 18 months
Typical diet:	Dung from herbivores

Rove Beetle

There are around 29,000 known species of rove beetle. This widespread family can be found wherever there is rotting vegetation or carrion. These predatory beetles do not feed directly on decaying matter, but on the grubs and insects that such food attracts. The most well known of the family is the devil's coach horse (*Staphylinus olens*). This large, black, European insect is usually found in graveyards and was thought to resemble the black horses which were used to pull hearses. Many members of the family Staphylinidae are unremarkable, medium-sized, dark beetles, but there are some striking exceptions. *Emus hirtus*, for example, looks like a piece of decaying vegetation, with large beaklike mandibles and a thorax covered in yellow hairs. This diverse family does share one characteristic: all are exceptionally mobile and can fly and run extremely well.

Family Staphylinidae

Where in the world:	All over the world
Habitat:	Adaptable; found, in woodlands, coasts and in polar regions
Size:	Up to 3cm (1.2in) long, depending on species
Reproduction:	Eggs laid in vegetation
Life span:	Averages 1 year
Typical diet:	Primarily insects

Fog-basking Beetle

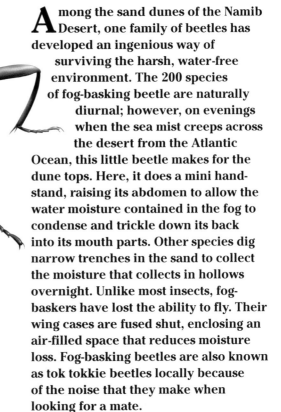

Among the sand dunes of the Namib Desert, one family of beetles has developed an ingenious way of surviving the harsh, water-free environment. The 200 species of fog-basking beetle are naturally diurnal; however, on evenings when the sea mist creeps across the desert from the Atlantic Ocean, this little beetle makes for the dune tops. Here, it does a mini handstand, raising its abdomen to allow the water moisture contained in the fog to condense and trickle down its back into its mouth parts. Other species dig narrow trenches in the sand to collect the moisture that collects in hollows overnight. Unlike most insects, fog-baskers have lost the ability to fly. Their wing cases are fused shut, enclosing an air-filled space that reduces moisture loss. Fog-basking beetles are also known as tok tokkie beetles locally because of the noise that they make when looking for a mate.

Family Tenebrionidae

Where in the world:	Atlantic coast of Southwest Africa
Habitat:	The Namib Desert
Size:	Up to 4cm (1.6in), depending on species
Reproduction:	Lays eggs in sand dunes
Life span:	Averages 3 years
Typical diet:	Larvae: plant matter. Adults: plants, dung and carrion

Giraffe Beetle

G iraffe beetles are found only on the island of Madagascar, which lies off the
eastern coast of Africa. Despite the name, this curious-looking insect is
actually a type of weevil. Weevils are beetles with elongated snouts as well as
powerful mandibles. Like their namesakes, giraffe beetles have incredibly long,
thin necks. They also have an additional neck joint, which allows them to bob their
heads up and down during mating displays. At the end of this neck is the giraffe
beetle's huge head, which is tipped with a pair of touch- and scent-sensitive
antennae. Giraffe beetles are conscientious mothers, and carefully wrap their
eggs in a rolled-up leaf. This gives the unhatched young some protection from
predators and a ready supply of food when the larvae grubs hatch. The same
leaves form a vital part of the diet of adult giraffe beetles.

Trachelophorus giraffa

Where in the world:	Madagascar
Habitat:	Wherever there is plentiful vegetation
Size:	1.4–2.2cm (0.9–0.6in) long; half of this length is head
Reproduction:	Lays eggs in carefully rolled leaves
Life span:	Unknown
Typical diet:	Leaves of shrubs and vines

Chagas Bug

Chagas bugs are also known as 'kissing bugs' because they typically feed on the skin around the mouth and eyes. By day, these tiny blood-suckers stay hidden in cracks and crevices, but at night they come out to feed. Like all bugs, Chagas bugs have sharp, hollow mouth parts, which are designed to pierce skin and remove fluids – a little like a hypodermic syringe. What makes these nocturnal feeders so dangerous is that they carry trypanosome, a type of parasite that lives on blood and attacks muscles and nerve cells. An average Chagas meal may last as long as 20 minutes, which is ample time for the bug to pass on any contaminants to its victim. The result is Chagas disease, which can cause fever and may, if left untreated, eventually kill. There are many different species of Chagas bugs, but the most virulent is *Triatoma infestans*.

Triatoma, Panstrongylus & Rhodnius species

Where in the world:	Southern USA; Latin America
Habitat:	Adaptable; found in rural and urban regions, wherever there are people
Size:	Up to 2cm (0.8in) long, depending on species
Reproduction:	Egg layer
Life span:	Averages 1 year
Typical diet:	Fresh blood

Tail-less Whip Spider

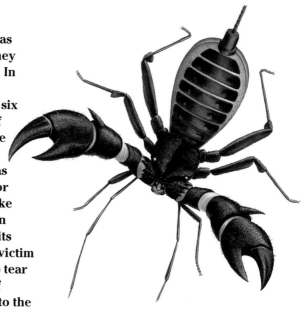

Whip spiders are also known as whip scorpions, although they are neither spiders nor scorpions. In common with solpugids, these distinctive arachnids walk on just six of their eight legs. The first pair of legs, which may be longer than the length of the creature's entire body, have been adapted for use as feelers. They have no silk glands or fangs, but hunt using these whiplike sensors to detect prey. Once within reach, the whip scorpion will use its enlarged pedipalps to restrain its victim while their powerful jaws begin to tear apart its flesh. In Latin, *amblypygi* means 'blunt rump', which refers to the fact that amblypygids lack a final tail segment on their abdomens. (Whip scorpions of the order Uropygi have a whiplike tail.) So far, approximately 136 species have been identified, although exact numbers are unknown. Preferred habitats are warm, moist environments.

Sub-order Amblypygi

Where in the world:	Tropical and subtropical regions
Habitat:	Forest, scrubland and deserts, depending on species
Size:	Up to 7.5cm (3in), depending on species
Reproduction:	Lays eggs; hatched young carried on mother's back
Life span:	Unknown
Typical diet:	Insects

Yellow Fat-tailed Scorpion

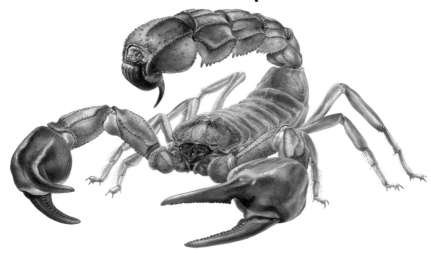

S corpion venom is held in two glands positioned just below the stinger – that barbed point at the tip of the tail. Their especially large venom glands make this species of scorpion's tail look 'fat'. Fat-tailed scorpion venom is especially designed to kill vertebrates. As most of its prey are invertebrates, this means that it was originally developed for protection, rather than as a hunting tool. This has not stopped this formidable predator from using this deadly toxin to get itself a meal, however. Small insects, such as locusts or beetles, are on its usual menu, but its toxin is so powerful that it can tackle mice and small lizards with relative ease. Once its prey has been incapacitated, the scorpion will dismember the body, using its razor-sharp pincers to cut the flesh into small enough pieces to eat.

Androctonus australis

Where in the world:	North Africa and Arabia
Habitat:	Arid, desert regions
Size:	Up to 10cm (4in) long; up to 25g (1oz) in weight
Reproduction:	Gives birth to live young, which are carried on mother's back
Life span:	Up to 5 years
Typical diet:	Locust, spiders, small lizards and mice

Dewdrop Spider

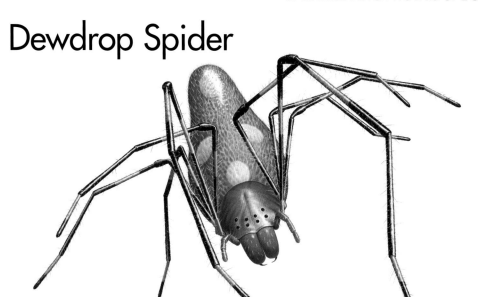

The numerous species of dewdrop spider are found as far afield as Australia (*Argyrodes antipodianus*) and the Southern United States (*Argyrodes elevatus*). This attractive arachnid owes its common name to its silvery-brown, domed abdomen, which reflects sunlight, giving it the appearance of a dewdrop. Dewdrops are a species of 'klepto-parasite'. This means that they live with and steal from other species. Dewdrops are often found living in the webs of other spiders, where they not only steal food, but, if the opportunity arises, will also mob the 'host' and eat it, too. They do this by waiting for the host to moult (shed their skin), at which point it is completely vulnerable until its new skin hardens. The web of a large spider such as an golden orb weaver may be home to several species of dewdrops, who take it in terms to feed from their host's 'larder'.

Argyrodes species

Where in the world:	Tropical and subtropical regions
Habitat:	The webs of other spiders
Size:	Females 3mm (0.1in) long; males smaller, depending on species
Reproduction:	20–40 eggs laid
Life span:	Averages 1 year
Typical diet:	Insects, other spiders and their eggs

Water Spider

The water spider is unique. There are many species of spiders which live and hunt on the water's edge, but this single species spends almost its entire life submerged. This amazing aquatic arachnid is able to do this because it makes its own watertight home. Construction begins with a sheet of silk, which is attached to floating vegetation. The spider has fine hairs on its legs and abdomen, which trap air. It uses this air to inflate its silken sheet, into a dome, in a process a little like filling a hot air balloon. Once this 'diving bell' is full, it climbs inside, with its legs hanging down into the water, to detect prey. Mating and egg-laying all take place underwater. If it needs to leave this refuge for any reason, then it spins a fine dragline of silk behind it, which helps it to find its way back.

Argyroneta aquatica

Where in the world:	Europe and Asia
Habitat:	Slow-moving ponds and lakes
Size:	Females up to 1.5cm (0.6in) long. Males smaller
Reproduction:	Mate and lay eggs in underwater 'diving bell'
Life span:	Averages 2 years
Typical diet:	Small fish, tadpoles, fish larvae and aquatic invertebrates

Purse-Web Spider

Purse-webs are related to trapdoor spiders, and both species build similar, elaborate underground burrows as refuges. These are lined with a silken cocoon. This extends up from the tunnel to form an overground, tube-shaped web. Inside, the purse-web spider hangs, upside down, waiting for prey. This secretive spider is virtually blind, but is able to detect approaching prey thanks to the touch-sensitive hairs on its legs, which pick up vibrations from the air. Once within reach, the spider strikes. In common with trapdoor spiders, the fangs of purse-webs point down, rather than face each other. This orientation allows trapdoor spiders to have longer fangs, so they effectively impale their victims on these huge hollow needles. They then cut through the silken 'purse' and haul their prey back into their burrow. The purse is later repaired, ready for another day's hunting.

Family Atypidae

Where in the world:	North America; Northern Europe; North Africa
Habitat:	Primarily grassland.
Size:	Up to 1.5cm (0.6in) long, depending on species
Reproduction:	Lays eggs in silk lined burrow
Life span:	Females up to 10 years
Typical diet:	Insects

Sydney Funnel-Web Spider

T he Sydney funnel-web spider is an evolutionary mystery. The venom of the
male of the species has relatively little effect on large mammals such as cats,
but is potentially fatal to both humans and monkeys. No one knows why this
should be, as the funnel-web's ancestors arrived in Australia long before humans
ever set foot on the continent. This large, blue-black arachnid typically makes its
home in any moist crack or crevice, although it also digs itself a shallow retreat
if there is no suitable hideaway. Here it builds a thick tubular web, and sits in wait
for prey. Most attacks on humans are made by aggressive males, who leave their
webs in search of a mate during the summer. Their venom, which contains
atraxotoxin, attacks the human nervous system, causing sickness and muscle
spasms, and – if left untreated – may be fatal.

Atrax robustus

Where in the world:	Within 160km (99-mile) radius of Sydney, Australia
Habitat:	Prefers moist conditions
Size:	Body length up to 5cm (2in); leg span up to 8cm (3.2in)
Reproduction:	Mates in summer; eggs laid
Life span:	10–20 years
Typical diet:	Insects, invertebrates, small lizards and frogs

Bird-eating Spider

Originally, the term 'tarantula' referred to a type of wolf spider that was found in Italy. Today this title is generally given to any large, hairy spider, including many species of Latin American bird-eaters. Despite their great size, the description – 'bird-eater' – is erroneous. Latin America is home to both the world's smallest and largest spiders. Tarantulas are officially the largest, and within this order, the Goliath bird-eating tarantula of Guyana is the giant of the species. Yet this monster is more likely to make a meal of mice or small lizards than fully grown birds, although fledglings may occasionally be on the menu. Bird-eaters are hunting spiders. This means that they hunt down their prey, rather than trap it in a web. They still use silk to make a fine 'dragline', which helps them to swing to the ground from high places, or escape from danger quickly.

Avicularia species

Where in the world:	Latin American rainforest
Habitat:	Nests in trees or on the ground, depending on species
Size:	Body length 6cm (2.4in); leg span 15cm (6in), depending on species
Reproduction:	Eggs laid in silk egg sac
Life span:	Females, up to 30 years in captivity
Typical diet:	Insects, reptiles, frogs and fledgling birds

Mexican Red-kneed Spider

Mexican red-kneed spiders are one of the most easily recognized species of 'tarantula'. In fact, they are so popular with the pet trade that they are now threatened in their native habitats. Most spiders are either free-roaming hunters or web-builders. Red-kneed tarantulas are hunters which live on a varied diet of insects and the occasional small reptile, amphibian or mammal. Like all spiders, they live on a liquid diet. Once a meal is caught, they inject their prey with enzymes, which 'pre-digest' their flesh. They then use short strawlike appendages to pierce the skin, and simply suck up their victim's body fluids, like soup. Using this technique, it is possible for a large tarantula such as a red-kneed to reduce a mouse to fur and bones in just 36 hours! Although generally harmless to humans, they shed 'urticating' hairs, which can cause a burning sensation, rashes and even blindness.

Brachypelma smithi

Where in the world:	Central Mexico
Habitat:	Arid, desert regions
Size:	Body length up to 10cm (4in) long; leg span up to 17cm (6.7in)
Reproduction:	Mates during wet season; 400–800 eggs laid in underground burrow
Life span:	Females up to 30 years
Typical diet:	Insects, small reptiles and mice

Old World Scorpion

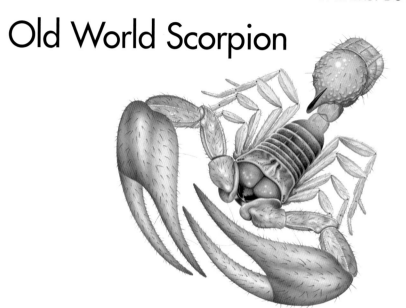

Although scorpions of the *Buthus* species are relatively small in size, they pack a powerful punch. *Buthus* have poor eyesight, but this is compensated for by touch-sensitive hairs on their legs, which allow them to detect even the minutest of movements, and home in on prey. Once the prey is in its powerful pincers, this tiny hunter arches its tail over its segmented body and injects the victim with a deadly cocktail of toxins. These are carried in a pair of venom glands, which feed into the barbed stinger found on the last segment of the scorpion's tail. *Buthus* scorpions are among some of the most dangerous members of the scorpion family. In secluded desert regions, where antitoxin is not readily available, their toxic sting is frequently fatal to humans. *Buthus* prefer warm, tropical and semitropical regions, and can be found throughout the Mediterranean coastline.

Buthus species

Where in the world:	Mediterranean Europe; North Africa and Arabia
Habitat:	Arid, desert regions
Size:	4–10cm (1.6in) long
Reproduction:	Gives birth to live young, which are carried on mother's back
Life span:	Up to 10 years
Typical diet:	Insects, small lizards, mice and scorpions

Bark Scorpion

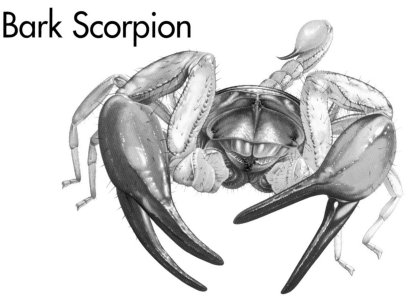

S corpions are the oldest order of arachnids. Species have been found in fossils that date back to the Silurian period, 400 million years ago. During this time, scorpions have adapted to a wide range of environments and are able to tolerate everything but the driest and coldest habitats. Bark scorpions, in common with many members of this order, are primarily nocturnal and spend much of the day in shaded spots. They do not dig burrows, but prefer to live above ground, hidden away in rock crevices or beneath vegetation. This is a small species, with a slender brown body and a tendency to hold its tail stinger to one side (rather than curled over its back) when at rest. The hollow sting in the segmented tail of the bark scorpion contains an extremely potent toxin, which is used for hunting, but can kill a human, if left untreated.

Centruroides species

Where in the world:	Southern USA; Latin America; the Caribbean
Habitat:	Warm, dry environments
Size:	5–10cm (2–4in) long, depending on species
Reproduction:	Gives birth to live young, which are carried on mother's back
Life span:	Unknown
Typical diet:	Insects and invertebrates

Yellow Sac Spider

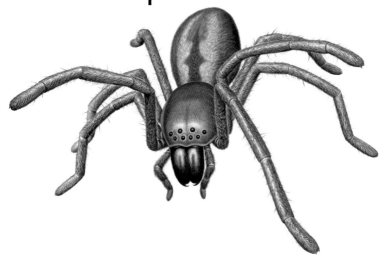

It is believed that yellow sac spiders may be responsible for more bites on humans than any other spider species, although many are misdiagnosed as brown recluse bites because their venom is cytotoxic and can take a long time to heal. These are eight-eyed, yellow to pale green arachnids, with an orange stripe on the abdomen of some species. Their common name refers to the thin, paper-like sacs of silk which they weave to hide in during the day. These refuges can often be found in gardens or homes, especially in out-of-the-way spots such as the corners of houses or behind shelves. Females make a similar sac to protect their eggs, which they guard until they hatch. Sac spiders hunt at night, using their front legs as feelers to search out prey among leaf debris and vegetation. Typically, small insects and other spiders are on the menu.

Cheiracanthium species

Where in the world:	All over the world, excluding Arctic and Antarctic
Habitat:	Adaptable
Size:	4–10mm (0.2–0.4in) long, depending on species
Reproduction:	Lays 30–48 eggs, depending on species
Life span:	Averages 1 year
Typical diet:	Insects and spiders

King Baboon Spider

When the king baboon was first identified in 1899, it was Africa's largest known species of spider. Some time later, the larger African Goliath tarantula (*Hysterocrates hercules*) was discovered. Therefore, despite its grand title, the king baboon is only Africa's second-largest spider. This large, rusty red arachnid is notoriously bad-tempered: when threatened or annoyed, it will rear up on its back legs to display its large fangs. King baboons construct extensive burrows, which can be as much as 60cm (24in) long. These underground refuges keep them sheltered from predators and the intense heat of the midday sun. They also make ideal spots from which to ambush prey. King baboons will readily tackle animals as large as, if not larger than, themselves. Insects and invertebrates, plus the occasional lizard, amphibian or ground-nesting bird, are all on the menu.

Citharischius crawshayi

Where in the world:	East Africa
Habitat:	Grassland and scrubland
Size:	Body length up to 15cm (6in); leg-span up to 20cm (8in)
Reproduction:	Eggs laid in underground burrow
Life span:	Female up to 30 years; males 10 years
Typical diet:	Insects, small invertebrates, lizards and frogs

Ant Mimic Spider

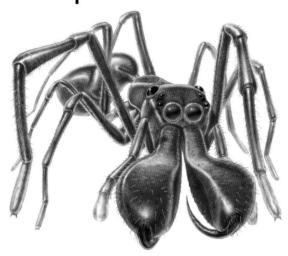

Mimicry is the ability of an animal to copy the appearance and behaviour of something else. Usually, in the animal kingdom, a harmless species will mimic a more dangerous one, for protection, as in the case of ant mimic spiders. Spiders mimic many insects, such as flies and wasps, but several groups within the families Clubionidae and Salticidae have evolved to look and act like ants. Ants are a useful species to mimic, as they are often toxic and are therefore avoided by many predators. Spiders are arachnids, which means that they have four pairs of legs, no antennae and no wings. So in order to look like an ant, they have to make some cunning adaptations. The Kerengga ant mimic spider (*Myrmarachne plataleoides*), for example, holds up its two front legs like antennae. It also has large black patches on its head to imitate the ant's compound eyes.

Families Clubionidae & Salticidae

Where in the world:	Tropical and subtropical regions
Habitat:	Primarily rainforests in Africa, Asia and Latin America
Size:	Up to 15mm (0.6in) long, depending on species
Reproduction:	Egg layers
Life span:	Up to 2 years
Typical diet:	Insects and other spiders

Trapdoor Spider

Trapdoor spiders are myglomorphs. This means their fangs point down, rather than face each other, which is usual with araneomorph spiders. This allows trapdoor spiders to have longer fangs than their araneomorph cousins. (Other myglomorphs include many species of large tarantula.) Trapdoor spiders get their name from their ability to construct 'traps' for catching prey. These medium-sized arachnids live in burrows. In fact, the females rarely venture outside. At the entrance to this arrangement of tunnels and interior doors is an outer 'door' made of compressed plant and soil material, and hinged with silk. The spider lies in wait behind this until prey approaches. It then shoots out, and pins its victim to the ground with its powerful front legs, while its large hollow fangs inject paralysing venom. It takes approximately 0.03 seconds for a spider to catch prey in this way.

Family Ctenizidae

Where in the world:	Tropical and subtropical regions
Habitat:	Adaptable; found in rainforest, grassland and desert
Size:	Up to 2.5cm (1in) long, depending on species
Reproduction:	Eggs laid in underground burrow
Life span:	Averages 20 years
Typical diet:	Insects and small reptiles

Central American Wandering Spider

There are 10 known species of *Cupiennius* spiders, all of which share similar characteristics. Most spider species either build silken webs in which to trap their prey, or hunt them down. Hunters need to be fast, strong and have excellent eyesight, and the wandering spiders of Central America possess all of these attributes. They also have amazingly touch-sensitive hairs on their body and legs. As nocturnal hunters, they cannot afford to rely on eyesight alone, so these fine filaments pick up any vibrations in the air made by the movements of prey. These hairs also have an important role to play during spider courtship. When looking for a mate, the male will tap out a series of rapid signals with his legs. These vibrations can travel more than 1 metre (40in) along tree branches and advertise the male's presence to any interested female in the area.

Cupiennius species

Where in the world:	Central American rainforest
Habitat:	Primarily arboreal
Size:	Body length up to 2cm (0.8in); leg span up to 12cm (4.7in)
Reproduction:	Sexually mature at 8–10 months; eggs held in silk cocoon
Life span:	Averages 2 years
Typical diet:	Insects and small frogs

Ogre-faced Spider

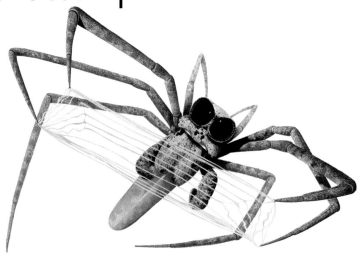

Ogre-faced spiders get their common name from the Greek 'deinos', meaning fearful, and 'opis', appearance. These slender arachnids have eight eyes, two of which point forwards like huge searchlights, which gives them a startling countenance. These eyes play a vital part in the spider's hunting technique. By day, these long-legged hunters remain hidden among the vegetation. Once night falls, though, they emerge to hunt. Unlike many spider species, ogres do not construct large static webs, but instead make small mobile 'nets'. They then hang upside down, from a strand of silk suspended close to the ground. They hold their net in front of them, grasped in their forelegs. Their huge eyes give them excellent vision, so when prey crawls past, they drop their net to ensnare them. Ogre-faced spiders are also known as net-casting spiders, in tribute to this unusual hunting technique.

Family Deinopidae

Where in the world:	Tropical regions
Habitat:	Among vegetation in grasslands or gardens
Size:	Females: up to 2.5cm (1in) long
Reproduction:	Mate in autumn; up to 4 eggs sacs laid
Life span:	Unknown
Typical diet:	Small insects

Dust Mite

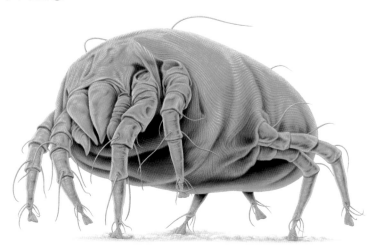

Invisible to the naked eye, dust mites can be found wherever there are people. These tiny arthropods occur in huge numbers in carpets, mattresses and anywhere that household dust gathers. Dust is made up of tiny particles such as dirt, plant pollen, dead skin and hair. It is this organic matter which dust mites find so irresistible. Mites do not have proper jaws to chew their food, but they are able to break down organic matter into a liquid meal by spraying it with digestive acids. In large numbers, dust mites are believed to be responsible for many of the more common diseases, such as asthma and dermatitis. This is because dust mite faeces contain an enzyme that causes strong allergic reactions in humans. *Dermatophagoides pteronyssinus* is common in Europe while its close relative, *Dermatophagoides farinae*, makes its home in North America.

Dermatophagoides species

Where in the world:	All over the world
Habitat:	Wherever there are people
Size:	0.15–0.3mm (0.005–0.01in) long
Reproduction:	Sexually mature in 1 day; tiny eggs develop into 6-legged larvae
Life span:	Averages 1 month
Typical diet:	Flakes of human skin and organic matter

European Raft Spider

The European raft, or fishing, spider can be found wherever there is stagnant water to attract insects. This attractive dark brown arachnid may be Europe's largest spider. It is not, as its name suggests, a raft-builder; instead it hunts for aquatic insects by stretching out its long legs over the water's surface to feel for minute vibrations made by approaching prey. It even 'fishes' by tapping the water to lure small fish and newts to the surface. The body of this long-legged spider is covered in water-repellent hairs, which prevent it from getting wet. However, it does occasionally intentionally drench itself – hiding underwater for short periods to escape predators. Despite its bulk, it can also walk across the water's filmlike surface. By spreading out its long legs, it can distribute its weight so that it does not break the water's surface tension. This stops it from sinking.

Dolomedes fimbriatus

Where in the world:	Europe and Asia
Habitat:	Cool, moist environments such as swamps and heath land
Size:	Body length up to 3.5cm (1.4in); leg span up to 8cm (3in)
Reproduction:	Female carries egg sac under her body until the eggs hatch
Life span:	Unknown
Typical diet:	Insects, tadpoles and small fish

Woodlouse Spider

Many spider enthusiasts find this small, widespread arachnid unappealing. With its reddish, hairless cephalothorax and cream abdomen, it is certainly distinctive. It is believed that woodlouse spiders originated in Europe, but they are now found throughout most of the world. This adaptable species makes its home wherever it finds its favourite prey – woodlice. It is not a web-builder, but does use silk to line the cracks and crevices which form its daytime retreat. It emerges at night to hunt, but even during the day these are aggressive spiders, which will readily bite anything that disturbs them. Their long fangs are powered by strong muscles at the base of each chelicera, which means that they close with enough force to penetrate the exoskeleton of a woodlouse. Although not usually fatal to humans, bites can be extremely painful, causing dizziness and nausea.

Dysdera crocata

Where in the world:	All over the world, excluding Arctic and Antarctic
Habitat:	Adaptable
Size:	Female body to 2cm (0.8in); leg span to 3cm (1.2in). Males half her size
Reproduction:	30–40 eggs laid in silk-lined refuge
Life span:	Averages 1 year
Typical diet:	Woodlice

Horned Orb Weaver

Spiders can be classified according to whether or not they build webs – and what type of web they build. Black widows construct elaborate 'tangled webs' which are complex, multi-layered traps. Trapdoor spiders do not spin webs at all, but use their silk to construct lined tunnels in which they lie in wait for prey. Orb weavers, such as the horned orb weaver, produce round webs, where threads of silk radiate out from the centre like the spokes of a wheel. These are often constructed between the branches of trees and some may be so strong that they can entangle small birds. The horned orb weaver is primarily found in warm, tropical forests, although they occasionally wander into urban gardens. Small flecks of loose silk are often woven into this web, probably as a lure to attract the interest of insects.

Gasteracantha falcicornis

Where in the world:	Southern and Eastern Africa
Habitat:	Primarily tropical forests
Size:	Females up to 8mm (0.3in) long
Reproduction:	Egg sacs kept in web
Life span:	Unknown
Typical diet:	Insects

Huntsman Spider

Huntsman spiders are distinguished by their elongated, almond-shaped abdomens and long legs, which are often held at the sides of the body, like a crab. Most species are hairy, with eight, equal-sized eyes, placed in two rows at the front of the head. Huntsman spiders tend to be brown or dark grey, although some have spectacular natural camouflage, such as the forest huntsman (*Pandercetes plumipes*) of Malaysia. This beautiful arachnid has banded brown legs and a pale green abdomen, which means it becomes virtually invisible among the trees. Other species, such as the olive-brown giant huntsman, have become a common sight in homes throughout Australia. Here, their camouflage is less effective, but the living is easier. Huntsmans get their name from their hunting prowess. These nocturnal predators are agile and powerful spiders able to pursue prey at incredible speeds.

Family Heteropoda

Where in the world:	Southeast Asia; Australia; New Zealand and New Guinea
Habitat:	Woodlands and rural areas
Size:	Body length 4cm (1.6in); leg span 16cm (6.3in), varying with species
Reproduction:	Eggs laid in egg sac; female guards young (spiderlings)
Life span:	Up to 3 years
Typical diet:	Flies, bugs and beetles

Hard Tick

There are believed to be 650 species of hard tick, which vary in colour from yellow to black. These flat, round-bodied arachnids have a flexible abdomen that stretches when the tick becomes engorged with fresh blood, on which it feeds. Ticks start their lives among vegetation, where the females lay their eggs. Once hatched, the larvae attach themselves to an animal host, where they begin to feed. After a few days, the larvae leave their host and find a secure place to moult. The emerging juvenile has just six legs and must feed and moult again before it adopts its final adult form. In some species of ticks, the male does not feed directly on the animal host, but attaches himself to the female and feeds off her. Hard ticks are a serious problem, as they transmit diseases to both animals and humans, including Lyme disease and tick typhus.

Family Ixodidae

Where in the world:	All over the world, excluding Arctic and Antarctic
Habitat:	Wherever there are host animals to feed on
Size:	2mm–3cm (0.08–1.2in) long, depending on species
Reproduction:	Lays eggs on vegetation
Life span:	Averages 2 years
Typical diet:	Blood

White-tailed Spider

The white-tailed spider's Latin name means 'mouse-grey' (murinus) 'cylinder' (cylindratus), which is a good description of this spider's body. Males of the species have a whitish hard plate towards the rear of their abdomen, which gives the spider its common name. There are two species of white-tail, both found in Australia – *Lampona cylindrata* is found in Southern Australia and Tasmania, while *Lampona murina* is more common in the northeast of the continent. The toxin of a white-tailed spider is commonly believed to be necrotic, or flesh-eating; however, recent research has suggested that the blistering effects caused by its bite are the result of an allergic reaction to bacteria carried in the soil and accidentally transferred to the wound by the spider's bite. White-tailed spiders typically make their homes in grassland, but have now made their way into rural parks, too.

Lampona cylindrata

Where in the world:	Southern Australia, including Tasmania; introduced to New Zealand
Habitat:	Woodlands, gardens and parks
Size:	1–2cm (0.4–0.8in) long
Reproduction:	Mates late summer; lays up to 90 eggs in egg sac
Life span:	Up to 2 years
Typical diet:	Insects and spiders

Australian Redback Spider

The Australian redback – or jockey spider, as it is also called – belongs to an infamous group of arachnids which includes the American black widow. This is a secretive species that hides itself in shady corners, including cars, houses and – famously – outside toilets. This predatory spider is well named. In Latin, 'latrodectus' means 'secret biter' and, if you are unlucky enough to be bitten by a female (the male's pincers are too small to break the skin), you are unlikely to notice until you start to feel unwell. No human has died from a redback bite since the introduction of an anti-venom in 1956, but they are still responsible for more serious animal bites than sharks and snakes put together. The male is three times smaller than the female, and just like the black widow, the female redback will usually make a meal of the tiny male after mating.

Latrodectus hasselti

Where in the world:	Australia, including Tasmania; introduced to Japan and New Zealand
Habitat:	Adaptable; found in all but the driest and coldest regions
Size:	Female body length up to 15mm (0.6in); males to 3.8mm (0.14in)
Reproduction:	Sexually mature at 2–3 months; lays 300 eggs in an egg sac
Life span:	Up to 1 year for females
Typical diet:	Bugs, insects and other spiders

Black Widow Spider

Black widows are closely related to the Australian redback and the European widow spider. In fact, for many years, it was believed that all three spiders belonged to the same, cosmopolitan species. In common with its cousins, the black widow is highly venomous and its bite can be extremely dangerous, if not fatal, to humans. Widows can be recognized by their unmistakably glossy, round black bodies, and the distinctive red hour-glass mark on their abdomen. These skilled hunters are 'tangle web' builders, constructing elaborate, layered traps, anchored at the floor or ceiling. During mating, males will tap out a signal along the threads of this web to warn the female that he is approaching. This does not always ensure his safety. After mating, the much smaller mates are often eaten, which is how the black widows earned their rather grisly name.

Latrodectus macatans

Where in the world:	From Northeast USA to Panama
Habitat:	Shady spots, in vegetation and leaf litter
Size:	Female up to 1.5cm (0.6in) long; male up to 5mm (0.2in)
Reproduction:	Eggs laid in silk egg sac
Life span:	Averages 2 years
Typical diet:	Insects and other spiders

Death Stalker Scorpion

T he aptly named death stalker is one of the deadliest species of scorpions known. Found mainly in dry, desert regions throughout the Mediterranean, Egypt, Israel and North Africa, this aggressive predator is a member of an ancient family that has been on Earth for 400 million years. Although scorpions are closely related to spiders, they are very different in appearance. In place of fangs, they have a barbed stinger in their tail, which is used to inject paralysing toxins into their prey. Two of their eight legs have been converted into powerful pincers for holding and crushing. They still have eight eyes, but only two are visible. The rest are so small that they are of little use for seeing. In fact, scorpions have poor eyesight and rely almost exclusively on touch-sensitive hairs on their legs to pick up vibrations in the air from prey or predators.

Leiurus quinquestriatus

Where in the world:	Southeast Europe; Arabia and North Africa
Habitat:	Arid desert environments
Size:	Up to 9cm (3.5in) long
Reproduction:	Gives birth to live young, which are carried on mother's back
Life span:	Averages 5 years
Typical diet:	Insects, mice and other scorpions

Dwarf Spider

Although it is not known exactly how many species of dwarf spider there are, nor how common each species may be, it is estimated that there are at least 4200 members of the family Linyphiidae. Coloration seems to depend on habitat and varies from pale yellow to black. The European *Floronia bucculenta* is able to change its colour at will to blend in with its surroundings. In Britain, dwarf spiders are commonly called money spiders because they are believed to be lucky. These tiny arachnids are mainly found in fields and open grassland, and often occur in plague numbers during late autumn in North America. If one area gets too crowded, however, this adventurous species simply takes to the air. By releasing thin strands of silk from its spinnerets and waiting for the breeze to pull them skywards, the dwarf spider is able to travel great distances.

Family Linyphiidae

Where in the world:	All over the world, excluding Arctic and Antarctic
Habitat:	Grasslands and gardens
Size:	Up to 7mm (0.3in) long, depending on species
Reproduction:	Eggs sacs are left in secluded spots to hatch
Life span:	Averages 1 year
Typical diet:	Small insects

Brown Recluse Spider

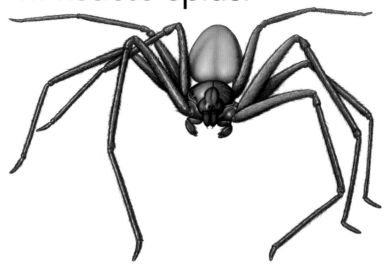

Spiders cannot chew their food, so they inject their victims with a complex cocktail of toxins. Some of these are designed to paralyse their prey; others act like stomach acids to break down the victim's flesh into a liquid sludge, which the spider can then suck up and digest. The brown recluse's toxin is especially potent. Its necrotic (flesh-destroying) properties mean that any human unlucky enough to be bitten may suffer a deep wound which, if untreated, can be fatal. The brown recluse is easy to identify because it has six eyes, arranged in pairs. Most US spider species have eight eyes, which are typically laid out in two rows of four at the front of the head. Many sources also mention the presence of a violin-shaped dark mark on the abdomen; however, this may not be present in young recluse spiders.

Loxosceles reclusa

Where in the world:	South Central USA
Habitat:	Dry shady spots in rural and urban areas
Size:	Body length 7–12mm (0.3–0.5in); leg span 2–5cm (1–2in)
Reproduction:	Lays up to 40 eggs in egg sac
Life span:	Up to 3 years
Typical diet:	Insects

Giant Whip Scorpion

Giant whip scorpions are not true scorpions. These dun-coloured arachnids actually belong to the order Uropygi, which contains 75 species. They do have a superficial resemblance to members of the order Scorpiones (scorpions), thanks mainly to their enlarged pedipalps, which look a little like a scorpion's pincers. Like whip spiders, these are flat-bodied creatures, with four pairs of legs, only three of which are used for walking. The first pair have become elongated and are used as 'feelers' to help the scorpion search for prey. Whip scorpions are also called 'vinegaroons' because they spray their victims with acetic acid, which is one of the ingredients of vinegar. They do this because they are unable to chew their food. Instead, they tear open their prey's flesh with their pedipalps, then the use acetic acid to break it down into a liquid form that they can digest.

Mastigoproctus giganteus

Where in the world:	Southwest USA to Northern Mexico
Habitat:	Dry arid regions
Size:	Up to 7.5cm (3in) long, excluding tail
Reproduction:	Eggs and young carried by mother
Life span:	Up to 4 years
Typical diet:	Insects, spiders, small rodents and frogs

Bolas Spider

Spiders can be classified according to whether or not they build webs – and what type of web they build. Black widows construct elaborate 'tangled webs', which are complex, layered traps. Orb weavers, such as the golden silk spider, create round webs, where threads of silk radiate out from the centre like the spokes of a wheel. Bolas spiders are considered to be orb-weavers, although they do not build true webs at all. Instead they create miniature, sticky balls of thread which hang from a line around 5cm (2in) long. When a meal is in sight, the bolas whirls this silken thread around and then, with perfect timing, releases it so that it hits the prey's body. The silk sticks fast, allowing the victim to be 'reeled' in. In the human world, a bolas is a Latin American weapon made of stones tied to the end of a long leather thong.

Mastophora, Cladomelea and other genera

Where in the world:	Africa; Asia; Australia and Central Latin America
Habitat:	Shady spots among the vegetation
Size:	Female 2cm (0.8in) long; male 5mm (0.2in), depending on species
Reproduction:	Eggs laid in silk egg sac
Life span:	Averages 3 years
Typical diet:	Moths and small invertebrates

Pirate Spider

There are roughly 200 species of pirate spider. These yellow-brown arachnids are also known as cannibal spiders, due to their preference for feeding on members of their own species. Members of the family Mimetidae are not web builders, and use other spider's webs when hunting. Their technique is to echo the movements of struggling prey. Some species will even mimic the courtship signals made by males to attract a mate. When the owner of the web comes to investigate these vibrations, this cunning predator captures, incapacitates and eats them. Members of the family Mimetidae are widespread, and make their homes in woodlands and grasslands all over the world. Part of the reason for this is that hatchlings are able to travel great distances by 'ballooning' – they spin fine silk threads, which are caught by the wind and carry the spider aloft.

Family Mimetidae

Where in the world:	All over the world, excluding Arctic and Antarctic
Habitat:	Woodland and grassland
Size:	2.5–7.5mm (0.1–0.3in) long, depending on species
Reproduction:	Female produces 3 cocoons, each containing around 8 eggs
Life span:	Unknown
Typical diet:	Spiders and spider eggs

Australian Mouse Spider

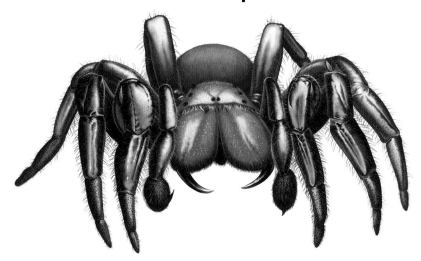

Thereare eight species of mouse spider in Australia. These are a widespread species, found in rural and urban environments. They are often confused with funnel-web spiders, and both are highly toxic. However, although they look similar, mouse spiders have a distinctly bulbous 'mousy' head, which may explain their common name. They also live in mouselike burrows, which they build with their powerful legs. These remarkable silk-lined constructions can be up to 55cm (21.7in) deep and provide the spiders with a safe refuge from predators and a place for the females to incubate and guard their eggs. These burrows also include two trapdoors, set at right angles to each other . These are designed to trap prey, which are then ambushed by the spiders waiting within. Mouse spiders have huge fangs, and these inject prey in a stabbing, downward movement.

Missulena species

Where in the world:	Mainland Australia
Habitat:	Adaptable; found in forest and arid regions
Size:	Body length up to 3cm (1.2in); leg span, up to 5cm (2in)
Reproduction:	Sexually mature at 6 years; eggs laid in underground burrows
Life span:	Females up to 20 years
Typical diet:	Small insects

Giant Orb Spider

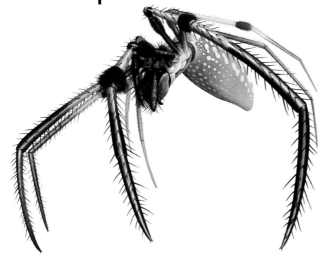

What makes the spiders of the *Nephila* genus so famous is not their great size, but the size of the webs they build. Orb spiders make the largest and strongest of all known webs. The golden orb (*Nephila maculata*) has been known to make spectacular golden traps as large as 6m (19.7ft) high and 2m (6.6ft) wide. These huge nets are designed to catch flying insects. They have even been known to catch small birds, although this is accidental and it is unlikely that the orb spiders intend to eat them. Unlike most webs, those of the giant orb are designed to last many years and are so strong that members of local tribes use them to fish with. Male orb spiders are many times smaller than the females and, in some instances, can live on the edges of her web, and may even remain undetected when mating with her.

Nephila species

Where in the world:	Tropical regions from Australia to Latin America
Habitat:	Primarily forest-dwellers
Size:	Female up to 5cm (2in) long. Males may be 1000 times smaller
Reproduction:	Silk egg sacs hidden in ground or web
Life span:	Averages 3 years
Typical diet:	Insects

Harvestman

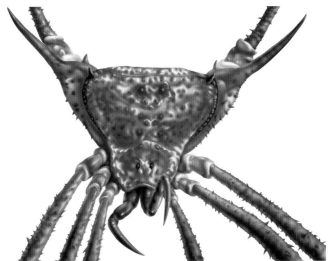

Harvestman may look like spiders, but they belong to the order Opiliones, which boasts around 5000 individual species. These vary in appearance and habits from region to region, although all of these curious arachnids share some physical similarities. They typically have four pairs of long, slender legs, a single pair of eyes at the front of their head (often raised) and elongated, segmented pedipalps. These may be so long that, should a Harvestman lose some of its legs, the pedipalps can be used in their place. Unlike spiders, which fertilize the female's eggs by transferring sperm to her body in their pedipalps, male Harvestman also have a penis. Their common name comes from their practice of gathering in large groups just before harvest time. Some Harvestman are mistakenly called 'daddy longlegs', a name which more accurately refers to the crane fly.

Order Opiliones

Where in the world:	All over the world, excluding Arctic and Antarctic
Habitat:	Adaptable
Size:	Body length up to 2cm (0.8in), depending on species
Reproduction:	Eggs laid in damp earth
Life span:	Averages 2 years
Typical diet:	Plants, invertebrates and carrion, depending on species

Emperor Scorpion

Despite its imposing title, the emperor scorpion is one of the more timid members of the scorpion family. When threatened, an emperor scorpion is more likely to barricade itself into its underground burrow – its pincers raised – than attack. They are, however, one of the largest species of scorpion and their impressive appearance, combined with their timid nature, has made them increasingly rare in the wild. Emperor scorpions are regularly sold to the pet trade, used as food or ground up to make traditional native medicines. As with all scorpions, emperors have poor eyesight and rely on touch-sensitive hairs on their claws to detect vibrations in the air from prey. With such large pincers, they have no need of powerful venom to subdue prey, as they are able to crush most small mammals and reptiles with ease.

Pandinus imperator

Where in the world:	West Africa
Habitat:	Adaptable; found in tropical rainforest to savannah
Size:	10–20cm (4–8in) long; up to 60g (2.1oz) in weight
Reproduction:	Give birth to up to 12 live young ('scorplings')
Life span:	Averages 8 years
Typical diet:	Insects, mice, small reptiles and other scorpions

Thick-tailed Scorpion

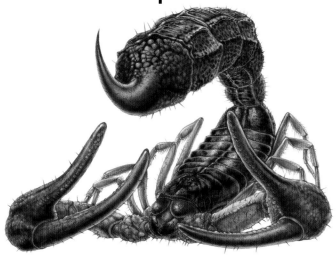

Thick-tailed scorpions belong to the phylum Arthropoda (anthropoid), class Arachnida (arachnid), order Scorpiones (scorpion). As with all arachnids, these powerful little predators are small but deadly opponents. Their body is divided into two sections. The front section is called the 'cephalothorax', which includes the head and chest (thorax). The hind part is called the 'abdomen'. At the end of the abdomen is a long, segmented tail, which contains two bulbous poison glands that feed into a hollow-tipped barb called a 'stinger'. Many of the toxins contained in their poison glands are designed simply to cause pain; however, at least two *Parabuthus* species have venom so potent that it can kill humans. This deadly species feeds mainly on invertebrates, but can kill mice and lizards, which it dissects with its powerful pincers.

Parabuthus species

Where in the world:	Southern and Eastern Africa
Habitat:	Savannah, grassland and desert
Size:	Up to 12cm (4.7in) long, depending on species
Reproduction:	Gives birth to live young, which are carried on mother's back
Life span:	Up to 6 years
Typical diet:	Invertebrates

Wolf Spider

All spiders are able to spin silk, which is drawn from silk glands via spinnerets on their abdomen. Many species use this to weave webs in which to trap prey, but hunting spiders, such as the wolf spider, do not make webs. These vagrant hunters stalk their prey and, when it is within reach, pounce. They use their silk for other nonlethal activities. The female wolf spider, for example, spins tough but lightweight sacks to protect her eggs, which she carries around with her until they hatch. Most wolf spiders are diurnal. This means that they are at their most active during the day, so they have well-developed vision. They also tend to be larger than other spiders, with powerful chelicerae, which are appendages located just above the spider's mouth opening, and are used to crush prey. All varieties of wolf spider are skilled, fast and powerful predators.

Pardosa species

Where in the world:	All over the world, excluding Arctic and Antarctic
Habitat:	Adaptable; found in a variety of habitats
Size:	Up to 1cm (0.4in) long, depending on species
Reproduction:	Eggs laid in egg sac
Life span:	Up to 2 years
Typical diet:	Small insects and invertebrates

Green Lynx Spider

Lynx spiders get their common name from the catlike way they pounce on prey. These skilled hunting spiders can jump up to 40 times their own body length, and will often leap into the air to catch flying insects. One of the exceptions is the American green lynx, which is a patient predator, preferring to lie in wait for prey, camouflaged among the green vegetation. However, not all of these attractive hunting spiders are grass-green. Some Californian species have yellow bodies, which allows them to blend in with the buckwheat fields where they make their home. Other species, which dwell in prickly pears (a cactus), have thornlike spikes on their legs. The green lynx's primary offensive weapons are its twin fangs, which it uses to inject toxin into its prey. When threatened, it is also capable of 'spraying' this venom at approaching predators, a little like a spitting cobra.

Peucetia species

Where in the world:	Australia; Asia; Africa; USA and Latin America
Habitat:	Bushes and low vegetation
Size:	Body length up to 2cm (0.8in); leg span up to 5cm (2in)
Reproduction:	Eggs laid in egg sac, which is guarded by female
Life span:	Up to 3 years
Typical diet:	Small insects

Brazilian Wandering Spider

This well-known species is fast and aggressive, has excellent eyesight and carries a deadly toxin. In the tropical rainforests, these attributes make this large arachnid a proficient hunter and a dangerous foe. As its common name implies, however, this widely travelled wanderer does not confine itself to the rainforest. It often turns up in homes in search of food, and has even made its way to Europe by stowing away on ships, although it cannot live for long in cold temperatures. If disturbed, the wandering spider's clawlike fangs act like pincers. These hollow needles are 4mm (0.2in) long and close against each other, which enables vast quantities of venom to be pumped into a victim. Brazilian wandering spiders have the largest venom glands of any spider, and a full dose is easily enough to kill any adult human unlucky enough to stumble across it in their home.

Phoneutria nigriventer

Where in the world:	Central Latin America; introduced to Europe and USA
Habitat:	Adaptable; found in rainforest and urban areas
Size:	Body length up to 3cm (1.2in); leg span 12cm (4.7in)
Reproduction:	Egg cocoons left under rocks
Life span:	10–15 years
Typical diet:	Large insects and small invertebrates

Indian Tiger Spider

Like all large, hairy tarantulas, tiger spiders are vagrant hunters. Rather than build webs, they actively seek out prey, relying on the touch-sensitive hairs on their legs to pick up vibrations from near-by animals. These large hunters make their homes in both rural and urban areas, although they are becoming increasingly rare in the wild. The reason is that tiger spiders are an especially attractive species and, despite their size, are relatively harmless to humans. They have therefore become very popular as pets. As nocturnal hunters, tigers spend much of the time hidden in small silk-lined tunnels. Young spiderlings may even share this refuge and have been known to hunt together in 'packs'. This spirit of cooperation lasts only as long as food is plentiful. In times of famine, baby tiger spiders will think nothing of making a meal of their brothers and sisters.

Poecilotheria species

Where in the world:	India and Sri Lanka
Habitat:	Primarily rainforest
Size:	Up to 22 cm (8.7in) long
Reproduction:	Eggs aid in underground burrows
Life span:	Females up to 15 years. Males average 5 years
Typical diet:	Inspects, small lizards and other spiders

Portia Spider

The 15 known species of Portia spider belong to the family Salticidae. This family group includes many species of jumping spider and mimic spider. Portias share both of these attributes. When hunting, they mimic dead leaves, creeping in slow, jerky motions towards their victims, as though they are being blown around by the wind. Once prey is in sight, they plunge forwards, fangs outstretched, to inject their fast-acting venom. A Portia's main diet is other spiders. They prey on species from as many as 11 different families, including other Portias. For each species, a different hunting technique is required, and Portias are skilled at learning and adapting. They may even mimic the sounds of struggling prey or courting males to entice their prey to come forward. Portias are found in Central Africa, Southeast Asia, New Guinea and Australia.

Portia species

Where in the world:	Central Africa; Southeast Asia; New Guinea and Australia
Habitat:	Primarily woodland and grassland
Size:	Up to 1cm (0.4in) long, depending on species
Reproduction:	Egg layers
Life span:	Averages 1 year
Typical diet:	Spiders

False Scorpion

In appearance, the 3300 members of the order Pseudoscorpiones look like miniature versions of full-grown scorpions, only lacking the characteristic tail and stinger. This adaptable order is well known for its tendency to hitch a lift on other species. They are rarely seen on their own, but can often be spotted on the backs of beetles, bugs and bees. This practice is called 'phoresy', and is one of the reasons why these tiny predators have become so widespread. Generally found amongst leaf litter and in damp vegetation, many of these 'pseudoscorpions' have also developed to live in specialized environments. *Neobisium maritimum*, for example, lives on the coast and avoids drowning at high tide by sealing itself in an airtight bubble. Pseudoscorpiones are also known as book scorpions, as they are often found among the pages of old books, where they feast on book lice.

Order Pseudoscorpiones

Where in the world:	All over the world, excluding Arctic and Antarctic
Habitat:	Highly adaptable, but prefer moist environments
Size:	1–7mm (0.03–0.3in) long
Reproduction:	Eggs incubated in silk nest
Life span:	Up to 4 years
Typical diet:	Small invertebrates

Jumping Spider

As their name suggests, the 5000 or so species of jumping spider are characterized by their tendency to pounce on their prey. They are able to do this because, compared to many spiders, they have superb eyesight. Their six small eyes are used primarily to judge distance and detect motion. The two enlarged, forward-facing eyes give the spider detailed images, which allow it to focus on prey, ready for attack. As diurnal hunters, good vision is vital, but it also plays an important part in mating rituals. Many species of jumping spider, especially those living in tropical regions, are brightly coloured, and this may help females identify the much smaller males. Jumping spiders are among the most intelligent spiders. Their brains, in proportion to their bodies, are large as a human's, and members of this family have shown themselves capable of puzzle-solving.

Family Salticidae

Where in the world:	All over the world, excluding Arctic and Antarctic
Habitat:	Adaptable; found in deserts and rainforest
Size:	4–10mm (0.2–0.4in) long, depending on species
Reproduction:	Eggs laid in silk sac, which is closely guarded
Life span:	Up to 3 years, depending on species
Typical diet:	Small insects

Scabies Mite

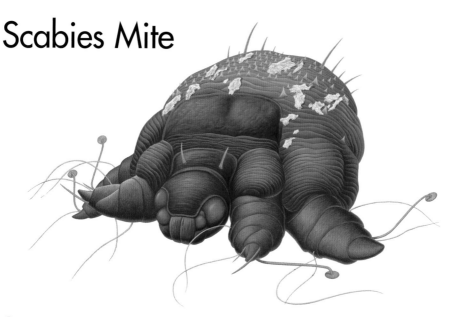

S cabies mites are parasitic – they get their nourishment by living off, or in, the body of a 'host' animal. This is usually harmful to the 'host'. The mites live in the 'subcutaneous' tissues of human skin. It takes around an hour for a pregnant female to burrow into the skin of her host. Here, she lays her eggs. Once hatched, larval mites dig their own burrows and remain beneath the skin until they begin to moult (shedding their skin in order to grow larger) and become adults. It is the faeces, saliva and mite corpses that cause an allergic reaction in the host. People afflicted with scabies typically develop red, itchy, scaly sores, which can cause serious infections if they are left untreated. Scabies is highly contagious, and close contact with an infected person is enough to spread scabies. Animals that are infected develop 'mange'.

Sarcopetes scabiei

Where in the world:	All over the world
Habitat:	Live on the skin of human hosts
Size:	0.20–0.45mm (0.008–0.02in) long
Reproduction:	Sexually mature at 10–20 days; lays up to 3 eggs per day
Life span:	Up to 60 days
Typical diet:	Dead skin

Spitting Spider

S pitting Spiders are nocturnal predators and have developed a unique method of hunting prey. All spiders have silk glands in their abdomen. When required, thin strands of silk can be drawn from these glands by up to three pairs of spinnerets, and used for everything from lining underground burrows to weaving eggs sacs. Spitting spiders have an enlarged cephalothorax, which is the combined head and middle body segment (thorax) of the arachnid. This houses additional silk glands, which are connected to its poison glands. Spitting spiders are extremely slow-moving, so, to capture a meal they spray their prey with a tangle of venomous silk. Spitting spiders are a widespread and adaptable species, which can be recognized by a distinctive 'leopard spot' pattern on their bodies. They count moths amongst their preferred prey, so are often a welcome addition in homes.

Scytodes thoracica

Where in the world:	All over the world, excluding Arctic and Antarctic
Habitat:	Typically beneath vegetation, but also in homes
Size:	Body length up to 8mm (0.3in); leg-span up to 12mm (0.5in)
Reproduction:	Female carries ball of eggs in jaws
Life span:	Averages 3 years
Typical diet:	Small insects

African Cave Spider

There are six known species of sicarius spider, which make their homes in Southern Africa. Of these, the cave spider – or six-eyed crab spider, as it is also known – is possibly one of the most toxic spider species in the world. Fortunately, *Sicarius hahnii* spends much of its life in secluded, sandy regions and is rarely encountered by humans. This shy spider is a genuine living fossil, the ancestors of which date back before the African and American landmasses separated. Similar species are therefore found in Latin America. The cave spider hunts by burying itself in the sand, with just its front legs uncovered. Here, it sits patiently and waits for prey to cross its path. Cave spiders will often make their homes close to antlion pits, where food is plentiful; however, if they need to, they can go without food and water for an entire year.

Sicarius hahnii

Where in the world:	Southern Africa
Habitat:	Dry, shady areas especially sandy caves
Size:	Body length up to 1.5cm (0.6in) long; leg span up to 5cm (2in)
Reproduction:	Eggs laid in cup-shaped egg sac, which is buried in sand to incubate
Life span:	Averages 12 years
Typical diet:	Small insects

Wind Spider

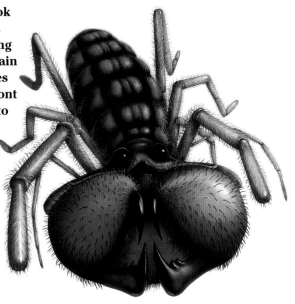

Solpugids, or wind spiders, may look like true spiders, but they are not. These straw-coloured arachnids belong to their own order – Solifugae. The main difference is that these ancient species run on six legs. The remaining two front legs have become adapted as feelers to detect prey. Their pedipali are greatly enlarged and much longer than their fourth pair of legs. There are around 1000 species of Solpugid, which are also known as camel spiders, thanks to an Arabian legend which credits them with being able to kill a camel with one bite. Although they have oversize and very powerful jaws, they do not have any poison glands. Their skill as hunters depends entirely on the incredible speed at which they move. Most Solpugids are nocturnal, but this is a widespread and adaptable order that has been introduced into many new environments as an ecofriendly means of pest control.

Solifugae Order

Where in the world:	Africa; Asia; Arabia; Southern USA; Central Latin America
Habitat:	Woodland, savannah and desert regions
Size:	2.5–7.5cm (1–3in) long, depending on species
Reproduction:	Lays 20–200 eggs in an underground burrow
Life span:	Averages 1 year
Typical diet:	Insects, small lizards and rodents, depending on species

Common House Spider

Fine sheets of silken web in the corner of a room mean that there is probably a house spider on the prowl. Some of Europe's largest spiders make their homes in our homes. *Tegenaria gigantea* can grow up to 10cm (4in) long, including its legs. Fortunately, for anyone who suffers from arachnophobia (a fear of spiders), the *Tegenaria domestica*, or common house spider, is one of the smaller and least active members of the species. The larger, long-legged females spend much of their time in the corner of their web, waiting for a meal. These triangular constructions are not sticky, but instead net their prey by entangling them in a mass of thin, silken threads. Males are more likely to be found 'wandering', especially during the summer months when they are busy searching for a potential mate. Male and females will share a web and their food while breeding.

Tegenaria domestica

Where in the world:	All over the world, excluding Arctic and Antarctic
Habitat:	Buildings and shady, secluded spots
Size:	Female body to 2cm (0.8in); leg span to 8cm (3.2in). Males smaller
Reproduction:	Egg layers
Life span:	Averages 3 years
Typical diet:	Flies and small insects

Crab Spider

Crab spiders are skilled ambush hunters. While many spiders spin webs to trap a meal, or actively hunt down prey, crabs are patient predators. These slow-moving arachnids spend much of their time hidden in leaves or flowers. Naturally, they come in such wide variety of colours that species identification is difficult. This is further hampered by the fact that they can change their skin colour to blend with their surroundings, although this may take many days. Once hidden, the crab spider will anchor itself in place, using its four back legs to grip the vegetation. Its remaining legs are longer than the rest and kept spread apart, ready to close on any prey that comes close. Crab spiders use their small hollow fangs to inject a powerful paralysing toxin, which means that their victims can be immobilized without the need of a web.

Family Thomisidae

Where in the world:	Tropical and temperate regions
Habitat:	Among vegetation, especially in flowers
Size:	Up to 1.4cm (0.6in) long, depending on species
Reproduction:	Eggs laid in silken sac, which is hidden in vegetation
Life span:	Averages 1 year
Typical diet:	Bees, butterflies and other spiders

Chigger Mite

These microscopic creatures begin their lives in damp soil and vegetation, where the female lays her eggs. Once hatched, the young larvae will find a 'host', attaching themselves to it and feeding off it – almost any passing animal will do. Using their sawlike chelicerae (modified food-eating claws), they penetrate the host's skin and begin to eat the dead tissue, which is rich in protein. They eventually work their way to the 'live' layers, which is when skin rashes and irritations set in. Once they have sated their appetites, the larvae drop off the host and moult. It is unknown how many species of chiggers there are, but these tiny parasites are well known throughout the world by a variety of common names, such as harvest lice or red bugs. Few species of chigger can live on humans, but those that do carry deadly diseases such as tsutsugamushi fever.

Trombicula & Eutrombicula species

Where in the world:	All over the world, excluding Arctic and Antarctic
Habitat:	Primarily warm, damp regions with thick vegetation
Size:	Less than 0.25mm (0.01in) long
Reproduction:	Lays eggs in damp soil
Life span:	Averages 2 months
Typical diet:	Animal skin

Death's Head Hawk Moth

The death's head moth belongs to the family of hawk moths known as Sphingidae. There are approximately 1100 species of hawk moth, of which the death's head is one of the most easily recognizable. On the top of its thorax is the famous 'death's head' skull pattern, which earned the moth a reputation in the Middle Ages as a bringer of death and bad fortune. Its forewings have a barklike patternation, but its hind wings and abdomen are designed to mimic the coloration of the queen honey bee. This large, elongated, moth's favourite food is honey, and, by carrying markings similar to the queen, it is able to enter the beehive without the soldier bees attacking. Once inside, it drinks its fill of sweet honey, using its long proboscis to suck up as much of the calorie-rich food as it can.

Acherontia atropos

Where in the world:	North Africa (excluding desert) and Southern Europe
Habitat:	Adaptable; wherever host plants are found
Size:	4–5cm (1.6–2in) long
Reproduction:	Lays up to 150 eggs
Life span:	Up to 6 months
Typical diet:	Larvae: leaves. Adults: honey, nectar and tree sap

Hawker Dragonfly

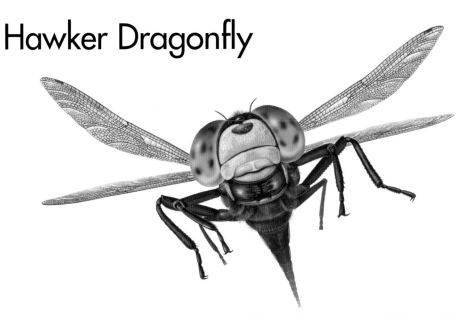

Hawker dragonflies are also known as darners in some parts of Europe. This strange common name is due to a folk tale which claims that they sew up children's lips during the night. The 420 known members of the family Aeshnidae include some of the largest species of dragonfly. These attractive and delicate-looking insects are typically blue, green or yellow, with bold black markings. They have exceptionally large eyes, which are comprised of more than 28,000 lenses. This gives them excellent vision. They are also accomplished aerial acrobats, which are able to drop, twist and turn in the air at speeds of up to 40km/h (24.9 mph). These attributes make them fearsome hunters. Larvae eat small fish and tadpoles, but adult dragonflies prey primarily on flying insects. This often includes prey much larger than itself, such as bees and wasps.

Family Aeshnidae

Where in the world:	All over the world, excluding the Arctic and Antarctic
Habitat:	Near still, freshwater ponds and streams
Size:	6–14cm (2.4–5.5in) long, depending on species
Reproduction:	Lays eggs on water plants
Life span:	Averages 3 years
Typical diet:	Larvae: insects, small fish and tadpoles. Adults: insects

Sand Wasp

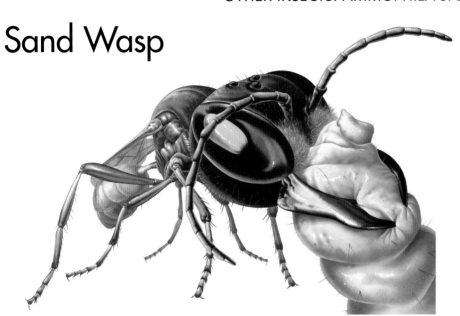

S and wasps belong to a group of insects which are known as digger wasps (family Sphecidae). In contrast to social insects such as paper wasps, which live in large colonies, sand wasps are a solitary hunters. Once a female has mated, she generally digs a nest in the soil, although some species also burrow into rotting wood or plant roots. She then begins to stock her larder with paralysed but still living food. This is usually a caterpillar or grub. The female will bury one or more grubs together with her eggs, so that when the newly hatched larvae emerge they have a ready supply of fresh food on which to feast. Some species continue to bring their rapidly growing young fresh food at regular intervals. Sand wasps can be found all over the world, excluding the coldest regions, although they prefer arid, sandy habitats.

Ammophila species

Where in the world:	All over the world, excluding the coldest regions
Habitat:	Dry, sandy regions
Size:	1.5–3.5cm (0.6–1.4in) long
Reproduction:	Eggs laid in live larvae
Life span:	Up to 6 months
Typical diet:	Larvae: grubs. Adults: nectar

Florida Walking-Stick

The Florida walking-stick is a stick insect of the family Phasmatidae, which boasts around 2450 individual species. These amazing-looking insects are examples of natural camouflage taken to the extreme. Like other members of its family, the Florida walking-stick is designed to resemble the twigs of a tree. Its body is extremely long and thin, with yellow and brown stripes running down the length. These allow it to blend in with its surroundings. The Florida walking-stick has many other common names, including the two-striped walking-stick, the palmetto walking-stick and the musk mare. This final name is particularly appropriate because *Anisomorpha buprestoides* sprays a foul-smelling chemical cocktail at its enemies. This fluid, which burns the skin and irritates the eyes, is directed at potential aggressors from a pair of jets on top of the insect's thorax.

Anisomorpha buprestoides

Where in the world:	Gulf of Mexico
Habitat:	Trees and shrubs
Size:	5.5–8cm (2.2–3.2in) long; antennae as long as the body
Reproduction:	Eggs, which look like seeds, laid on ground
Life span:	Unknown
Typical diet:	Tree leaves, especially oak

Malarial Mosquito

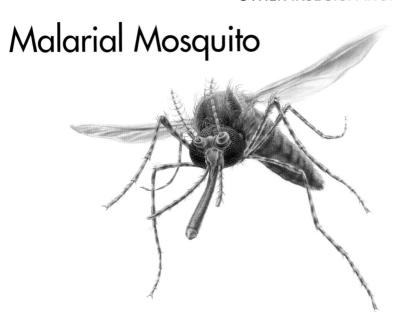

Mosquito is a Spanish word that means 'little fly', and this is exactly what mosquitoes are. There are around 3100 known species, of which members of the genus *Anopheles* are the most dangerous. These are the species that carry malaria and a host of other potentially fatal diseases, including yellow fever. Female malarial mosquitoes feed on blood, by inserting their sharp snout into their victim's skin, like a hypodermic syringe. They inject saliva into the wound to prevent the blood from congealing, which makes it easier to feed. It is this saliva which carries disease. Once a mosquito has fed on someone with malaria, it will pass the infection on to its next victim. Only female malarial mosquitoes drink blood, as they need this rich food source to nourish their eggs. Male malarial mosquitoes feed exclusively on nectar.

Anopheles species

Where in the world:	Tropical regions
Habitat:	Warm, damp areas, such as swamp land
Size:	Up to 6mm (0.2in) long
Reproduction:	Up to 300 eggs laid
Life span:	Females: up to 1 month
Typical diet:	Females: blood. Males: nectar

Killer Bee

Killer bees look similar to the European honey bee. These furry brown bees have distinctive black stripes on their abdomen, two large bulbous compound eyes and a stinger in their tail. Yet their history is very different. They were developed by selective breeding in Brazil in 1956 by geneticist Warwick Kerr. The Brazilian government wanted to increase its production of honey and, as African bees produce around four times more honey per hive than the European variety, queens were brought from South Africa to Brazil. In 1957, around 26 of these 'modified' bees escaped and interbred with local species. They have since proved to be a particularly aggressive species. Their sting is less potent than that of the European honey bee, but they attack en masse and will determinedly pursue any intruders. Killer bees are also known as 'the Africanized honeybee'.

Apis mellifera scutellata

Where in the world:	Southern Africa; introduced to Latin America and Southern USA
Habitat:	Adaptable
Size:	Queen: up to 2cm (0.8in) long. Worker: up to 1.5cm (0.6in)
Reproduction:	Queen lays eggs all year round
Life span:	Queen: up to 5 years
Typical diet:	Nectar and pollen

Tiger Moth

Tiger moths are among the most attractive members of the order Lepodoptera. However, their bright colours – reds, oranges and yellows – are more than just aesthetically pleasing. They warn predators that they are poisonous. Like many species, Tiger moth larvae feed on toxic plants and are able to absorb their poisons for their own defence. When these hairy caterpillar larvae (known as 'woolly bears') pupate, these toxins are often retained by the adult moth. Some species, such as the foaming tiger moth (*Amerila crokeri*), even produce a bubbling toxic foam and use this to cover their bodies when in danger. Bats are a tiger moth's biggest enemy. If poison does not deter, members of the family Arctiidae have an additional defence mechanism. They are able to detect the sounds made by hunting bats and block them with noise-producing organs in their abdomens.

Family Arctiidae

Where in the world:	All over the world, excluding the Antarctic
Habitat:	Adaptable
Size:	2–7cm (0.8–2.8in) long, depending on species
Reproduction:	Eggs laid on vegetation
Life span:	Averages 1 year
Typical diet:	Larvae: plants. Adults: nectar

Robber Fly

Robber flies belong to a diverse group of insects which have adapted to a broad range of habitats. Many members of this 5000-strong family feed exclusively on just one species. Some have evolved to look similar to their prey, in order to get closer to them while hunting, while others are opportunists, eating whatever food comes their way. Robber flies typically have long, tapered bodies, large eyes, a visible divot on the top of their head and long, bristly legs. Both larvae and adults are voracious hunters. The former, which live and pupate in the soil, feed on eggs and the larvae of other insects. The latter specializes in plucking small insects out of the air. These are quickly immobilized with an injection of chemical cocktails that paralyses their prey and breaks down its flesh into a liquid meal.

Family Asilidae

Where in the world:	All over the world, excluding coldest regions
Habitat:	Adaptable, but especially on dry, sandy grasslands
Size:	3mm–3cm (0.1–1.2in) long, depending on species
Reproduction:	Eggs laid in soil or under leaf litter
Life span:	Up to 3 years
Typical diet:	Larvae: grubs. Adults: insects

German Cockroach

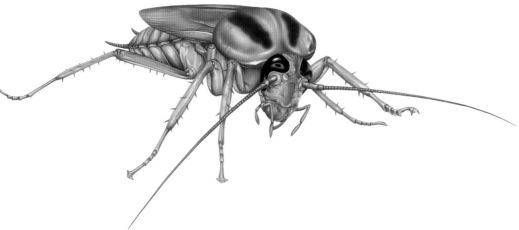

G erman cockroaches belong to the family Blattellidae, while common cockroaches belong to the family Blattidae. It is the German variety which has given the other species of cockroach such a bad name. *Blattella germanica* make their homes in our homes. In fact, studies have shown that they cannot survive in areas without human activity, probably because they rely exclusively on humans for their food. The German cockroach's life cycle is very fast. From egg, to nymph, to adult takes around 100 days, and females will breed continuously if conditions are right – a warm, moist environment with plentiful food. This means that a cockroach infestation can reach plague proportions extremely quickly. This is a real problem in densely populated urban areas, as these adaptable insects also spread diseases such as asthma, skin rashes and gastroenteritis.

Blattella germanica

Where in the world:	All over the world, excluding the coldest regions
Habitat:	Wherever there is human habitation; preferably warm and moist
Size:	1–1.5cm (0.4–0.6in) long
Reproduction:	Eggs carried in egg case (ootheca) until they are due to hatch
Life span:	Up to 2 years
Typical diet:	Almost any organic or inorganic matter

Bluebottle

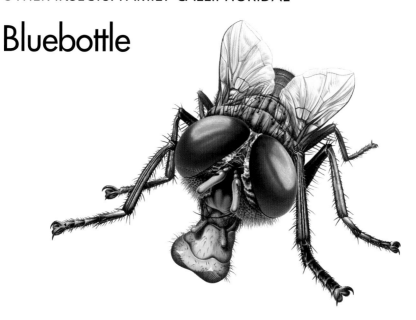

There are around 1200 known species of bluebottles, which are also known as blow flies. These familiar insects are larger than the common house fly. Their bodies have a blue-ish sheen, with a bristly thorax and two large, prominent wings. Bluebottles are excellent fliers, thanks in part to a pair of sticklike organs, which replace the hind wings. These organs, called 'halteres', contain sensors that help the bluebottle to fly straight and steady. Bluebottles lay their eggs on rotten meat (including corpses), human excrement and occasionally live animals, which form the diet of the growing maggot larvae. Adult bluebottles continue to feed on the same food sources that they were fed when young, but supplement this with nectar and any sweet foodstuffs. A bluebottle may go directly from a meal of rotting flesh to snacking on a doughnut, which is how they spread disease.

Family Calliphoridae

Where in the world:	All over the world
Habitat:	Adaptable
Size:	Up to 1.5cm (0.6in) long
Reproduction:	Eggs laid on meat
Life span:	Up to 1 month
Typical diet:	Larvae: rotting meat and dung. Adults: nectar and rotting meat

Puss Moth

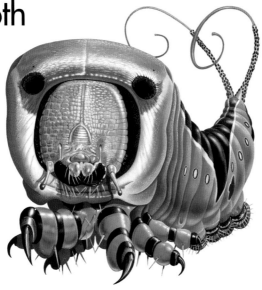

The puss moth is one of the most distinctive and attractive members of the 3000-strong family Notodontidae. These large, hairy insects have a bulbous, furry abdomen, greyish zigzag markings on their wings and furlike scales over their head. It is this 'fur' which is responsible for the moth's common name – at rest, it could easily be mistaken for a small cat. In its larval caterpillar stage, the puss moth is quite different in appearance. Puss moth larvae are flightless and usually slow-moving, which makes them vulnerable to predators, so as a result they use intimidation to scare away hunters. Green in colour, with large false eye spots and bright red heads, these large larvae are a frightful sight. Nor is their threatening appearance all bluff. They also have two whiplike tails, and can spray predators with formic acid from glands in their 'necks'.

Cerura vinula

Where in the world:	Across Europe into Siberia
Habitat:	In trees, especially aspen, poplar and willow
Size:	Adult wing span up to 7cm (2.8in) long
Reproduction:	Eggs laid on leaves
Life span:	Up to 16 months
Typical diet:	Leaves of aspen, poplar and willow

Cuckoo Wasp

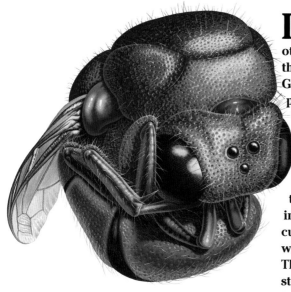

In common with the infamous cuckoo bird, female cuckoo wasps rely on others to raise their young. They lay their eggs in the nests of other wasps. Generally, they secrete just one egg per nest, leaving the unsuspecting surrogate mother to provide the food for their larvae. Many species of wasp seal their eggs up with a supply of fresh food for the emerging young to eat, so the mother is unlikely to notice the presence of the cuckoo invader. There are three distinct types of cuckoo wasp. The first are 'parasitoids', which feed on the larvae of the host. The second are 'klepto-parasites', which steal the food intended for the host's larvae. The third eat both the food and host larvae. Cuckoo wasps are a brilliant metallic green, blue or red colour, which has earned them the names gold wasp, ruby wasp and jewel wasp.

Family Chrysididae

Where in the world:	All over the world, excluding the Arctic and Antarctic
Habitat:	Wherever hosts are found
Size:	Up to 2cm (0.8in) long, depending on species
Reproduction:	Lays eggs in other wasps' nests
Life span:	Unknown
Typical diet:	Larvae: wasp grubs. Adults: nectar

Common Lacewing

Common lacewings belong to the family Chrysopidae, which includes around 1600 species. Most of these delicate, four-winged insects are a pale green in colour, with large, golden eyes and long antennae. A few species are brown. As adults, lacewings feed mainly on plant sap, but their larvae are voracious hunters. Females may lay several batches of eggs through the spring and summer. These hatch into the grey-brown larvae, which have well-developed pincers for subduing prey. The larvae's favourite food are aphids, and females usually lay their eggs where there is a good supply. From larvae to adult, there are three stages (called 'instars'), during which the rapidly growing young insect sheds its skin in order to grow larger. On the third stage, the larvae cocoons itself in a parchment-like roll of silk while it pupates. After five days, the adult – complete with wings – emerges.

Family Chrysopidae

Where in the world:	Everywhere, excluding New Zealand and the far north
Habitat:	Wherever there are aphids
Size:	1–5cm (0.4–2in) long, depending on species
Reproduction:	Lays 100s of stalked eggs among vegetation in spring
Life span:	Averages 3 months
Typical diet:	Larvae: insects. Adults: plant sap and insects

Cicada

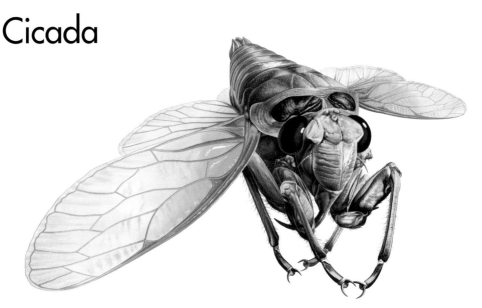

There are 2500 species of cicada, which live in the world's warmer regions. Cicadas vary in size, from an average of 2cm (0.8in) to the massive Malaysian empress cicada (*Pomponia imperatoria*), which grows up to 20cm (8in) long. They also come in a range of colours, which allows this four-winged insect to blend with its surroundings. Despite these physical differences, all species are known for their loud buzzes and chirrups, which they use to defend territory and attract a mate. The 'song' of the cicada emanates from a pair of plates in the abdomen, called 'tymbals'. These are housed in a large air chamber and held on a ring of muscle. As the muscle is flexed, these plates vibrate to produce sounds which are then amplified in the air chamber. The result is so loud that a cicada in search of a mate can be heard over a distance of 500m (1640ft).

Family Cicadidae

Where in the world:	Warm regions
Habitat:	Shrubs and trees
Size:	2.5–5.5cm (1–2.2in) long, depending on species
Reproduction:	Eggs laid in leaves
Life span:	Up to 17 years
Typical diet:	Tree and plant sap

Hickory-horned Devil

The hickory-horned devil is the larvae of the regal moth, which belongs to the family Saturniidae. Saturniid moths are also known as moon or atlas moths. This huge, horned, spiky green caterpillar starts its life as a tiny egg, which the female moth lays, in small clusters of two or three, underneath a leaf. When it is born, the hickory-horned devil is small and brown, but it changes colour as it matures. Fully grown horned devils may be larger than the adult moth. Huge spikes and 10 reddish-orange horns on its head provide this bouncing baby with much needed protection from predators. At the end of the year, the fully grown caterpillar falls to the ground, where it burrows underground to pupate. It may take as much as two years for the beautiful, orange-striped adult regal moth to finally emerge from its cocoon.

Citheronia regalis

Where in the world:	Eastern USA
Habitat:	Wooded areas
Size:	Up to 17cm (6.7in) long
Reproduction:	Up to 3 eggs laid underneath leaves
Life span:	Averages 1 year
Typical diet:	Tree leaves, especially hickory

Thick-headed Fly

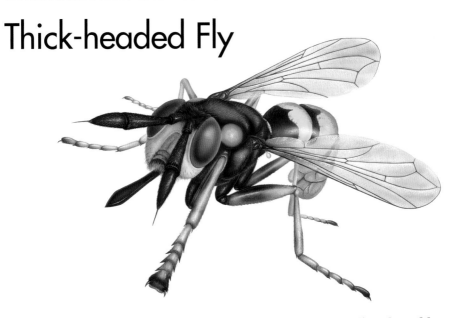

Thick-headed flies can be found all over the world, excluding the coldest regions. Adults of the species feed on nectar, but they still need a plentiful supply of insects on which to lay their eggs. They are therefore typically found in warm, dry regions where there are both flowers and the insects that they attract. These distinctive, two-winged flies have large, bulbous heads, a long proboscis and prominent, yellow compound eyes. Their antennae are usually short and flat, with a tapered tip. Many species of thick-headed flies have evolved to resemble the insects in which they lay their eggs (and which the larvae eat, from the inside, once they hatch). Some, for example, have narrow 'waists' and yellow and black stripes on their abdomen to resemble a wasp. Such coloration not only gives them protection from predators, but also allows them to get close to their prey.

Family Conopidae

Where in the world:	All over the world, excluding the coldest regions
Habitat:	Dry regions where food is plentiful
Size:	3mm–2.6cm (0.1–1in) long, depending on species
Reproduction:	Eggs laid in bodies of live host insects
Life span:	Averages 1 month
Typical diet:	Larvae: insects. Adults: nectar and honeydew

Wart Biter Cricket

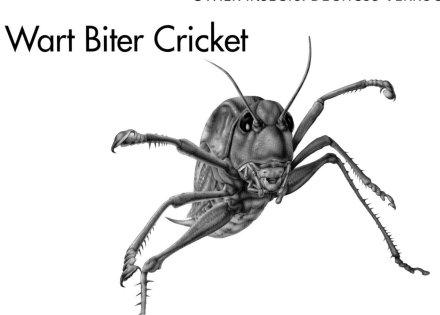

Wart biter crickets get their curious common name from an ancient belief that these large grassland dwellers could be used to bite off warts. This bizarre 'natural remedy' may even have been used in reality. It is true that wart biters do have extremely powerful and sharp mandibles, but these are used to tear through tough vegetation, rather than flesh. Wart biter crickets are increasingly rare in parts of Europe, due mainly to loss of habitat. When they hatch, these voracious eaters will spend several months feeding in their nymph form. Four moults are necessary before they finally transform into adults. This incomplete metamorphosis requires lots of grassland vegetation, and this is becoming increasingly scarce. Programmes to reintroduce this popular insect have been initiated in some parts of the UK, but the species is still a rare sight in Northern and Southern Europe.

Decticus verrucivorus

Where in the world:	Central Europe
Habitat:	Dry grasslands
Size:	Up to 4.5cm (1.8in) long; up to 2.5g (0.08oz) in weight
Reproduction:	Eggs laid in sandy soil
Life span:	Averages 6 months
Typical diet:	Any vegetable matter

Giant Weta

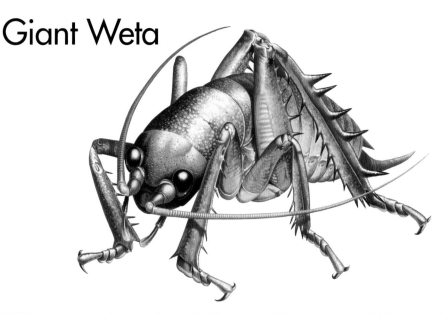

The name 'weta' comes from the Maori word 'wetapunga', which means 'God of ugly things'. There are 11 species of giant weta in New Zealand, most of which are now threatened with extinction due to the introduction of rats, cats and other non-native predatory species. Not all wetas are giants – the name is given to the species, regardless of size. Some, such as the Nelson alpine weta, weigh only an average of 7g (0.2oz). In contrast, the Little Barrier Island weta is one of the largest and heaviest arthropods in the world. Weta are generally shy herbivores, which spend much of the day hidden under rocks or among plant debris. Giant wetas take at least two years to become sexually mature. Once they are ready to breed, the female may lay up to 300 eggs. Both parents generally die before the young hatch.

Deinacrida species

Where in the world:	New Zealand
Habitat:	Under rocks and plant debris
Size:	Up to 10cm (4in) long; up to 50g (1.8oz) in weight
Reproduction:	Sexually mature at 2 years; lays 100–300 eggs
Life span:	Up to 3 years
Typical diet:	Leaves, ripe fruit and carrion

Stalk-eyed Fly

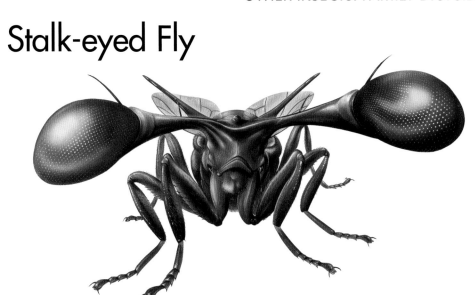

There are 180 species of stalk-eyed flies. These narrow-bodied, two-winged insects can be found primarily in tropical Africa and in parts of the Indian subcontinent. So far, only one species has been identified in the New World, and its range is restricted to a few states in Southern USA. Male stalk-eyed flies have their eyes on long, sticklike projections which can span up to 2cm (0.8in) from eye to eye. The purpose of these amazing features is to intimidate other males during the breeding season. The larger the eye stalks, the more likely the male is to win the right to mate. Furthermore, this process of 'selective breeding' ensures that only males with the longest eye stalks pass on their genes to the next generation. Female stalk-eyed flies lack these impressive 'ornaments', and look similar to many other species of fly.

Family Diopsidae

Where in the world:	Africa; Asia; Southern USA
Habitat:	Primarily rainforest, but also found on rice plants
Size:	3–20mm (0.1–0.8in) long, depending on species
Reproduction:	Eggs laid on foliage
Life span:	Up to 2 years
Typical diet:	Larvae: tree bark and plants. Adults: nectar

Giant Millipede

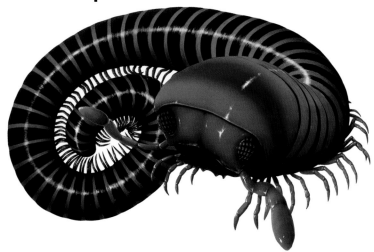

Millipedes belong to the class Diplopoda, which includes around 10,000 species. Not all of these widespread myriapods are, however, giants. They vary in size from 2mm (0.08in) to 30cm (12in) in length. This successful order can be found virtually all over the world, but the giants, which belong mainly to the family Spirostreptidae, originate in the tropics. These brightly coloured millipedes are surprisingly slow-moving, considering their legendary numbers of legs. They do not, of course, have a thousand legs (in Latin, 'milli' means a thousand and 'pede' legs) – just 100 to 400, depending on the species and their age. Unlike centipedes, which have one leg per body segment, giant millipedes have two. Millipedes generally have bad eyesight and, despite their size, make poor hunters. They feed instead on the organic matter contained in leaf litter or soil.

Class Diplopoda

Where in the world:	Giants found mainly in tropical regions
Habitat:	In soil
Size:	Up to 30cm (12in) long, depending on species
Reproduction:	Mate during rainy season; up to 300 eggs laid in underground burrow
Life span:	Up to 10 years
Typical diet:	Organic matter extracted from soil

Driver Ant

Army ants are fierce, nomadic hunters and live above ground. These predatory insects live in huge colonies. Within each are workers, soldiers and the queen. The workers feed and care for the queen and her young. Army ants found in Africa are known as driver ants, and their colonies can comprise 10–20 million workers. These massive groups need so much food that they are permanently on the move, so they have no permanent nest site. Instead, they form a mobile column. Inside are the queen and her young. Next come the workers, then the soldiers, which flank the column and protect it with their huge jaws. These ant columns can turn into an unstoppable, swarming mass, which clears entire swathes of forest of life. When columns rest at night, they create a living, protective sheet for the queen by grasping each others arms and legs. This temporary refuge is called a 'bivouac'.

Dorylus species

Where in the world:	Sub-Saharan Africa
Habitat:	Warm, moist regions, especially rainforest
Size:	Queen: up to 5cm (2in) long. Worker: up to 7mm (0.3in)
Reproduction:	Queen lays up to 300,000 eggs in a few days
Life span:	Unknown
Typical diet:	Any small insects, mammals and reptiles

Burchell's Army Ant

Army ants are fierce, nomadic hunters, which live above ground. Traditionally, Latin American army ants are called legionary ants. Burchell's ants are one of the best-known Latin American species. These predatory ants live in huge colonies. Within each are workers, soldiers and the queen. The workers, who are all blind, feed and care for the queen and her young. In place of a nest, they create a living, protective sheet by grasping each other's arms and legs. The soldiers, equipped with huge sickle-shaped jaws, forage for food. These colonies need so much to eat that they must constantly be on the move. However, once the young ants pupate and no longer need food, the ants will build a temporary nest, where the queen lays more eggs. After they hatch, in three weeks, the column sets off once more in search of food.

Eciton burchelli

Where in the world:	South and Central Latin America
Habitat:	Tropical and deciduous forests
Size:	Queen: up to 2.5cm (1in). Workers: up to 1.2cm (0.5in) long
Reproduction:	Queen lays 100,000–300,000 eggs
Life span:	Unknown
Typical diet:	Any small insects, mammals and reptiles

Dance Fly

Dance flies belong to the family Empididae, which contains around 3500 species. Within this group, members of the genus *Hilara* fly with a low, spiralling, bobbing motion, which makes it look like they are dancing. However, the name 'dance fly' is not exclusive to the *Hilara*. All members of this family perform elaborate acrobatics during the mating season. Male *Empis borealis* flies, for example, inflate their abdomens and stretch out their legs and wings to make themselves as big as possible, trying to impress a female. Others species perform elaborate aerial stunts before presenting their mate-to-be with a gift. A dead insect is an acceptable token, but some males wrap their offerings in leaves or cotton cocoons. Some, more cunning suitors, present empty leaves and cocoons, and mate with the female before she discovers the deception.

Family Empididae

Where in the world:	All over the world, excluding the Arctic and Antarctic
Habitat:	Woodland, marsh land and scrub
Size:	1.5mm–1.5cm (0.06–0.6in) long, depending on species
Reproduction:	Eggs laid in soil or in vegetable matter
Life span:	Unknown
Typical diet:	Small flying insects and nectar, depending on species

Ornate Mantis

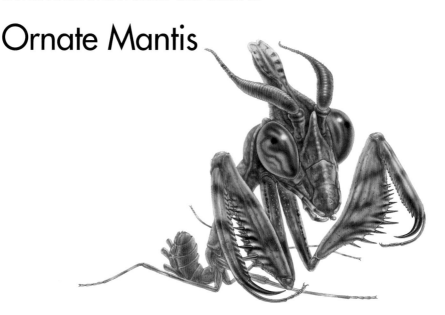

There are 2000 species of mantis in the order Mantodea. This includes around 30 members of the family Empusidae, which is found in warm, tropical regions across Africa, along the Mediterranean coast of Europe and into India. These elongated, insects typically have long, slender antennae, leaflike extensions on their abdomens and irregular growths on top of their heads. The mantis is a patient predator, which lies in wait for prey, using its natural camouflage to remain hidden until the last possible moment. It has excellent eyesight and is able to turn its head to look behind it. This enables it to stay almost immobile, yet still track the movements of prey precisely. Once a meal is within reach, it pounces, slamming its spiked forelegs closed on prey within a tenth of a second. Insects form the bulk of its diet, although the mantis has also been known to eat its own kind.

Family Empusidae

Where in the world:	Africa; the Mediterranean and Asia
Habitat:	On vegetation and among foliage
Size:	4.5–15cm (1.8–6in) long, depending on species
Reproduction:	Eggs laid in egg case
Life span:	Unknown
Typical diet:	Insects, including other mantis

Macleay's Spectre

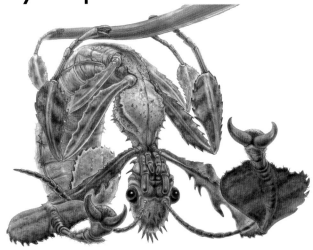

Macleay's spectre is a stick insect of the family Phasmatidae, which boasts around 2450 individual species. Around 150 species of these phasmids are natives of Australia. The family name comes from the Greek for phantom ('phasm'), due to the seemingly spectral ability of these highly camouflaged insects to appear and disappear among the foliage. Young Macleay's spectres start their lives inside ant's nests. The eggs of the species contain a nodule of nutrients, which ants find irresistible. They therefore carry the spectre's eggs back to their nests, eat the nodule and discard the rest. When the young nymphs hatch, they look and behave just like their ant hosts. Once they are able to find their way out of the nest, they begin to climb up into the tree canopy. Once safely among the foliage, they moult into the familiar form of the adult green or brown leaf mimic.

Extatosoma tiaratum

Where in the world:	Australia and New Guinea
Habitat:	Forest-dweller
Size:	Females: up to 12cm (4.7in) long. Males: up to 9cm (3.5in)
Reproduction:	Lays up to 12 eggs every day of adult life
Life span:	Females: up to 2 years. Males: averages 1 year
Typical diet:	Primarily eucalypt leaves

Common European Earwig

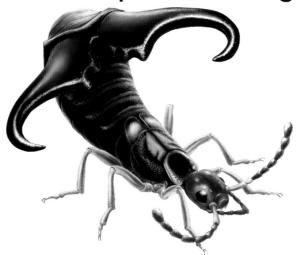

The name 'earwig' comes from the Old English 'earwicga', which means ear beetle. It used to be believed that these flat-bodied, reddish-brown insects would crawl into the ear of a sleeping human at night and lay their eggs in their brain. In reality, earwigs are totally harmless to people, although they may give a nasty nip if they are picked up. The common European earwig is the most widespread and numerous of the 450 species which make up the common earwig family, Forficulidae. Unlike most earwigs, the common European variety has two incomplete sets of wings, which makes them flightless. These are relatively slender insects, with a long and segmented antenna, which they use to 'taste' the air for food. At their rear are a pair of large pincers (these are curved in males), which can open and close.

Forficula auricularia

Where in the world:	All over the world, excluding the Arctic and Antarctic
Habitat:	Damp crevices, such as in wood piles or under stones
Size:	Up to 1.8cm (0.7in) long
Reproduction:	20–50 eggs laid in spring
Life span:	Averages 1 year
Typical diet:	Any organic matter

Pond Skater

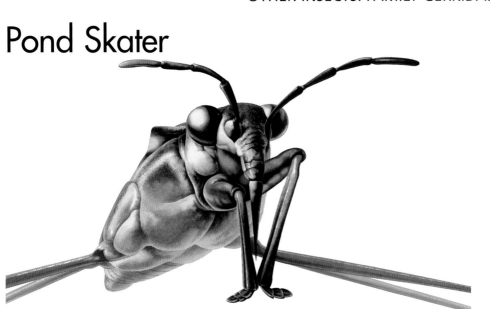

Pond skaters can be found all over the world, except in Antarctica. These small insects are typically dark in colour, with fine hairs on their bodies to repel water and six pairs of legs – two elongated legs at the rear, two smaller legs at the front and two in the middle. The molecules holding water together create a thin film. It is this film, known as 'surface tension', which the pond skater uses to support itself. When it wants to move across the water, it simply rows, using its middle pair of legs like oars, to propel itself forward at great speed. As it moves, the pond skater spreads out its long legs to redistribute its weight, so that it does not break through the water's surface. Its shorter legs are used to catch prey. Pond skaters are also known as water skimmers and water lopers.

Family Gerridae

Where in the world:	All over the world, except Antarctica
Habitat:	Still or slow-flowing water
Size:	0.2–3.5cm (0.08–1.4in) long, depending on species
Reproduction:	Eggs laid on submerged plants
Life span:	Up to 2 years
Typical diet:	Small insects

Tsetse Fly

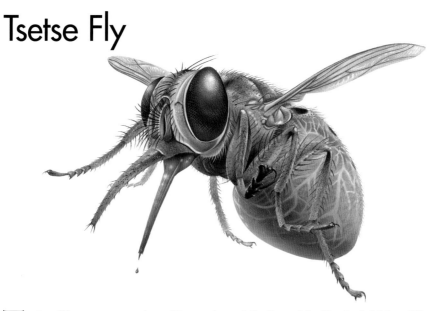

Tsetse flies are a species of two-winged fly found in Central Africa. There are around 22 known species of these stocky brownish insects, of which all but three carry parasites called trypanosomes, which cause sleeping sickness in humans and nagana in cattle. These diseases are spread in a similar way to malaria, in that an infected fly passes on the parasite when it feeds on the blood of its host. Unlike malarial mosquitoes, however, both male and female tsetse flies are blood drinkers, and both are capable of passing on infection. Tsetse flies breed slowly. The female produces one egg at a time, which hatches inside her body and is deposited on the ground when the larva is big enough to pupate. Despite this, they still present a serious health problem in much of Africa and attempts are ongoing to eradicate the species.

Glossina species

Where in the world:	Central Africa, excluding desert regions
Habitat:	Woodland and savannah
Size:	6mm–1.8cm (0.2–0.7in) long, depending on species
Reproduction:	Gives birth to a single, live young
Life span:	Up to 3 months
Typical diet:	Fresh blood

Madagascar Hissing Cockroach

Madagascan hissing cockroaches are wingless, ground-dwelling insects, which spend much of their time foraging for food among the leaves and organic debris on the forest floor. On every segment of this giant cockroach's body are a pair of openings, called 'spiracles'. During territorial disputes with other males, or when they are threatened by predators, the hissing cockroach squeezes air out of these spiracles. The remarkable 'hissing' sound they produce is so loud that it can be heard almost 4m (13.1ft) away. Female hissing cockroaches are devoted mothers and tend to their young for several months after birth. These young are white in colour until their outer exoskeleton hardens. Apart from this, they look like mini versions of their parents. Their exoskeletons cannot stretch, so they must moult several times as they grow, until they reach maturity, at around nine months.

Gromphadorhina portentosa

Where in the world:	Madagascar
Habitat:	Ground-dwellers; found among vegetation in tropical rainforests
Size:	2.8–7.5cm (1.1–3in) long
Reproduction:	Sexually mature at 9 months; gives birth to 30–60 live young
Life span:	Up to 5 years
Typical diet:	Fruit and fungi

Mole Cricket

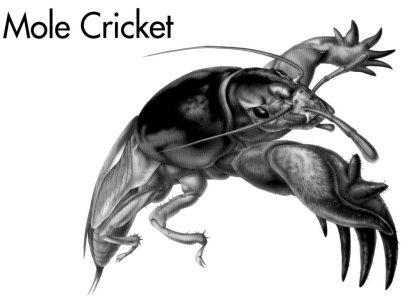

These brownish insects have many features in common with real moles. The most noticeable is the layer of fine hair over their bodies, which gives them a velvety appearance. They also have large, spadelike forelegs, used for digging through the soil. Mole crickets live in underground burrows, but also travel rapidly below the surface of the soil, by pushing a trail of dirt out behind them. Mated females lay their eggs in burrows, and the nymphs remain underground until they mature. There may be as many as 10 development stages (called 'instars') before the fully formed adult emerges. Most of the 20,000 members of the order Orthoptera, which includes grasshoppers and crickets, are famed for the 'songs' they produce by rubbing their forewings together. Mole crickets are no exception, and their burrows may even be designed to amplify the calls of the males.

Family Gryllotalpidae

Where in the world:	All over the world, excluding coldest regions
Habitat:	Primarily in damp soil
Size:	2–4.5cm (0.8–1.8in) long, depending on species
Reproduction:	Eggs laid in underground burrows
Life span:	Unknown
Typical diet:	Grass roots and insects

Armoured Ground Cricket

The armoured ground cricket is known by many different names: the armoured bush cricket, the gobabis prawn and the wheat cricket (or koringkriek). The last of these names refers to the cricket's habit of feeding off cereal crops, which has turned this spiky little insect into Public Enemy Number One in much of its native Africa. Female armoured ground crickets lay their eggs in small batches, during the summer, but these remain dormant until the wet season. This is exactly the same time that most farmers plant their crops. This ensures that its young have a fresh supply of vegetation to eat when they hatch. Young armoured ground crickets are voracious eaters. They are unable to fly, but swarms of newly hatched young can devastate a whole season's crops as they march across the savannah in search of a meal. They will even eat the bodies of other, dead armoured crickets.

Sub-Family Hetrodinae

Where in the world:	Africa, excluding desert regions
Habitat:	Anywhere there is abundant vegetation to feed their young
Size:	4–6cm (1.6–2.4in) long, depending on species
Reproduction:	15–30 eggs laid in foam 'pods'; these lie dormant until rain comes
Life span:	Up to 1 year
Typical diet:	Plants and carrion

Louse Fly

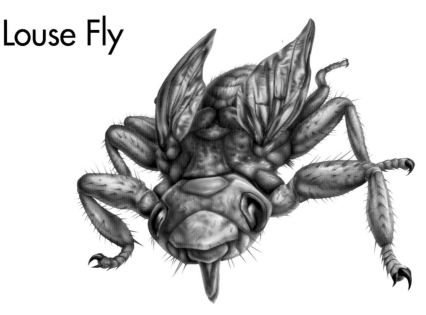

There are around 200 known species of louse flies belonging to the family Hippoboscidae. These stocky, armoured parasites are found all over the world – wherever there are suitable host animals. Most species live off feathered or furred hosts, but a few have also been known to bite humans. One of the most widespread is the sheep ked (*Melophagus ovinus*), which feeds off the blood of sheep. Female louse flies incubate their eggs inside their body and give birth to live young, which resemble white or yellow maggots. In some species, these larvae burrow into the ground to pupate, but others, such as sheep keds, pupate on the host's body, among the sheep's wool. Once they pupate, the louse flies take up residence on a suitable host. Their clawed feet are extremely powerful, which makes these blood sucking pests extremely hard to remove.

Family Hippoboscidae

Where in the world:	All over the world
Habitat:	Wherever there are host animals
Size:	0.2–12mm (0.008–0.5in) long, depending on species
Reproduction:	Gives birth to live young
Life span:	Up to 1 year, depending on species
Typical diet:	Fresh blood

Ichneumon Wasp

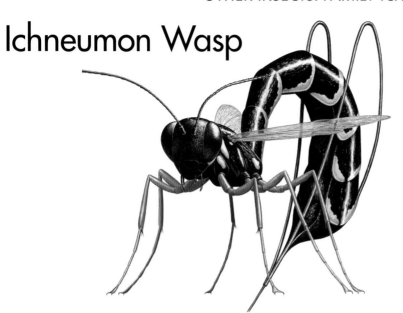

There are around **60,000** species of ichneumon wasp. These slender-bodied insects are 'parasitoids', which means that their young feed on the larvae of other species. These widespread wasps use their antennae to track down host larvae. The female then uses her long, tubelike 'ovipositor' to pierce the skin of the larvae and lay her eggs inside. These ovipositors are extremely tough, and can bore through wood to pierce the bodies of wood-dwelling grubs hidden inside. Females of species such as *Rhyssa persuasoria* have ovipositors, which are longer than their entire bodies, and tipped with manganese and zinc – a little like a precision-made drill. Some species lay their eggs on the skin of the larvae, but the result is the same. When the eggs hatch, the young ichneumon wasps eat their host. Adult wasps, in comparison, feed almost exclusively on plant nectar.

Family Icheumonidae

Where in the world:	All over the world, excluding the coldest regions
Habitat:	Adaptable; found wherever there are suitable hosts
Size:	0.3–4cm (0.1–1.6in) long, depending on species
Reproduction:	Lays eggs on or inside hosts
Life span:	Up to 3 years
Typical diet:	Larvae: beetle larvae. Adults: nectar

Dry Wood Termite

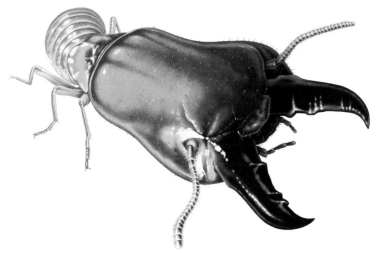

Termites, in common with ants, live in large, stratified and well-ordered colonies. These are headed by a reproductive pair – a king and queen. The workers are smaller in size, blind and sterile. They form the bulk of the termite colony and are responsible for feeding the rest of the community. The final 'caste' are the soldiers. These are also blind and sterile. It is the soldiers' job to protect the colony from predators, and they are ideally equipped for the job. These large ants have enormous heads and powerful jaws and forelegs. They are, however, unable to look after themselves and are cared for by the workers. Dry wood termites make their nests in dead wood. Their presence can often be detected by small piles of faecal pellets, which the worker termites kick out of the nest at regular intervals.

Family Kalotermitidae

Where in the world:	Tropical and subtropical regions
Habitat:	In wood
Size:	Queen: up to 2.2cm (0.9in) long. Worker: up to 2cm (0.8in)
Reproduction:	Reproductive king and queen mate; eggs laid in wood
Life span:	Worker: average 1 year. Queen and king: up to 50 years
Typical diet:	Wood

Firefly

There are around 2000 species of fireflies, which are also called lightning bugs. In reality, they are neither flies nor bugs, but a type of long, flat-bodied beetle. During the mating season, these spectacular insects use the light-emitting organ in their abdomen to make dramatic displays in the night sky to attract a mate. It is not just the brightness of the firefly's glow which impresses the female, but also the speed and complexity of his display. In some species, the females are wingless, so they watch the flashing display from nearby foliage, and signal their approval with flashes of their own. Firefly larvae are commonly called 'glow worms' because they share their parent's light-emitting abilities. As they have yet to grow wings, this would seem to make them an easy target for predators. However, the same chemicals which produce the appealing light show also make them taste terrible.

Family Lampyridae

Where in the world:	Temperate and tropical regions
Habitat:	Warm, damp environments such as riverbanks
Size:	0.5–3cm (0.2–1.2mm) long, depending on species
Reproduction:	Eggs laid in vegetation
Life span:	Averages 4 years
Typical diet:	Larvae: invertebrates. Adults: nectar

Silverfish

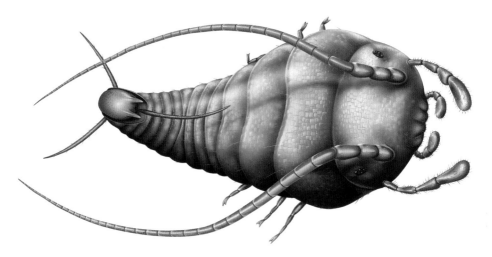

Silverfish belong to an ancient family of wingless insects whose ancestors date back more than 300 million years. It is believed that silverfish were one of the earliest insects to evolve and, remarkably, they have changed little over the millennia. Their common name refers to the silvery scales covering their flat bodies, combined with the swimming motion they use to move. Silverfish can be found all over the world, but, as their bodies cannot retain moisture, they favour damp, warm environments. Species can be found anywhere from tree canopies to birds nests, but the varieties that we are most familiar with are likely to be found near water sources, in kitchens and bathrooms. Silverfish are ametabolous, which means that young nymphs change into adults without any obvious metamorphosis. This is a trait that they share with their close relative, the bristletails.

Family Lepismatidae

Where in the world:	All over the world, except the Arctic and Antarctic
Habitat:	Adaptable
Size:	0.8–2cm (0.3–0.8in) long, depending on species
Reproduction:	Sperm deposited on ground to fertilize eggs
Life span:	Up to 5 years
Typical diet:	Almost anything organic

Common Praying Mantis

Common praying mantises get their name from the way they hold their spiked forelegs when at rest, which makes them look as if they are praying. This species belongs to the family Mantidae, most of which are found in areas of lush vegetation in the world's tropical and subtropical regions. European and Chinese species were introduced to the USA around 75 years ago in an attempt to control garden pests. These distinctive-looking insects are the favourite food of several species of bird and bat, so rely on camouflage for protection. Common mantises are generally green or brown, while flower mantises of the family Hymenopodidae are usually brightly coloured to blend in with the flowers on which they rest. For added protection, some species of mantis have a hollow chamber inside their bodies, which enables them to detect the ultrasound used by bats when hunting.

Family Mantidae

Where in the world:	Southern Europe; North Africa; introduced to USA
Habitat:	On vegetation where prey is plentiful
Size:	2–15cm (0.8–6in) long, depending on species
Reproduction:	Clusters of eggs laid in autumn; nymphs emerge following summer
Life span:	Up to 8 months
Typical diet:	Small insects, lizards or frogs, depending on species

Velvet Ant

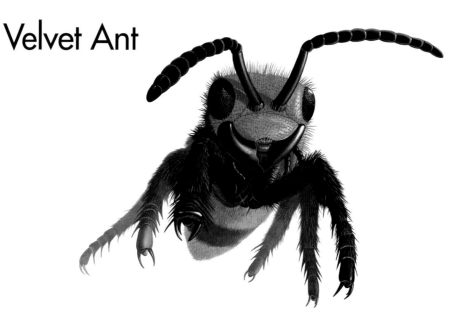

Velvet ants are a species of solitary hunting wasp. Their common name comes from the fact that the wingless females are covered in a fine, velvety fur and resemble ants. Males are more 'wasplike', with fully developed wings and bands of red or yellow hair on their black abdomens. Velvet ants are one of the most pernicious of predators. As adults, they live on a diet of nectar, but their larvae feed on the young of other wasps or bees. The female lays her eggs in the nests or burrows which other species have prepared for their own young. In some cases, the original occupant hatches and munches its way through the grub which has been left for it to feed on, and is then itself eaten. Female velvet ants have a powerful stinger, which farmers have claimed is capable of killing cattle – hence their other common name, cow-killer.

Family Mutillidae

Where in the world:	All over the world, excluding the coldest regions
Habitat:	Warm dry, sandy regions
Size:	0.3–3cm (0.1–1.2in) long, depending on species
Reproduction:	Lays eggs on the larvae of other wasps
Life span:	Unknown
Typical diet:	Larvae: grubs. Adults: nectar

Giant Bulldog Ant

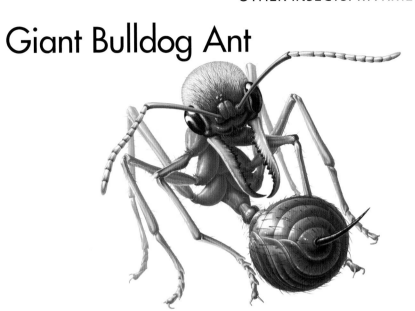

The giant bulldog ants of Australia belong to a primitive group that has a much less organized social structure than most other species of ant. Generally, ant colonies are highly stratified communities, with workers and soldiers all dedicated to protecting the queen and her young. Bulldog ant colonies, in comparison, are founded by a single queen, which tends and feeds her own young. The first brood to hatch are females; the second are males. These two groups form the basis for the next colonies. Bulldog ants are closely related to wasps and still have a stinger in their rear, which most species of ants have lost over time. They use this stinger, in conjunction with their large, serrated jaws, to subdue prey. Most other species of ant work together to find food, so do not need to be as large or aggressive.

Myrmecia species

Where in the world:	Australia, including Tasmania; New Guinea
Habitat:	All but the driest desert regions
Size:	Queen: 2.9cm (1.1in) long. Worker: 2.6cm (1in), depending on species
Reproduction:	Queen lays eggs all year round
Life span:	3–4 years
Typical diet:	Plants, small insects and nectar

Honeypot Ant

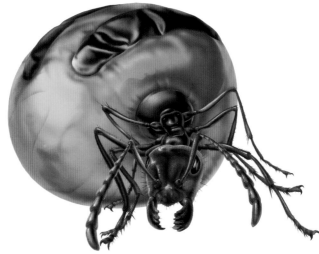

Honeypot ants have devised a remarkable way of surviving the dry season. They live on the fringes of some of the world's driest deserts – in Australia, South Africa, Mexico and Southern USA. Here, food can be scarce. So, immediately after the wet season, when plants in these arid regions temporarily bloom, the colony's largest workers (who are called 'repletes') turn into living storage units. The colony's workers gather in the dwindling reserves of plant nectar and 'empty' their supply into the repletes. As the repletes' abdomens swell up with food, they become so large that they are unable to move properly. They therefore attach themselves, upside-down, to the roof of special galleries within the colonies. When the fresh food starts to run out, other members of the colony visit these galleries to 'milk' the repletes, which keep the queen and her larvae fed during times of famine.

Myrmecocystus, Camponotus & other species

Where in the world:	Southern USA to Mexico; Australia; Southern Africa
Habitat:	Arid, semi-desert regions
Size:	Up to 1cm (0.4in) long, depending on species
Reproduction:	Queen lays eggs all year round
Life span:	Queen: up to 10 years. Worker: 2 months
Typical diet:	Plant nectar, honeydew and insect protein

Antlion

Antlion larvae are some of the most remarkable engineers in the insect kingdom. Soon after birth, the fat, hairy antlion begins to dig its first pit. This ingenious grub has three pairs of spiked legs, which are designed to hold it in place in the sand. This design means that the larvae can only walk backwards, so they must use their rear end like a plough, to dig down, in a circle, to create a funnel-shaped trap. This is where the antlion will spend the next three years, feeding on any insects that fall into the pit. It leaves its home only three times during this period to moult. Once they reach their adult form, antlions look like dragonflies. These delicate adults may live only a few weeks until they mate. This means that some species of mature antlion do not need to eat at all.

Family Myrmeleontidae

Where in the world:	Tropical and subtropical regions
Habitat:	Dry, sandy soil
Size:	Up to 4.5cm (1.8in) long, depending on species
Reproduction:	Eggs laid in soil or vegetation, depending on species
Life span:	Up to 3 years
Typical diet:	Larvae: insects and arachnids. Adults: plant sap or nothing at all

Damsel Bug

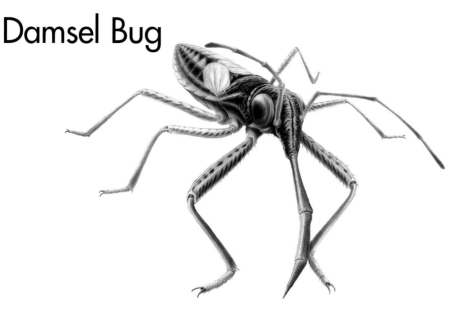

Damsel bugs belong to the family Nabidae. These varied insects can be found throughout Latin America, into the USA and Canada, and across Central Europe to Asia. They tend to be absent from colder northern extremes as well as desert regions, where low-lying vegetation is in short supply. Some species also make their homes among the trees and in swamp lands. Damsel bugs are mainly carnivores, who feed on small soft-bodied insects, especially aphids. However, they will eat members of their own species if food is scarce. A damsel bug's main offensive weaponry is its elongated, needle-like mouth parts, called 'stylets'. When the bug feeds, it uses its strong forelegs (called 'raptorial legs') to grip and hold prey while its mouth parts are injected into the victim's soft underbelly. At this point, the stylets begin to grind up the flesh to create an easily digested liquid meal.

Family Nabidae

Where in the world:	Latin America; USA; Central Europe into Asia
Habitat:	Low-lying vegetation
Size:	5–7mm (0.2–0.3in) long
Reproduction:	25–40 eggs laid; up to 3 broods a year
Life span:	Averages 5 months
Typical diet:	Small insects, especially aphids

Weaver Ant

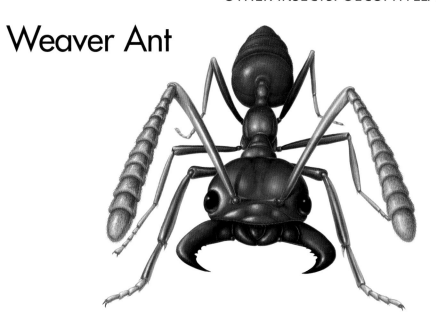

In common with many families of ants, weavers display a remarkable ability to utilize their environment. These ingenious ants build their nests out of living leaves. Working together, the ants form a chain along the edges of the leaf. Gradually, they remove one ant from the chain until the edges have been pulled together. They then squeeze one of their larvae so that it produces thin strands of silk. This is stronger than the silk produced by other species of ant larvae and acts like glue to seal the nest. A typical weaver ant colony may span a number of trees, with the queen safely hidden in one nest, and her workers in the others. Weaver ants have been used as a natural form of pest control in China since AD 300. This is so effective that they are now being introduced into many other regions.

Oecophylla species

Where in the world:	Old World tropics, from Africa to Indian subcontinent
Habitat:	Primarily rainforest
Size:	Up to 2cm (0.8in) long, depending on species
Reproduction:	Queen lays eggs all year round
Life span:	Queen: up to 5 years
Typical diet:	Insects and plant nectar

Bot Fly

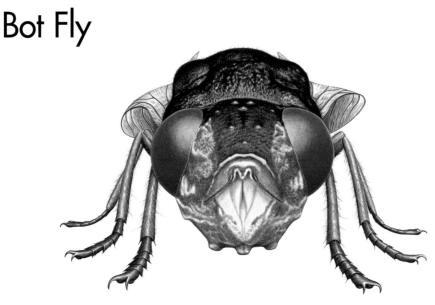

There are approximately 80 species of bot fly in the family Oestridae. These large, bluish insects are a species of parasitic insect that can be found all over the world, wherever there is a suitable host. Mammals such as rabbits, sheep and rats are the flies' usual targets, but the torsalo, or human bot fly (*Dermatobia hominis*) regularly lays its eggs on a human host. The flies' lifecycle begins with the female capturing a small insect, such as a mosquito. She lays her eggs on her tiny captive, then releases it. Once the mosquito lands on a warm body, the eggs begin to hatch and the maggot larvae quickly burrow into their host's flesh. They feed for around 10 weeks, until fully grown, when they fall to the ground to pupate. The fully developed adult bot fly emerges some weeks later.

Family Oestridae

Where in the world:	Tropical and subtropical regions
Habitat:	Wherever hosts can be found
Size:	Up to 2.5cm (1in), depending on species
Reproduction:	Lays eggs in live hosts
Life span:	Averages 1 year
Typical diet:	Body fluids of living animals

Common Scorpion Fly

Scorpion flies belong to the family Panorpidae. This large insect grouping has more than 360 members. These can be found in almost every part of the world, excluding desert and polar regions, although their preferred habitat is well-shaded vegetation. These are slow-moving insects that feed on nectar, fruit, or dead and dying insects, which are often 'stolen' from spiders' webs. Scorpion flies generally have long, elongated bodies and pointed, beaklike snouts. Females and males can be easily distinguished from one another, as the females have tapered abdomens, while in males the second or third segment of the abdomen is bulbous and can be curved over the body, in a similar way to a scorpion's tail stinger. Most species typically have broad white or brown bands across their wings. Common scorpion flies are often mistaken for crane flies, which usually have clear wings.

Family Panorpidae

Where in the world:	All over the world, excluding desert and polar regions
Habitat:	Among vegetation; prefers the shade
Size:	0.9–2.5cm (0.4–1in) long, depending on species
Reproduction:	Eggs laid in damp soil or on leaf litter
Life span:	Up to 2 years
Typical diet:	Larvae: leaves. Adults: Insects, fruit and nectar

Bullet Ant

In common with the Australian bulldog ant, the giant tropical bullet ant of Latin America has a fairly primitive social structure. There are no workers or soldiers to feed or protect the community. Instead, the relatively small colonies seem to divide labour on size. The smaller ants tend to act as nursemaids to care for the young, while the larger forage for food. The rapidly growing young will eat any scavenged animal matter, but adults prefer plants and nectar, which is brought back to the nest. Typically, nest sites can be found at the base of trees, where there is a ready supply of fallen matter, but occasionally the bullet ants venture into the tree tops, to occupy cavities in the trunk. Although not naturally aggressive, bullet ants have a large stinger, which packs a powerful enough punch to have earned them their common name.

Paraponera clabata

Where in the world:	Atlantic coast of Central Latin America
Habitat:	Rainforests.
Size:	Worker 1.8–2.5cm (0.7–1in) long
Reproduction:	Queen lays eggs all year round
Life span:	Unknown
Typical diet:	Larvae: animal matter. Adults: nectar

Human Louse

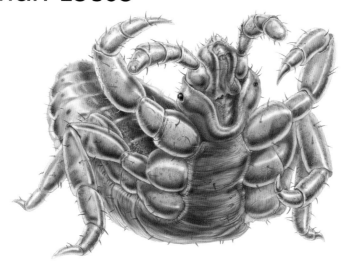

There are two species in the family Pediculidae. The most widespread is the human louse (*Pediculidae humanus*), of which there are two sub-species: head (*Pediculidae humanus capitis*) and body louse (*Pediculidae humanus corporis*). The second species is found only on apes. Body lice lay their eggs in the fibres of clothing, while head lice deposit their eggs (called 'nits') in hair. Both sub-species take around 20 days to develop from egg to adult. These tiny insects are parasites and feed on their host's blood. Head lice are common in children, as they can pass from head to head during any close contact. Despite the stigma of head lice, they are not attracted to dirty hair – in fact, exactly the opposite. Hair lice can be removed fairly easily with specialist shampoos. Body lice are more persistent and can transmit serious diseases such as typhus, relapsing fever and trench fever.

Family Pediculidae

Where in the world:	All over the world
Habitat:	Wherever there are human hosts
Size:	2–4mm (0.08–0.2in) long
Reproduction:	Lays up to 300 eggs
Life span:	Up to 4 weeks
Typical diet:	Fresh blood

Tarantula Hawk Wasp

The tarantula hawk wasp is the largest member of the 4000-strong family Pompilidae – the spider-hunters. Unlike social wasps which live in large colonies, these insects are solitary predators. Male and females live and hunt separately and come together only to breed. Once a female has mated, she goes in search of food. As the name suggests, this species hunts the large spiders known as tarantulas. Although female tarantulas spend much of their time in burrows (unlike the free-roaming males), they are larger and are therefore the preferred prey of the female wasp. Combats between the two can be fierce, but, once the tarantula rears up to bite, the wasp inserts her stinger. This paralyses the spider, which is then dragged to her nest, where an egg is laid on the captive's abdomen. When the eggs hatch, the emerging larvae feed on the still-living tarantula.

Pepsis species

Where in the world:	Latin America and USA
Habitat:	Warmer regions, from rainforest to open grasslands
Size:	Up to 8cm (3.2in) long, depending on species
Reproduction:	Egg laid on body of tarantula
Life span:	Up to 3 years
Typical diet:	Larvae: tarantula. Adults: nectar

Bee-Killer Wasp

These large insects are vegetarian as adults, but their young begin life in a cocoon of living flesh. The bee-killer, or wolf, wasp female is a skilled predator, using her sensitive antennae to 'taste' the air for prey. Bee-killers hunt only honey bees, so, once the identity of their victim has been confirmed, the female strikes. Using her powerful forelegs, she pins her victim down while she injects it with a paralysing toxin from her stinger (which is on her rear). Once the drug begins to take effect, the bee-killer takes to the air, with its victim clamped securely in place by her middle pair of legs. This fresh food supply is then dragged into the wasp's underground burrow. Once she has a larder of three or four bees, she begins to lay her eggs – one in each bee. These will feed the growing larvae when they hatch.

Philanthus triangulum

Where in the world:	Throughout Europe, excluding the coldest regions
Habitat:	Prefers warm, dry sandy regions
Size:	Up to 2cm (0.8in) long
Reproduction:	Eggs laid in the bodies of live bees
Life span:	Adult lives just a few months
Typical diet:	Larvae: bees. Adult: nectar and pollen

Leaf Insect

T here are 30 known species of leaf insect in the family Phyllidae. These insects
have evolved to look like the leaves and foliage which are most common in
their rainforest habitats. This ability is called 'phytomimesis'. Most are green or
brown in colour, with flat abdomens, small heads and leaflike body patternations.
Some species also mimic the movements of leaves as they sway in the breeze. This
camouflage even extends to the leaf insect's unhatched eggs, which look like small
seeds. Some insects go through a complete metamorphosis (change) during their
lives – from egg, to larvae, to pupa, to adult. Many others, including the leaf insect,
have an incomplete metamorphosis. From egg, they develop into a nymph that
looks very like the adult, except it usually has no wings. After several moults, the
nymph develops into a fully formed adult, which is ready to mate.

Family Phyllidae

Where in the world:	Southeast Asia; Southern Australia; New Guinea
Habitat:	Primarily tropical rainforests, but wherever there is plentiful vegetation
Size:	Up to 11cm (0.4in) long, depending on species
Reproduction:	Eggs laid on ground
Life span:	Unknown
Typical diet:	Green leaves

Harvester Ant

There are more ants than any other type of insect. Part of the reason for their success is their ability to both adapt to and use their environment. Some ants are weavers, making nests from leaves. Others are fungus growers and grow a mouldlike yeast to eat. Harvester ants collect seeds, which they store in their nests. The worker ants then reduce these seeds to a soft pulp by grinding it up with their jaws and mixing it with their saliva. The resulting mush is called 'ant bread'. A supply of ant bread ensures that the colony has sufficient food to survive during times of drought and famine. Harvester ants can be found all over the world, but *Pogonomyrmex* live mainly in Southern and Western USA. A typical harvester ant colony can contain as many as 90,000 ants, and a mature nest may measure as much as 1m (40in) across.

Pogonomyrmex species

Where in the world:	Southern and Western USA
Habitat:	Plains and grasslands
Size:	5–12mm (0.2–0.5in) long
Reproduction:	Queen lays eggs all year round
Life span:	Queen: up to 15 years. Worker: up to 1 year
Typical diet:	Seeds and small insects

Paper Wasp

The name 'paper wasp' is given to numerous species of medium-sized, black, brown or reddish wasps that build nests out of 'paper', in common with some species of hornet. Nest building begins with a single mated female queen in the early spring. Using a combination of chewed wood mixed with saliva, the queen constructs her papier-mâché nest, which resembles an upside-down umbrella. This fragile-looking construction holds her first brood, which consists entirely of sterile female workers, which help the queen to enlarge the nest and feed the next generation of young. As the colony matures, the founding queen will produce a brood of males and additional queens. Once mated, these new queens will fly off to form colonies of their own. Adult paper wasps drink nectar and fruit juices, but their larvae generally eat insects, so they play an important link in pest control.

Polubia, Polistes, Melanogaster & others

Where in the world:	Tropical and subtropical regions
Habitat:	Adaptable; builds nests in trees and houses
Size:	Worker: up to 2.5cm (1in) long
Reproduction:	Queen lays eggs all year round
Life span:	Queen: up to 3 years. Worker: 1 year
Typical diet:	Larvae: insects. Adults: nectar and fruit

Slavemaker Ants

Slavemaker ants steal the pupae of neighbouring ants – often members of the species *Formica fusca*, which are smaller and less heavily armoured than other ants. Once the larvae emerge from their cocoon, they believe that their captor's colony is their own, and begin to work for it. Some species of slavemaker are so reliant on their servants that, in experiments, they starve to death without them. Occasionally, a newly mated female, wanting to establish her own colony, will invade a neighbouring nest, kill the queen and take her place. She will use the captive workers to rear her own young, until they outnumber the original colony members and must go in search of more slaves to maintain their (almost) work-free lifestyles. Little is known about how many species of slavemaker there are, but species have been found in the USA and in Northern Europe through to Asia.

Polyergus species

Where in the world:	USA; Northern Europe into Asia
Habitat:	Warm, dry regions
Size:	8–10mm (0.3–0.4in) long, depending on species
Reproduction:	Queen lays eggs all year round
Life span:	Queen: up to 2 years. Worker: 2 months
Typical diet:	Insects and honeydew

Spider-hunting Wasp

Unlike social wasps which live in large colonies, spider-hunters are solitary predators. Male and females live and hunt separately, and come together only to breed. Once a female has mated, she goes in search of food. As their name suggests, this varied and widespread species hunt spiders, which they paralyse by using powerful chemicals injected into their prey via the needle-like stinger in their rear. Prey is then dragged to the nest or burrow, where eggs are laid on the spider's abdomen. When the eggs hatch, the emerging larvae feed on the still-living spider. It is believed that the size of the spider meal provided may influence whether a male or female wasp is born. Larger spiders produce the larger female wasp. Some pompilids may also lay their eggs on mobile spiders. These eggs hatch only when the spider eventually dies.

Pompilus species

Where in the world:	All over the world
Habitat:	Warm regions, wherever there is a plentiful supply of food
Size:	1.5–2.5cm (0.6–1in) long
Reproduction:	Eggs laid on captured spider
Life span:	Unknown
Typical diet:	Larvae: spiders. Adults: nectar

Acacia Ants

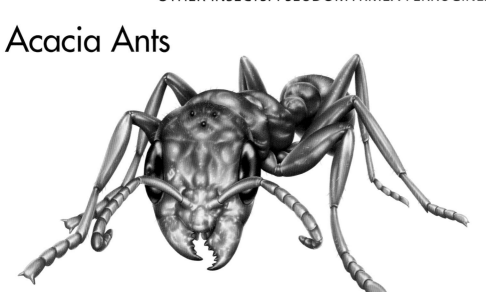

There are more ants than any other type of insect. Part of the reason for their success is their ability to both adapt to and use their environment. Some ants are weavers, making nests from leaves, while others are farmers, 'farming' insects that provide them with food. Acacia ants are the gardeners of the ant world. Acacia bushes are a species of thorny shrub found in arid regions from Southern USA through to Mexico, Venezuela, Colombia and Ecuador. Acacia ants have a symbiotic relationship with these bushes. The bush provides the ants with a safe home among its thorns, and a regular supply of nectar. The ants, in return, protect the bush from animals and even other plants, by chewing up any nearby shrubs with which the bushes would otherwise have to compete. Without their resident gardeners, the bushes die within a year. With them, they may live for 20.

Pseudomyrmex ferruginea

Where in the world:	Southern USA; Mexico; Venezuela; Colombia and Ecuador
Habitat:	Acacia bushes
Size:	6mm (0.2in) long
Reproduction:	Queen lays eggs all year round
Life span:	Queen: up to 20 years. Worker: 2 months
Typical diet:	Plant nectar and insects

Snakefly

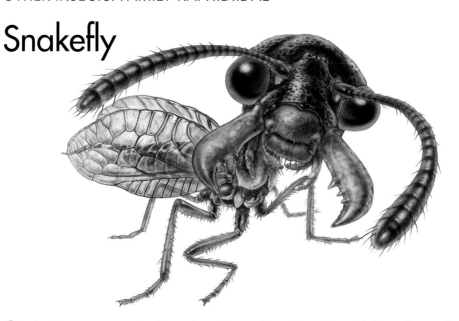

Snakeflies are an ancient species of two-winged insects, which can be easily identified by their elongated 'neck' and triangular head. There are two snakefly families in the order Raphidioptera. The second – Inocellidae – has 65 species. These look very similar to the Raphidiidae snakeflies, but have longer antennae. Snakeflies get their common name from the serpentine way in which the adults raise their heads before striking out at prey. Fossilized snakeflies have been found dating back 300 million years. It is believed that their ancestors may have been the first species of insect to develop a pupa stage (insects that undergo an incomplete metamorphosis, evolved from an earlier, more primitive insect group). Snakeflies are increasingly rare across much of their range, due to the destruction of many natural woodlands, which is where this delicate insect makes its home.

Family Raphidiidae

Where in the world:	All over the world, except Australia and Antarctica
Habitat:	In woodlands
Size:	0.6–3cm (0.2–1.2in) long, depending on species
Reproduction:	100s of eggs laid in bark
Life span:	Averages 2 years
Typical diet:	Larvae: beetle grubs. Adults: grubs and insects

Predatory Bush Cricket

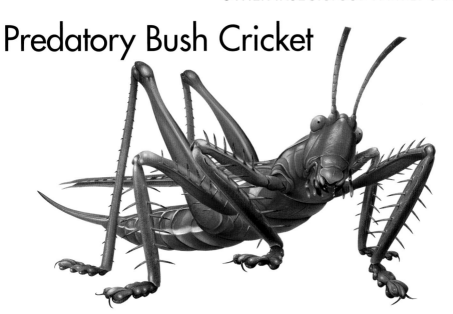

Predatory bush crickets are among Europe's largest insects. The giant of the family is the rare Saga pedo. The insect can grow up to 12cm (4.7in) long, and may be parthenogenetic, which means that females reproduce without mating. Bush crickets are found on warm, dry grasslands throughout Mediterranean Europe, Northern and Sub-Saharan Africa and Australia. Some species may also occur in Asia and China, although these have not yet been classified. Predatory bush crickets are actually grasshoppers, but, unlike most of the order, they are carnivores and feed on other grassland insects. Bush crickets have powerful forelegs, which are spiked to enable them to hold onto prey effectively. They also have large, sharp mandibles for cutting and dissecting their food. Most species are brown or green in colour, which enables them to blend in with their surroundings.

Sub-family Saginae

Where in the world:	Europe; Africa; Australia; possibly Asia
Habitat:	Warm, dry habits, especially grasslands
Size:	Up to 12cm (4.7in) long, depending on species
Reproduction:	Eggs laid deep in soil
Life span:	Up to 3 years
Typical diet:	Small insects

Flesh Fly

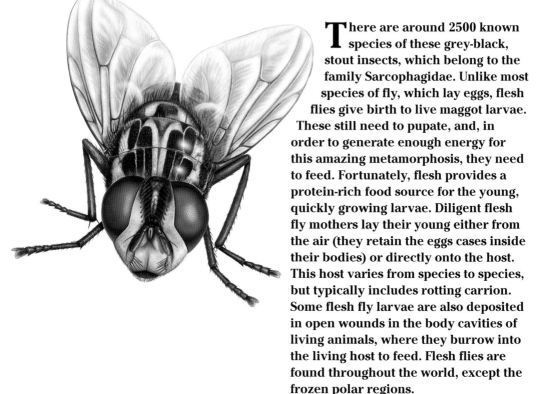

There are around 2500 known species of these grey-black, stout insects, which belong to the family Sarcophagidae. Unlike most species of fly, which lay eggs, flesh flies give birth to live maggot larvae. These still need to pupate, and, in order to generate enough energy for this amazing metamorphosis, they need to feed. Fortunately, flesh provides a protein-rich food source for the young, quickly growing larvae. Diligent flesh fly mothers lay their young either from the air (they retain the eggs cases inside their bodies) or directly onto the host. This host varies from species to species, but typically includes rotting carrion. Some flesh fly larvae are also deposited in open wounds in the body cavities of living animals, where they burrow into the living host to feed. Flesh flies are found throughout the world, except the frozen polar regions.

Family Sarcophagidae

Where in the world:	All over the world, excluding the Arctic and Antarctic
Habitat:	Adaptable
Size:	6–20mm (0.2–0.8in) long, depending on species
Reproduction:	Gives birth to live maggot young
Life span:	Averages 2 weeks
Typical diet:	Any organic matter

African Desert Locust

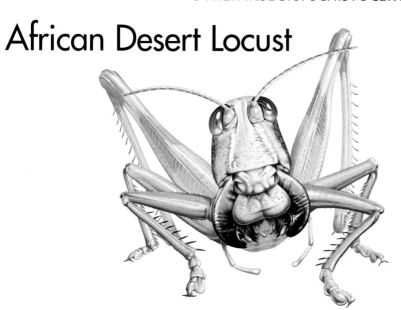

Locusts are a type of migratory grasshopper and belong to the family Acridodae. These voracious insects have short antennae, long hind legs and two pairs of wings. They also have a small opening in their head, which is surrounded by a set of powerful grinding jaws called 'mandibles'. A second pair of less powerful jaws, called 'maxillae', lie behind. Together, these jaws enable the locust to munch its way through just about anything. A swarm, which can contain 150 billion insects, can eat 90,720 tons (100,000 tonnes) of food a day. In The Bible, desert locusts were one of the 10 plagues sent by God to punish the Egyptians, and the devastation they bring can be aptly summed up by a quotation from Exodus (10:150): 'They covered the ground, until it was black; they ate everything ... including all the fruit on the trees. Not a green thing was left ... in all the land.'

Schistocerca gregaria

Where in the world:	North Africa; Arabia and Asia
Habitat:	Wherever there is plentiful food
Size:	Up to 9cm (3.5in) long
Reproduction:	Eggs laid in soil
Life span:	Up to 6 months
Typical diet:	Any vegetation

Scarab-Hunter Wasp

Scarab-hunters are also called mammoth wasps due to their large size. Like the tarantula hawk wasp, the scarab-hunter is a solitary wasp and does not live in cooperative colonies with others of its kind. Scarab-hunter females are larger and more aggressive then the males – and they need to be. The female has sole responsibility for ensuring that the next generation of scarab-hunters survive. After mating, she hunts for beetle larvae beneath the vegetation. These are paralysed and dragged back to her nest or burrow, where an egg is laid on each of the grub's abdomens. When the egg hatches, the emerging larvae are able to use the still living grub to fuel their own metamorphosis from larvae to adult wasp. Some scarab-hunters, such as *Scolia maculata*, specialize in specific prey, which means that, as their numbers fall, so, too, do those of the wasps which feed on them.

Family Scoliidae

Where in the world:	All over the world, except Antarctica
Habitat:	Wherever there are plenty of flowers and beetles
Size:	1–5cm (0.4–2in) long, depending on species
Reproduction:	Eggs laid on beetle larvae
Life span:	Unknown
Typical diet:	Larvae: beetle grubs. Adults: nectar and pollen

Giant Centipede

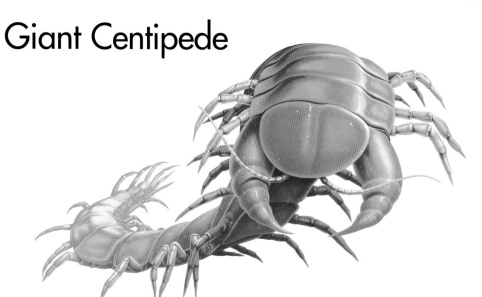

Despite their name, giant centipedes do not have 100 legs. They have a pair of legs for each section of their body. This adds up to between 15 and 23 pairs for an average giant. This is far too many to qualify as an 'insect', which have just six legs. In fact, these huge predators are myriapods, which are terrestrial arthropods with long, segmented bodies and many legs. Giant centipedes are fast and active hunters, which have been observed to rear up and snatch flying insects from the air. Members of the *Scolopendra* species are typically brightly coloured, with dark bands down their bodies. In place of eyes are four light-receptive organs called 'ocelli', which are typically found in a formation on top of the head. Most giant centipedes also have backward-facing hind legs, which act as pincers for defence. They are also able to deliver a venomous bite.

Scolopendra species

Where in the world:	Tropical and subtropical regions
Habitat:	Adaptable; found in forests and deserts
Size:	Up to 30cm (12in) long, depending on species
Reproduction:	Eggs laid in clusters, under soil or vegetation
Life span:	Up to 10 years in captivity
Typical diet:	Insects, invertebrates, small reptiles, mammals and frogs

Fire Ant

Fire ants are so called because they inflict painful, burning stings. These are aggressive insects and sting several times, holding their victim in their jaws, and injecting their toxin in a circular pattern around the mandibles. Naturally, both *Solenopsis invicta* (red imported fire ant) and *Solenopsis richteri* (black imported fire ant) are natives of Latin America. However, these adaptable species are now found in at least nine southern US states, and are a considerable pest. Fire ants are attracted to electricity sources and will build huge underground nests in factories or by electricity pylons. These colonies contain up to 300,000 workers, and may leave mounds above ground which are 60cm (24in) high. Such 'infestations' cost US businesses hundreds of millions of dollars every year. There are four other US species of fire ant, and these are generally less destructive.

Solenopsis invicta & Solenopsis richteri

Where in the world:	Latin America; imported to Southern USA
Habitat:	Adaptable; found in rainforest and urban areas
Size:	Queen: up to 1.2cm (0.5in) long. Worker: up to 3mm (0.1in)
Reproduction:	Queen lays eggs continually
Life span:	Queen up to 20 years, depending on species
Typical diet:	Nectar, fruit and small insects

Cicada-Killer Wasp

Cicada-killers are solitary insects, unlike the more social species, such as the paper wasp. They are easily recognized by their large size and coloration, which makes them look more like hornets than wasps. Their black bodies are marked with a yellow band across the thorax and on the first three parts of the abdomen. Their heads are a dark red, while their legs and wings are a rich yellow colour. Adult cicada-killer wasps drink nectar, but their young feed on the live bodies of cicadas, which the female paralyses and drags back to her underground burrow. The males of the species may look aggressive, but, unlike the females, they do not have a stinger and are relatively harmless. Killer wasp burrows are generally built in dry, sandy soil, which means that they are often found in golf courses, driveways and any urban, well-drained garden.

Sphecius speciosus

Where in the world:	Eastern USA
Habitat:	Sandy soil, close to cicada populations
Size:	Up to 3.5cm (1.4in) long
Reproduction:	Eggs laid on live cicadas
Life span:	Averages 1 year
Typical diet:	Larvae: cicadas. Adults: nectar and tree sap

Lobster Moth

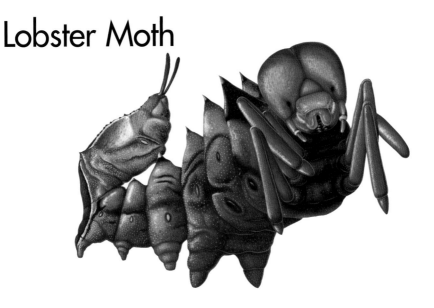

Mimicry is the ability of an animal to copy the appearance and behaviour of something else. Usually, a harmless species will mimic a more dangerous one for protection, as in the case of lobster moth larvae. When they first hatch, these larvae are small, with dark bodies and two elongated forelegs, which makes them look like ants. Ants are a useful species to mimic, as they are often toxic and are avoided by many predators. As they grow, they turn red and develop an enlarged, lobster tail. If threatened, they arch this tail over their back, in a similar way to scorpions. If this fails to scare off a predator, they can also squirt formic acid from special glands in their rear. As adults, the lobster moth's camouflage is a little less dramatic, but equally effective. Their hairy brown bodies are perfectly designed to help them remain inconspicuous among trees.

Stauropus fagi

Where in the world:	Northern Europe
Habitat:	Deciduous woodlands
Size:	Wing span up to 7cm (2.8in) across
Reproduction:	Eggs laid on underside of leaves
Life span:	Up to 1 year
Typical diet:	Larvae: leaves. Adults: nectar

Hoverfly

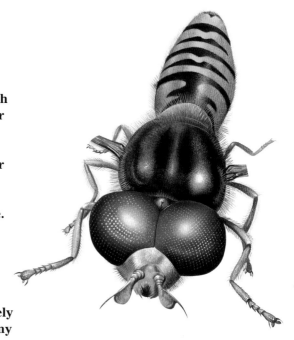

Hoverflies are often confused with bees or wasps, as many species have yellow-and-black striped abdomens. This characteristic is an example of Batesian mimicry, by which one species imitates the appearance or behaviour of another, often more dangerous animal, for protection. Hoverflies are also known as flower or drone flies because they feed on the nectar from plants. They also make a characteristically loud 'droning' noise. This is caused by their wings, which vibrate at such high speeds that they produce a musical tone. Unlike bees, they have large eyes and one, rather than two pairs, of wings. Young hoverflies (called 'maggots') vary widely in appearance and feeding habits. Many are carnivorous, some feed on wood pulp, and others, such as the rat-tailed maggot (*Erisralis tenax*), feed in stagnant waters, and have a specially adapted breathing tube to enable them to spend time hunting underwater.

Family Syrphidae

Where in the world:	All over the world, excluding the coldest regions
Habitat:	Wherever food (i.e. flowers) is plentiful
Size:	3–4mm (0.1–0.2in), depending on species
Reproduction:	Eggs laid where larvae feed
Life span:	Varies with species
Typical diet:	Larvae: some eat insects. Adults: honeydew and nectar

Rolling Wasp

There are approximately 1600 members of the family Tiphiidae. This shiny-bodied wasp starts life as an egg laid in the live body of a beetle larva. This larva must first be immobilized by the female wasp, the toxic sting of which paralyses the helpless grub. She then lays her egg in the larva's body and uses her long, powerful forelegs to bury it in the soil. This ensures that, when the egg hatches, the wasp larva has a ready-made supply of fresh food to eat. Once the wasp larva pupates, the adult may live only a few weeks, so it must find a mate quickly. Female rolling wasps are usually wingless and males often carry them from flower to flower – attached tail to tail – while mating. In some species, the males actively feed the females. This ensures that she receives enough protein to provide nourishment for her eggs.

Family Tiphiidae

Where in the world:	All over the world, excluding the coldest regions
Habitat:	Found wherever there is plentiful food
Size:	0.4–3cm (0.2–1.2in) long, depending on species
Reproduction:	Eggs laid in live beetle larvae
Life span:	2 weeks as an adult
Typical diet:	Larvae: beetle grubs. Adults: nectar

Jigger Flea

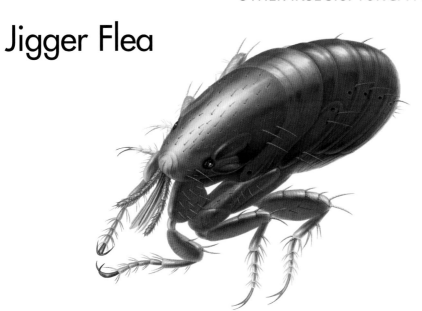

The jigger flea is also known as the sand, or chigoe, flea. This is the smallest species of flea and is especially unusual in that, rather than simply biting their host, they dig into its skin. Typically, a newly mated female will burrow into the soft skin beneath the toenail. Just the tip of her abdomen remains exposed. Once safely hidden, she begins to feed, using the host's blood to nourish her eggs. As the eggs grow, her abdomen may swell to the size of a garden pea. It takes two weeks until the eggs are ready to be laid. The female's exposed abdomen means that the eggs are not laid in the host, but fall to the ground, where they hatch a few days later. The female dies once the eggs have been laid. The flea's rotting body causes further infection in the host, which may result in gangrene.

Tunga penetrans

Where in the world:	Tropical and subtropical regions
Habitat:	Wherever their is a suitable host
Size:	1–8mm (0.04–0.3in) long
Reproduction:	Lays up to 200 eggs, then dies
Life span:	Up to 1 year
Typical diet:	Fresh blood

European Hornet

In common with ants, a European hornet colony is founded by a single queen. The mated queen begins to build her nest in the spring. A hornet's nest is made out of paper, which the queen constructs using chewed-up wood pulp. Typically, these nests are made in trees or the eaves of houses. The nest begins with a series of hexagonal cells, into which the queen lays her eggs. This first brood will consist entirely of female workers, which help the queen to enlarge her nest and feed the next generation of young. The colony will stay in the nest for only a year – the last two broods include males and more queens. After the new queens have mated the males, they hibernate for the winter. They then fly off to form their own colonies. The males and workers die as the winter approaches.

Vespa crabro

Where in the world:	From Southern England to Mongolia
Habitat:	Nests in trees or houses
Size:	Queen: up to 3.5cm (1.4in) long. Worker: up to 2.5cm (1in)
Reproduction:	Queen lays eggs all year round
Life span:	Queen: up to 5 years. Worker: 1 year
Typical diet:	Larvae: insects. Adults: insects, nectar and plant sap

Common Wasp

Wasps are divided into social and solitary species. The common wasp belongs to the family Vespidae, which are social, colony-building insects. Like ants, these colonies are complex structures, based around the protection of the queen and her offspring. All colonies are founded by a solitary female, which rears the first generation of sterile female workers herself. These continue to enlarge the nest while the queen gives birth to more colony members. The nest is constructed in a thin, paper-like material made from chewed plant fibres. Eventually the queen will produce larger, fertile females and males, which will go on to found new colonies. With their yellow-and-black striped bodies and narrow waists, common wasps are the archetypal wasp. This large species was originally a native of Europe, but has now made its way to Asia, the Americas and Australia.

Vespula vulgaris

Where in the world:	Europe; Asia; Australia; USA; Central Latin America
Habitat:	Wherever there is vegetation
Size:	Queen: 1.5–2cm (0.6–0.8in) long. Worker: 1–1.5cm (0.4–0.6in)
Reproduction:	Queen lays eggs all year round
Life span:	Queen: averages 1 year. Worker: 2 weeks
Typical diet:	Larvae: insects. Adults: nectar

Plague Flea

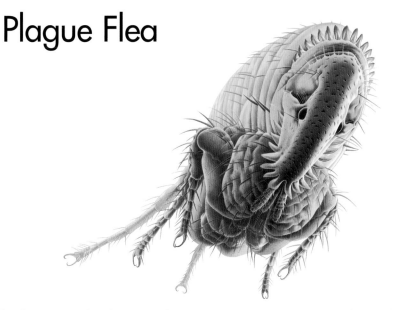

The plague flea is probably one of the biggest killers in history. These tiny insects spread disease as they feed – sucking the blood of their victims and passing bacteria from host to host as they do so. Common fleas can transmit a range of infectious diseases, including the tape worms that affect dogs, cats and humans. However, plague fleas, which carry the bacterium that causes the bubonic plague (or 'the Black Death', as it is known), are typically carried by rats. In the fourteenth century, an outbreak of this virulent disease was responsible for the death of more than a quarter of the entire population of Europe. Today, there are around 2000 reported cases of bubonic plague worldwide every year. This deadly infection can now be treated quite successfully with antibiotics; however, if left untreated, it is still fatal in 50–90 per cent of cases.

Xenopsylla cheopis

Where in the world:	Tropical and subtropical regions
Habitat:	Wherever there are hosts
Size:	Up to 2mm (0.08in) long
Reproduction:	Eggs laid in host burrows
Life span:	Averages 1 year
Typical diet:	Fresh blood

Elegant Grasshopper

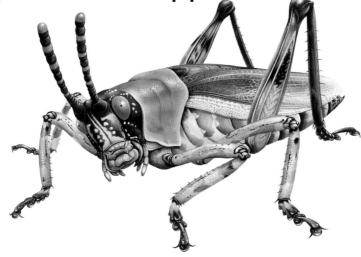

The elegant grasshopper is found throughout Central and Southern Africa. *Zonocerus elegans* ranges from South Africa through to Mozambique, Zaire and Angola. *Zonocerus variegatus* is more common in the west and east of the continent, below the Sahara Desert. This numerous and widespread species is named after its brightly coloured body, which looks attractive but is designed as a warning to predators to stay well away. In the animal kingdom, bright colours, especially reds, often mean that a species is poisonous. This is certainly true in the case of the elegant grasshopper, the body of which contains toxic alkaloids. These come from the Siam weed, which the grasshopper munches in vast quantities. This weed has little nutritional value, but is rich in the toxins which the grasshopper needs to protect itself. Elegant grasshoppers are considered a serious pest by farmers.

Zonocerus elegans & Zonocerus variegatus

Where in the world:	South to Central Africa
Habitat:	Adaptable; found in rainforest, savannah and domestic gardens
Size:	Up to 3.5cm (1.4in) long
Reproduction:	Lays eggs in soil
Life span:	Averages 1 year
Typical diet:	Siam weed, sweet potato, coffee and millet

Pistol Shrimp

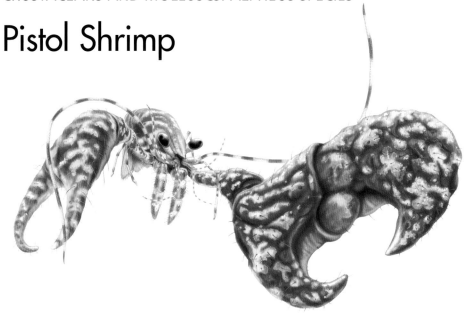

Pistol shrimp are also known as snapping, or symbiosis, shrimp. The first of these common names derives from the incredible noise they make when hunting. Pistols have one enlarged claw, which they use to generate shock waves in the water. This massive pincer – which is often bigger than the whole of the shrimp's body – is designed like the hammer of a gun. When the shrimp opens this gigantic claw, sticky pads at the base lock together. When the shrimp flexes its muscles, these pads suddenly give way, bringing the pincers together with an audible snap. The vibrations produced travel through the water and stun prey. The second of its popular names comes from its interdependent relationship with the goby fish. Shrimp have very poor eyesight, so the little goby keeps watch for predators and, in return, is allowed to share the shrimp's burrow and food.

Alpheus species

Where in the world:	From the Caribbean to Pacific Ocean
Habitat:	Warm, shallow waters, especially coral reefs
Size:	Up to 5cm (2in) long, depending on species
Reproduction:	Couples pair for life; female lays millions of eggs
Life span:	Unknown
Typical diet:	Small fish, shrimp and crabs

172

Robber Crab

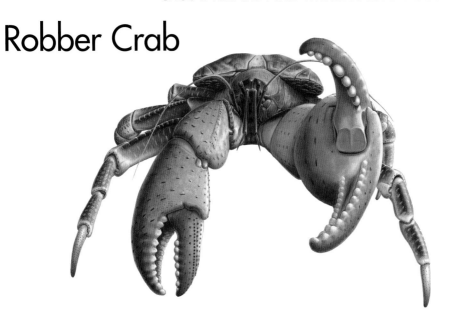

Robber crabs are the world's largest land crab. Like the Christmas Island red crabs, these huge crustaceans spend their entire adult lives on land, although females must lay their eggs in the sea, where the larvae hatch. Robber crabs still have gills, but they can absorb oxygen directly from the air as long as they keep them moist. They therefore spend much of their time in damp burrows along the shoreline or in mangrove swamps. They come out to feed at night, and often climb trees in search of ripe fruit to eat. They have a particular fondness for coconuts, but, contrary to popular myth, even their huge pincers are not strong enough to crack open these giant nuts. They must wait for one to fall from the tree and crack open by itself. Robbers get their common name from their habit of stealing shiny objects from houses and camp sites.

Birgus latro

Where in the world:	Indian and Pacific oceans
Habitat:	Primarily mangrove swamps
Size:	Up to 60cm (24in) long; up to 3kg (6lb 8 oz) in weight
Reproduction:	Female carries eggs on abdomen, then releases them into sea to hatch
Life span:	Averages 10 years
Typical diet:	Fruit, especially coconuts, and carrion

Cone Shell

T hese snail-like predators are well known for the striking patternation on their shells, which has made them popular with collectors. Worldwide, there are around 400 different species, most of which have adapted to hunt specific prey, such as shellfish or aquatic worms, depending on what is plentiful. Found mainly in shallow waters, cone shells are patient predators and often bury themselves in the mud to lie in wait for a meal. The rasping 'radular' teeth, which are common in other gastropods, have been adapted in cone shells into toxin-filled harpoons. These are thrust into prey, by the cone's proboscis, or feeding tube. Venom is then pumped into the victim until it is subdued and can be pulled into the cone mouth. Cone shell venom includes a series of powerful neurotoxins, which are quite capable of killing a human, so cones should always be handled carefully.

Family Conidae

Where in the world:	Tropical and subtropical oceans
Habitat:	Mud and sand in warm shallow waters
Size:	25cm (10in) long; 2kg (4lb 8 oz) in weight, varying with species
Reproduction:	Up to 700 eggs deposited in purselike capsules
Life span:	Unknown
Typical diet:	Small fish, molluscs, aquatic invertebrates

Christmas Island Red Crab

Christmas Island is home to 13 species of land crab, and the most abundant of these are the large, bright red crabs that have been known to bring the island to a virtual standstill during their annual migration to the sea shore to breed. There are an estimated 100 million of these extremely successful crustaceans, and they still follow the same migration routes that their ancestors used before humans arrived on the island – regardless of what obstacles now lie in their path. Red crabs live in underground burrows, which they dig into the rainforest floor, although they are so plentiful that they can also be found in domestic gardens. In order to keep their gills damp, they plug these burrows with moist vegetation. Although they need this wet environment, the red crab is a true land crab and will drown if immersed in water.

Gecarcoidea natalis

Where in the world:	Christmas Island
Habitat:	Primarily rainforest
Size:	Up to 12cm (4.7in) long
Reproduction:	Lays eggs in sea at high tide; 100,000 eggs at each spawning
Life span:	Up to 10 years
Typical diet:	Leaves, fruit, flowers or carrion

Blue-ringed Octopus

Blue-ringed octopi are found around shallow coastal waters in Australia, the Philippines and Indonesia. It is unclear how many species there are, but three have been identified: the greater blue-ringed, the lesser blue-ringed and the blue-lined octopus. Despite having no outer shell, octopuses are classed as molluscs. In fact, their bodies are entirely boneless, so their internal organs must be protected by a sheet of muscular tissue called a 'mantle'. When alarmed, the skin of the blue-ringed octopus, which contains chromatophores, changes colour to flash blue warning rings. The greater the danger, the brighter and faster the flashes. Should this warning fail to deter, few animals can survive its bite, as blue-ringed octopi are one of the world's most poisonous species. In fact, a single bite is capable of killing a human in minutes.

Hapalochlaena species

Where in the world:	Indo-Australian oceans
Habitat:	Warm shallow waters
Size:	*Hapalochleana lunulata* is the largest species, at 20cm (8in) long
Reproduction:	Female lays eggs in water, which are cared for until they hatch
Life span:	Up to 2 years
Typical diet:	Fish and crustaceans

Harlequin Shrimp

It is the bold patterns on the body of the harlequin shrimp which are responsible for its unusual name: in the Middle Ages, harlequins were a type of clown, famous for their bright, mutli-coloured clothing. Harlequin shrimp are shy creatures and emerge from their burrows only at night to hunt. These small reef-dwellers mate for life, and males and females will hunt together. Most shrimp are opportunistic feeders and will eat anything, but harlequins hunt only starfish, and they have especially grim feeding habits. Once prey has been found, the hunting pair work together to turn over the starfish. This renders it immobile, but does not kill it. The shrimp then proceed to feed off the fleshy undersides of their prey. It can take many weeks for a pair to eat a starfish, working their way from leg to leg. They will even feed the starfish to keep it alive – and fresh.

Hymenocera picta

Where in the world:	Tropical oceans
Habitat:	Warm waters, especially rocky coastlines and coral reefs
Size:	Up to 6cm (2.4in) long
Reproduction:	Couples pair for life; eggs kept in burrows by female until they hatch
Life span:	Unknown
Typical diet:	Starfish

Opalescent Squid

Only in the darkness of the ocean depths is it apparent why the opalescent squid has such an evocative name. This intelligent and social member of the mollusc family communicates with other opalescent squids using the luminous cells in its body (called 'chromatophores') to send messages. By varying the strength of the electric pulses sent to the chromatophores, the squid can produce a dazzling display of light and shade. This method of communication is so sophisticated that a squid may change colour a dozen times in a few seconds. Each combination of colours is believed to transmit very specific messages – about hunting, mating or even how they are feeling. Opalescent squid are highly intelligent animals and hunt in groups (called a 'school'), and this light display may help members of the assembly to identify each other and keep in formation in the darkness.

Loligo opalescens

Where in the world:	Pacific Ocean
Habitat:	Food-rich waters off the western coast of the USA and Latin America
Size:	Body length up to 25cm (10in) long
Reproduction:	Sexually mature at 3 years; mates once and dies soon after laying eggs
Life span:	Averages 3 years
Typical diet:	Small crustaceans and fish

Spider Crab

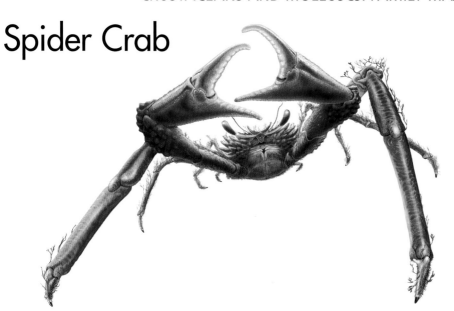

S pider crabs form the second-largest family of crabs. There are more than 900 species in this widespread and adaptable group, and members can be found throughout the world's oceans, excluding only the coldest waters of the Arctic and Antarctic. Typically, spider crabs have a triangular carapace and extremely long thin legs. The Japanese spider crab (*Macrocheira kaempferi*), which lives in the ocean depths off Japan, is a true giant of the species, with a recorded leg span of 2m (78.7in). In place of a skeleton, crustaceans have an external exoskeleton. This does not grow with the animal, so most crustaceans shed their shells regularly. Spider crabs may 'moult' several times a year while they are growing. Once mature, however, the spider crab keeps its existing shell and, over time, this may become encrusted with algae and seaweed, which helps to camouflage it.

Family Majidae

Where in the world:	The world's oceans, excluding Arctic and Antarctic regions
Habitat:	Seabed, often in shallow waters
Size:	Body 45cm (17.7in) long; leg span 2m (78.7in), varying with species
Reproduction:	Egg-laying
Life span:	Unknown
Typical diet:	Algae, small invertebrates and carrion, depending on species

179

Horseshoe Crab

Horseshoe crabs have changed little since their ancestors roamed the oceans 300 million years ago. These unique creatures are the sole survivors of a group that was once abundant in the waters of the Palaeozoic era. There are now only four remaining species: the American horseshoe (*Limulus polyphemus*), *Tachyphelus tridentatus*, *Tachyphelus gigas* and *Carcinoscorpinus rotundicauda*, which are found in coastal waters from Japan to Indonesia. The horseshoe crab has light blue, copper-based blood; a tough, rounded exoskeleton; five pairs of jointed legs; and a long tail, which it uses as a rudder and to turn itself back over if flipped upside down. These nocturnal crustaceans are called crabs, but are more closely related to scorpions and spiders. Part of the reason for their continued survival is that they tolerate a range of temperatures and water conditions.

Class Merostomata

Where in the world:	Eastern coast of North America; Southwestern Asia
Habitat:	Shallow bays and estuaries
Size:	Up to 60cm (24in) long, depending on species
Reproduction:	Sexually mature at 9–12 years; lays green eggs on beaches
Life span:	Up to 19 years
Typical diet:	Shellfish and aquatic invertebrates

Nautilus

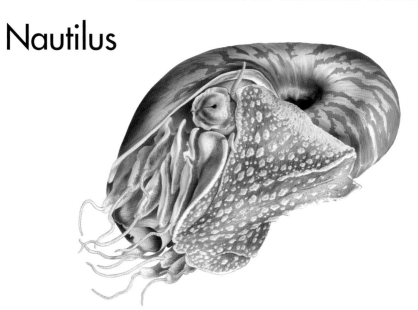

Nautilus are cephalopods – a group that includes squid and octopus. These creatures have remained virtually unchanged for 500 million years, when their ancestors dominated the world's oceans. Today there are believed to be only six species remaining. The pearly nautilus (*Nautilus pompilius*) and the king nautilus (*Nautilus scrobiculatus*) both have the characteristic coiled, chambered shell out of which protrude feeding tentacles. As the nautilus grows, it adds new chambers to this shell. It lives in the outermost chamber. Those at the rear are filled with water and nitrogen, which the nautilus uses to control its buoyancy. When speed is required, this mollusc blasts jets of water from a breathing tube to propel it forwards suprisingly quickly. Other species, including the paper nautilus, do not have a chambered shell and are more closely related to the octopus.

Nautilus species

Where in the world:	Indian and Pacific oceans
Habitat:	Around coral reefs, at depths to 600m (1968ft)
Size:	Up to 25cm (10in) across, depending on species
Reproduction:	Egg-laying
Life span:	Unknown
Typical diet:	Small crustaceans and carrion

Dog Whelk

The dog whelk – or Atlantic dogwinkle, as it is also known – is one of the ocean's many species of sea snail. Like its land-bound counterparts, the dog whelk is a slow but proficient hunter. Using its large muscular 'foot' to creep across the sea bed, the whelk is able to follow prey over great distances. It tracks them by tasting the water for their chemical 'scent'. Once a meal is within reach, this tenacious carnivore literally 'softens' up its victims by secreting a toxin on their shells. It then extends its tubular 'proboscis' and bores through, using its sawlike tongue (the radula) to grind up its prey's flesh. The whelk's own shell has a distinctive spiral shape, pointed at the tip, and is often decorated in brown or cream, or bands of both. Whelks have disappeared from some areas due to pollution from TriButyl tin, which is used on ship's hulls.

Nucella lapillus

Where in the world:	Eastern USA; Northwest Europe; Iceland
Habitat:	Rocky, coastal shallows
Size:	Up to 5cm (2in) long
Reproduction:	Lays 100s of eggs; few develop; young eat undeveloped eggs
Life span:	Unknown
Typical diet:	Muscles, barnacles and other dog whelks

Sea Slug

There are around 3000 known species of sea slug. Despite their pedestrian common name, most of these soft-bodied molluscs – which are effectively shell-less snails – are incredibly brightly coloured. These voracious hunters often sport spectacular stripes or spots, with particularly bright colours reserved for the horn-like lumps (called 'cerata') protruding from their backs. Sea slugs have the unusual ability of being able to eat highly toxic creatures such as the Portuguese man-of-war, and absorb their stinging cells for their own protection. These recycled cells are contained in the cerata and can often be just as deadly as they were on the original 'owner'. Like all gastropods, sea slugs have one muscular foot which they use to walk. However some species of this extremely widespread and diverse order can also swim, by rippling the soft tissue around their bodies like wings.

Order Nudibranchia

Where in the world:	The world's oceans, excluding the Arctic and Antarctic
Habitat:	Shallow coastal waters
Size:	Up to 30cm (12in) long, depending on species
Reproduction:	Lays thousands of eggs in ribbon-like strands
Life span:	Up to 2 years
Typical diet:	Coral, sea anemones, sponges and other sea slugs

Ghost Crab

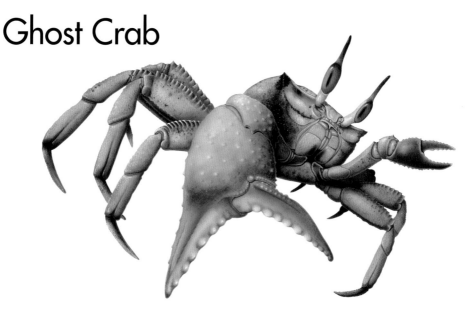

G host crabs live anywhere there is a suitable sandy beach or mud flat in which to dig an underground burrow. They emerge at low tide to scavenge for food, often feasting on fish and jellies that have been stranded on the beach by the retreating waters. However, they are an extremely adaptable species. Depending on their environment, ghost crabs may dig up turtle eggs, eat seaweed or survive on the flesh of rotting sea birds. In mangrove swamps, they have even been known to climb trees in search of arboreal insects. Ghosts are extremely fast movers, which can appear and disappear so quickly that its easy to see why they were believed to be supernatural. This speed has earned them another common name – the racing crab. During the mating season, these crabs are easier to locate thanks to the rasping noise they make by rubbing their legs together, to warn away rivals.

Genus Ocypode

Where in the world:	Tropical and subtropical waters
Habitat:	Beaches, mudflats and mangrove swamps
Size:	Up to 6cm (2.4in) wide, depending on species
Reproduction:	Lays eggs in the sea
Life span:	Averages 3 years
Typical diet:	Small animals, plants and carrion

Hermit Crab

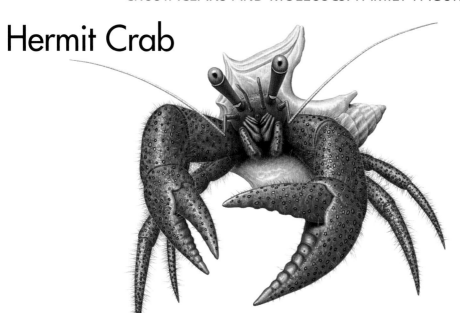

U nlike true crabs, hermits lack the protection of a carapace over their abdomen. They solve this deficiency by making their homes in discarded shells, especially those of whelks. This protects the vulnerable parts of their body and also gives the hermit a ready-made place to retreat to when danger threatens. It is possible that at some point in the past hermits lived in rock crevices, but they are now so well adapted to life in these stolen homes that their abdomens are bent to match the spiral shape of the shell. As exoskeletons cannot expand, most crustaceans need to shed their shells regularly as they grow. Hermits simply have to find a larger shell and eject its current occupant. There are around 500 species of hermit. Family Paguridae hermits are ocean dwellers; family Coenobitidae Hermits live entirely on land, although females must return to the water to mate.

Family Paguridae

Where in the world:	The world's oceans
Habitat:	From shallow waters to deep seas
Size:	Up to 30cm (12in), depending on species
Reproduction:	Female carries eggs in shell until they hatch as free-floating larvae
Life span:	Depends on finding a suitable shell
Typical diet:	Animal or plant matter, depending on species

Spiny Lobster

Like all crustaceans, lobsters have a thick exoskeleton protecting them from predators. The spiny lobster goes one step further. Its tough outer 'shell' is lined with thornlike spines, which make it a prickly prospect for would-be predators. In some species, these spines even extend to the antennae, which can be used, whiplike, for defence when the lobster is threatened. Each of these long feelers can also move independently, which is especially useful for warding off the attacks of trigger fish, which often hunt in male–female pairs. If this impressive arsenal does not deter a predator, though, the spiny lobster has 10 legs, which lets it run at speeds of up to 28km/h (17.4 mph). During stormy weather, spiny lobsters often migrate to calmer waters. These migrating columns march in a defensive line, head-to-tail, and can cover more than 100km (62 miles) in a week.

Panulirus species

Where in the world:	Tropical and subtropical oceans
Habitat:	Warm, coastal waters, in caves and rock crevices
Size:	50cm (20in) long; 14kg (30lb 13 oz) in weight, varying with species
Reproduction:	Female carries up to 1 million eggs under her tail
Life span:	Up to 50 years
Typical diet:	Starfish, crabs and carrion

Common Woodlouse

Woodlice are one of the few species of crustaceans that have adapted to a life spent entirely on land. Even land crabs, which still have gills, need to return to the sea to lay their eggs. The common woodlouse is dark grey with a flat, oval, segmented body divided into three fused sections. They have seven pairs of legs, and very distinctive sharp points at the rear of their exoskeleton. Woodlice of the family Porcellionidae share many characteristics with the pill woodlouse of the family Armadillidae. However, members of the family Armadillidae are able to curl themselves up into a tight ball when threatened by predators. Porcellionidae woodlice cannot do this – they can manage only a half-moon. These numerous and widespread crustaceans feed mainly on rotting vegetation, and can often be found beneath leaf piles and in compost heaps.

Porcellio scaber

Where in the world:	From Western Europe to North Africa
Habitat:	Cool, damp conditions, especially in leaf litter
Size:	1–1.5cm (0.4–0.6in) long
Reproduction:	Up to 200 eggs carried in brood patch until they hatch
Life span:	Up to 3 years
Typical diet:	Plant and animal matter

Slipper Lobster

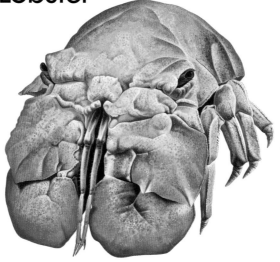

Most lobsters are equipped with two huge claws, which they use for both defence and offence. Slipper lobsters are unusual in that they do not have these pincers, but instead use their large, flattened antennae to dig through the mud and sand of the sea bed in search of food. Slipper lobsters are not fussy eaters. They will make a meal of any tasty scrap, including aquatic worms and crustaceans. As they do not have powerful, crushing pincers to tear up prey, their stomachs do much of the work. Inside is a series of hard ridges, which act like teeth to grind up food. Carrion is a favourite dish, but some of the 70 or so known species are entirely vegetarian, and live on a diet of algae and underwater plants. Without its pincers for protection, the slipper lobster relies on its rough, mottled, shell to help it blend in with underwater rocks.

Family Scyllaridae

Where in the world:	Tropical and subtropical oceans
Habitat:	Warm coastal waters, to depths of 600m (1968ft)
Size:	15–50cm (6–20in), depending on species
Reproduction:	Female carries clusters of eggs on her back
Life span:	Up to 15 years, depending on species
Typical diet:	Varies with species from algae to carrion

Cuttlefish

Cuttlefish belong to the same class of animal as the squid and octopus, and, like their aquatic cousins, these intelligent creatures have been shown to be capable of solving complex puzzles in captivity. The 100 or so species in the family Sepiidae are commonly found throughout the world's oceans, although they favour shallow waters. Cuttlefish have eight sucker-laden arms and two long feelers. These are usually held in pockets behind the eyes, but can be deployed at great speed to grasp passing prey. While octopus crawl along the seabed, cuttlefish are able swimmers. Cuttlebone, which is often fed to canaries, is an internal shell used by the cuttlefish to control their buoyancy. When threatened, these adaptable cephalopods will often release an inky pigment into the water. This helps to confuse predators. In the past, this pigment was used to make 'sepia' ink.

Family Sepiidae

Where in the world:	The world's oceans
Habitat:	Highly adaptable, but prefer shallow waters
Size:	2–50cm (0.8–20in) long, depending on species
Reproduction:	Adults gather along coasts to breed and die soon after laying eggs
Life span:	Unknown
Typical diet:	Small fish, crabs, shrimp, aquatic invertebrates

Arrow Crab

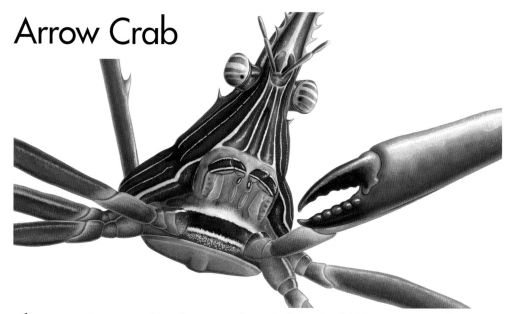

Arrow crabs are nocturnal, so spend most of the day hidden among rocks or in crevices in the coral. They come out at night to hunt and are particularly found of feather duster worms, which live among the reefs. The arrow gets its common name from its barbed beak, which it uses to spear and hold prey, while its sharp pincers deftly tear the flesh apart. Arrow crabs, like most crustaceans, start life as one of many millions of eggs carried by the female. Once hatched, the young go through several changes before they take on the physical characteristics of the adults. Arrow young (zoa) are shrimplike and spend much of their time floating near the water's surface. As they grow, arrows must 'moult', as their exoskeleton cannot expand. They may do this several times during the early months and, once mature, will continue to moult once a year.

Stenorhynchus species

Where in the world:	Tropical oceans
Habitat:	Shallow, warm waters, to depths of 1500m (4920ft)
Size:	Body up to 3cm (1.2in) long; 1cm (0.4in) wide; 7cm (2.8in) long legs
Reproduction:	Female carries eggs on abdomen until the young (zoa) hatch
Life span:	Unknown
Typical diet:	Carrion and small invertebrates

Mantis Shrimp

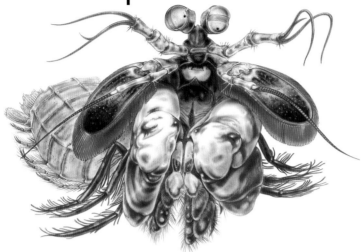

Mantis shrimp belong to the subclass Malacostraca, which includes some of the largest and most familiar crustaceans. Within this grouping are around 20,000 marine and terrestrial species, which share many characteristics. This includes a segmented body that is divided into three main parts: the head, the thorax and the abdomen. Most crustaceans also have a pair of antennae, which extend from the head, and a tough outer casing, called an 'exoskeleton', which protects the internal organs. Mantis shrimp have two pairs of antennae, which are used to taste the water to locate food. Mantis live mainly in warm oceans. By day, they live in burrows in the seabed, but come out to hunt at night. They are well known to fishermen as 'thumb choppers' because they are aggressive hunters and will lunge at any potential prey with their huge barbed claws.

Order Stomatopoda

Where in the world:	The world's oceans
Habitat:	Warm waters, to depths of 1000m (3280ft)
Size:	Up to 30cm (12in) long, depending on species
Reproduction:	Eggs kept in burrows by female until they hatch
Life span:	Unknown
Typical diet:	Small fish, crustaceans, molluscs and aquatic invertebrates

Axolotl

In the Aztec language, axolotl means 'water monster', and, while this unique amphibian may not be exactly monstrous, it certainly is curious. Most amphibians start their lives in the water. This is where the adults lay their eggs, and where they ultimately hatch. For the first few months of their lives, these juveniles are fully equipped for an aquatic existence, having gills and long tails for powering through the water. Over time, however, they grow lungs and legs, and move onto the land. The axolotl is unusual because it remains in its juvenile, or 'larval', form all its life. This may have something to do with the low levels of iodine in the lake where they live. Iodine aids the production of thyroxin, which is the hormone that helps juveniles grow into adults. Axolotls can be induced to adopt their adult form in captivity.

Ambystoma mexicanum

Where in the world:	Mexico
Habitat:	Lake Xochimilco
Size:	Up to 30cm (12in) long; 300g (10.5oz) in weight
Reproduction:	Sexually mature at 12–18 months; lays 400 eggs a year on lake bottom
Life span:	Up to 25 years in captivity
Typical diet:	Small insects and invertebrates

Fire-bellied Toad

There are six species of this small warty toad: the European, the yellow-bellied, the guangxi, the giant, the hubei and the Oriental. Of these, the European is the most widespread, although the smallest, rarely reaching more than 4cm (1.6in) in length. The Oriental, with its racing green body and vivid red and black underbelly, is perhaps the most colourful. There is some evidence that much of this colour is dependent on the toad's diet, as all species lose their natural vibrancy in captivity unless they are fed a specific type of aquatic crustacean, the bodies of which contain a natural red dye. As is common in the animal kingdom, such bright colours are used to warn away potential predators. Should this fail to deter, the fire-bellied toad will also excrete a foul-tasting mucus, which is enough to convince even the hungriest hunter to spit this little toad out.

Bombina species

Where in the world:	Europe and Southern Asia, depending on species
Habitat:	Prefers wet environments
Size:	4–8cm (1.6–3.1in), depending on species
Reproduction:	Lays eggs in rivers and lakes during the spring and summer
Life span:	Up to 30 years, depending on species
Typical diet:	Insects, invertebrates and small crustaceans

Cane Toad

Cane toads are also known as marine toads, although they do not live in oceans, but prefer the brackish, slightly saline waters where river estuaries meet the sea. These huge, bloated amphibians are natives of Latin America, but have been introduced into various parts of the world in an attempt to control pests on plantations. In Australia, this policy has been disastrous. The cane toad, which is one of the largest toads in the world, has devastated local wildlife. The problem is heightened by the fact that it has no natural predators in Australia, is highly toxic, will poison both anything trying to eat it and the water sources it inhabits, and breeds all year round. From an initial batch of 102 cane toads, there are now estimated to be more of these voracious predators in Australia than in Latin America – and numbers are still growing.

Bufo marinus

Where in the world:	Latin America; introduced into Australia
Habitat:	Widespread and adaptable, but prefers brackish waters
Size:	Up to 24cm (9.4in) long; up to 2.5kg (5lb 8 oz) in weight
Reproduction:	Mates all year round; lays up to 33,000 eggs per spawning
Life span:	Up to 20 years
Typical diet:	Mainly reptiles and amphibians, but will eat almost anything

Giant Salamander

S alamanders look like lizards, but are actually a species of slender, long-tailed amphibian. Like other amphibians, salamanders prefer moist habitats. Some species are wholly aquatic and lay their eggs in water, where the larvae spend their early months. Others live in burrows dug in damp soil, while some are happy among the tree tops. The giants of the order Caudata are the Chinese great salamanders (*Andrias davidianus*), which can grow to almost 2m (6ft 6in) long. The champions of the New World are the hellbenders (*Cryptobrachus alleganiensis*), which live in mountain streams in the eastern USA. These large, stocky salamanders belong to an ancient group, in which the male fertilizes the female's eggs outside her body. In comparison, the grandly named Pacific giant salamanders, which are found in the USA and Canada, grow to only 45cm (17.7in).

Order Caudata

Where in the world:	USA; China and Japan
Habitat:	Primarily damp environments, such as mountain rivers
Size:	Chinese up to 1.8m (6ft) long; up to 65kg (143lb 5oz) in weight
Reproduction:	Lays eggs in water or on land, depending on species
Life span:	Unknown
Typical diet:	Varies with species. Larvae generally carnivorous

Ornate Horned Frog

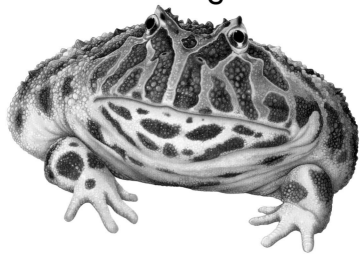

The ornate horned frog is a resident of the dense, lush rainforests of Latin America. This plump-bodied amphibian makes its home in damp burrows, beneath the thick leaf litter on the forest floor. These distinctive-looking frogs grow extremely quickly and may metamorphosize into an adult within two weeks of hatching. Part of the reason for this accelerated growth is undoubtedly due to the frog's huge appetite. Ornate horned frogs are equipped with an extremely large mouth, which enables them to make a meal of almost any small- to medium-sized rainforest mammal or reptile. They generally hunt during the day. Frogs do not chew, but instead use their powerful forearms to cram in food, which they swallow whole. Their common name comes from the hornlike folds of skin over their eyes. Ornate horned frogs are also known as Bell's horned frog.

Ceratophrys ornata

Where in the world:	Argentina; Uruguay; Paraguay; Brazil
Habitat:	Primarily rainforest
Size:	Up to 20cm (8in) long; up to 480g (1lb 1oz) in weight
Reproduction:	Sexually mature at 18–24 months; lays 1000s of eggs in still water
Life span:	Averages 6 years
Typical diet:	Insects, lizards, mice and frogs

Poison-Dart Frog

Seeping from the skin of these sumptuously coloured frogs is one of the most toxic poisons known to man. Just a few drops of the venom from the skin of the green poison-dart frog is 10 times more deadly than the tetrodotoxin produced by the infamous puffer fish. In the rainforests of Latin America, local tribes have used these toxins for centuries when hunting. When daubed on the tip of a dart, just a drop is enough to kill a large monkey. While these small amphibians may be deadly, though, they are dedicated parents. Unlike most frogs, who lay batches of several hundred eggs at a time, poison-dart frogs lay only a few, fairly large eggs. When they hatch, these are carried on the parent's back to small pools of water that collect in the hollows of leaves. Here, the tadpoles are fed by their parents until they mature.

Dendrobates species

Where in the world:	Latin America
Habitat:	Primarily rainforest
Size:	Up to 5cm (2in), depending on species
Reproduction:	2–10 large eggs; female cares for young
Life span:	Up to 5 years for most species
Typical diet:	Small insects, invertebrates and fruit

Budgett's Frog

Frogs and toads do not chew their food. Like snakes, they swallow it whole. So the size of a meal is limited only by the size of the amphibian's mouth – and some species have a legendary reputation for their eating capacity. With their huge mouths, Budgett's frogs will attempt to eat whatever comes their way, even other Budgett's frogs. This cannibalistic tendency is particularly apparent during their youth. Huge numbers of eggs are laid, but only a relatively small number make it to adulthood, as aggressive juveniles will happily make a meal of any weaker siblings. Once mature, Budgett's frogs spend much of their time submerged in the mud at the bottom of ponds, lying in wait for prey. When eating, this powerful amphibian uses its unwebbed forearms to cram food into its mouth, restraining its victim with two toothlike projections that jut from its lower jaw.

Lepidobatrachus laevus

Where in the world:	Northern Argentina; Western Paraguay; Southeast Bolivia
Habitat:	Small semi-permanent ponds on grasslands
Size:	Female up to 14cm (5.5in) long; male up to 10cm (4in)
Reproduction:	Up to 1200 eggs can hatch within 2 days of being laid
Life span:	Up to 10 years in wild
Typical diet:	Insects, invertebrates and other frogs

Mantella Frog

The tiny mantella frogs of Madagascar are characterized by their vivid skin tones, large forward-facing eyes, rounded snouts and long, delicate limbs. In their native rainforests, they hunt by day, with little fear of attack from predators. The reason for this apparent lack of concern is simple. They may be small, but, like the Latin American poison-dart frogs, they are highly toxic. When threatened, they excrete a noxious mucus from their skin, which is enough to make any predator spit them out. In common with the fire-bellied toad, this toxin seems to be produced as a result of the frog eating a specific native ant, as they gradually lose this ability in captivity. These attractive amphibians are popular as pets, and this, combined with the destruction of much of their habitat, has reduced the number of all species considerably in recent years.

Mantella species

Where in the world:	Madagascar
Habitat:	Primarily rainforest
Size:	1.5–3cm long (0.6–1.2in); averages 2g (0.07oz) in weight
Reproduction:	Lays eggs in water pools; in some species, females care for the tadpoles
Life span:	Unknown
Typical diet:	Small insects and invertebrates

Malaysian Horned Toad

Animals use camouflage to both hide themselves from enemies and potential prey. The Malaysian horned toad is a true master of the art. Its name comes from the hornlike projections over its eyes. (The Latin 'megophrus' means 'big eyebrows'.) Yet it is also known as the leaf toad because it can hide itself among leaf litter and be virtually invisible. The shape of its body, as well as the cryptic camouflage patterns of green, brown and black covering its flat, angular body, make it the perfectly designed rainforest predator. Like most toads, the horned toad is not especially active, but takes a patient approach to hunting. Lying buried under leaves on the forest floor, the toad simply waits for prey to pass by. Small reptiles, mammals and insects are all on the menu, but the horned toad will attempt to eat anything it can fit into its mouth.

Megophrus montana

Where in the world:	Southeast Asia; across the Malay Peninsula
Habitat:	Primarily rainforest
Size:	Female up to 16cm (6.3in) long; male up to 9cm (3.5in)
Reproduction:	Lays small eggs on the underside of submerged logs and rocks
Life span:	Unknown
Typical diet:	Small reptiles, mammals, insects and invertebrates

Pipa Toad

The Naturalist Gerald Durrell (1925–1995) famously described the pipa toad as 'looking … as though [it] had been dead for some weeks and was already partially decomposing'. In fact, the seven species of this mainly Latin American toad are striking in appearance. These unappealing amphibians have extremely flat, dark, rectangular bodies, small black eyes and long spidery fingers, which are used for catching prey. This design is ideal for lying in the sluggish, leaf-clogged 'black waters' of the Amazon River system, where the pipa toad lives and hunts. Generally slow-moving, the pipa nevertheless performs amazing gymnastics during the mating season. The breeding pair will perform loop-the-loops over each other as the female releases her eggs. These land on the her back and sink into the skin. They remain there, protected by a film of mucus, until the tadpoles hatch.

Pipa species

Where in the world:	Latin America and parts of Trinidad
Habitat:	Slow-moving 'black water' streams
Size:	4–120cm (1.6–47.2in), depending on species
Reproduction:	*Pipa pipa* (Surinam toad) is famous for its acrobatic mating displays
Life span:	Up to 6 years
Typical diet:	Dead fish and small, slow-moving water invertebrates

Paradoxical Frog

Sometimes truth is stranger than fiction, and this is certainly the case with the paradoxical frog. When tadpoles emerge from their eggs, they are not fully formed adults, but resemble tiny fish – complete with gills and a tail. As they grow, feeding on the algae in the water, they slowly metamorphosize into adults, exchanging their tails and gills for legs and lungs. The paradoxical frog spends much longer as a tadpole than other species of frog, and so grows to a remarkable 25cm (10in) in length. It would be expected that such a bouncing baby would grow into a huge adult; however, as it begins to change, the paradoxical frog also shrinks in size. Fully grown, it measures just a quarter of the length it did as a tadpole, which is why it is also known as the shrinking frog.

Pseudis paradoxa

Where in the world:	Latin America; Trinidad
Habitat:	Primarily humid environments; swamps; rainforests; wetlands
Size:	As tadpole, up to 25cm (10in) long; adult up to 7cm (2.8in)
Reproduction:	Lays eggs in water on a platform of floating foam
Life span:	Unknown
Typical diet:	Mainly insects as an adult

African Bullfrog

Most amphibians spend their lives in or close to fresh water, but the African bullfrog has adapted to an existence on the dry grasslands of Africa. For much of the year, it spends its time underground, where it is protected from the ravages of the sun. It emerges from its burrow at night to hunt, using its powerful unwebbed front legs to hold and subdue prey. It also has three sharp 'teeth' in its bottom jaw, which can exert a vicelike grip. The African bullfrog is a notoriously big eater and will attempt to make a meal of anything it can fit into its mouth, even poisonous snakes. During the dry season, it digs down into the soil, where it forms a cocoon of shed skin and mucus around itself. It then waits for the rains to come. This is its cue to come up for food and to mate.

Pyxicephalus adspersus

Where in the world:	Southern, Eastern and Central Africa
Habitat:	Savannah and open grasslands
Size:	Up to 24cm (9.4in) long; up to 2kg (4lb 8oz) in weight
Reproduction:	Lays up to 4000 eggs (frog spawn) in puddles during the wet season
Life span:	Up to 40 years
Typical diet:	Small reptiles, mammals and insects

Crested Newt

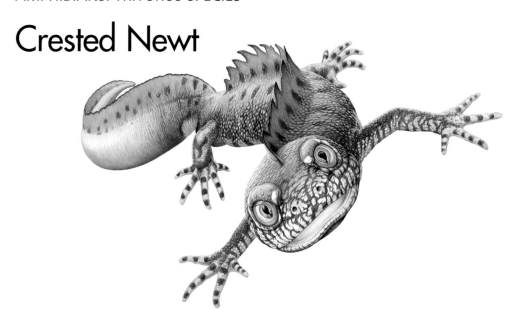

Crested newts range throughout Europe and into Northern Iran. Until recently, all crested newts were considered to belong to the same species, but they have now been reclassified as four separate species. This includes the Italian, the northern, the Danube and the southern, or Turkish, crested newt. Like all newts, crested newts begin their lives in the water. At around four months, they lose their gills and grow legs, ready to venture out onto dry land. They return to the water to mate, to hunt and occasionally to hibernate, spending the winter hidden safely in the mud at the bottom of the river. Despite their name, it is only during the breeding season that the mature males develop the distinctive crest along their back. This is used to attract a female, and is absorbed back into the newt's body once the breeding season is over.

Triturus species

Where in the world:	Europe, excluding Ireland; Spain and Portugal
Habitat:	Tolerant of a range of habitats
Size:	Up to 20cm (8in), depending on species
Reproduction:	Female lays up to 1200 eggs which hatch within a few days
Life span:	Up to 7 years in the wild; 27 in captivity
Typical diet:	Invertebrates; frog spawn, small newts

Crown of Thorns Starfish

Unlike most starfish, which have five 'arms', the crown of thorns can have up to 23 – all covered with sharp, protective spines. These are loaded with venom, giving the starfish added defence from predators such as shrimp and crabs. The crown's preferred food are the microscopic polyps that 'build' coral reefs. Crawling over the coral on its large sucker-like feet, the crown of thorns pours digestive juices over these polyps and sucks up their dissolved flesh. This leaves behind dead, white coral. In the 1970s, the Australian Government became so concerned about the numbers of crown of thorns preying on the Great Barrier Reef that it began a campaign to reduce their numbers. Now it is known that such 'swarms' are natural and present little long-term threat. In fact, crowns prefer to eat the faster growing species of corals, which help the slower ones to compete.

Acanthaster planci

Where in the world:	Indian and Pacific oceans
Habitat:	Primarily around coral reefs
Size:	Up to 80cm (32in) long
Reproduction:	Spawning takes place when waters reach correct temperature
Life span:	Unknown
Typical diet:	Mainly coral and algae

Sea Anemone

Sea anemones, in common with jellyfish, belong to the phylum Cnidaria. 'Cnidae' are the stinging cells that members of this group use to capture prey and defend themselves from attack. Sea anemones spend much of their time fixed to rocks on the sea bed (meaning that they are described as 'benthic'). However, they are able to walk, and even swim, by moving their tentacles backwards and forwards, and flexing their cylinder-shaped bodies. When hunting, these tentacles are used as bait. By wriggling them, like worms, the sea anemone is able to attract fish. Once within reach, the anemone's tentacles spring forwards, injecting the fish with toxic barbs that paralyse it. The fish is then drawn towards the anemone's mouth, which stretches to allow it to swallow its prey whole. It is not unusual for a sea anemone to eat a meal as big as itself. Any 'indigestible' parts of the meal are ejected later.

Order Actiniaria

Where in the world:	The world's oceans
Habitat:	Fixed to rocks or reefs, often in deep waters
Size:	1cm–1m (0.4–40in) across, depending on species
Reproduction:	Varies from asexual 'budding' to egg-laying
Life span:	Up to 70 years, depending on species
Typical diet:	Small fish, crustaceans, molluscs and plankton

Spotted Eagle Ray

The eagle ray is one of the most attractive species of ray. These large, graceful fish are powerful swimmers, using their enlarged pectoral fins like wings to glide through the ocean. When pursued by predators, they have even been known to leap out of the water and glide for a short distance over the surface. Unlike many rays, which are bottom-dwellers, eagles are most often seen in the shallows, especially in warm, tropical waters. An estimated 100 species of rays are stingrays. These have long, tapering tails, tipped with poisonous spines. The eagle ray has three to five sharp spines, which are lined with thornlike barbs. At the base of these spines are poison glands. When a stingray is disturbed or threatened, these spines are thrust towards an attacker, causing a deep, lacerated cut. Venom is then injected into the wound, causing enough pain to warn off any planned attack.

Aetobatus narinari

Where in the world:	The world's oceans
Habitat:	Warm, shallow waters, coral reefs and estuaries
Size:	2m (6ft 6in) long with 6cm (2.4in) tail; weight up to 225kg (496lb)
Reproduction:	Up to 4 pups born in each litter
Life span:	Unknown
Typical diet:	Mainly molluscs and crustaceans

Wolf Fish

The wolf fish – or sea cat, as it is sometimes called in Europe – is an ancient species of fish that can be found in fossil records dating back over 50 million years. With its elongated scale-less body, and long dorsal fin, which runs from its head to tail, this Arctic-dwelling species looks more like an eel than a fish. This is a powerful predator with excellent vision, thanks to eyes placed well forward on the top of its head. Unlike many fish, it relies on sight, rather than sound or vibrations in the water, as its prime hunting tool. Its preferred food are crustaceans, molluscs and starfish, and it makes short work of them in its powerful jaws. In fact, the wolf fish typically eats its prey whole – shells and all – and uses its large canine-style teeth to break its meal into more manageable chunks.

Anarrhichas lupus

Where in the world:	Northern Arctic oceans
Habitat:	Seabeds in cool coastal waters, to depths of 500m
Size:	1.3m (4ft 3in) long; 25kg (55lb) in weight, varying with species
Reproduction:	Male builds 'nest' and vigilantly guards eggs and young (fry)
Life span:	Unknown
Typical diet:	Bottom-dwellers

Frogfish

Almost all of the 50 or so species of frogfish belong to the suborder Antennarioidei. Frogfish are anglerfish, which get their name from their unique method of catching prey. Attached on a bony spine between their eyes is a flexible 'rod', tipped with a fleshy lure that is used to 'fish' for food. When prey attempts to eat this fake bait, the angler simply opens its mouth and sucks in its prey, whole. Frogfish can do this in about one-hundredth of a second. Unlike its relative, the goosefish, the frogfish is less compressed, with a larger, more bulbous head. It can also change colour at will. The naturalist William Swainson (1789–1855) best described these bizarre-looking creatures when he said, 'they are the most grotesque ... the most hideous ... of all the fishes and, as their vernacular name ... implies, they have nearly as much the appearance of frogs or toads as fish.'

Antennarius species

Where in the world:	The world's oceans
Habitat:	Prefers tropical and subtropical waters, to depths of 100m (328ft)
Size:	3.5–40cm (1.4–16in), depending on species
Reproduction:	Lays 1000s of eggs in a floating 'raft'
Life span:	Varies with species
Typical diet:	Fish and crustaceans

Deep Sea Hatchetfish

The deep sea hatchetfish is a 'mesopelagic' species, which means that it can be found in the deep oceans, at depths of 200–1000m (656–3280ft). As is common with many deep-sea species, hatchetfish cannot afford to waste valuable energy. Food in the depths is scarce, so their bodies come in a very basic design. They are small, with compact fins, and a huge gaping, mouth, which they use to hoover up any debris falling from above. To help them search for food, hatchetfish have large, luminous eyes, which point slightly upwards. They also have light-producing organs, called photophores, which are dotted along their axe-shaped under-bellies. These give out an eerie blue light, which the hatchetfish can adjust to match the level of sunlight that filters through the waters from sky above. This helps them to blend with their surroundings and hunt virtually unseen.

Argyropelecus species

Where in the world:	The world's oceans
Habitat:	Cooler waters, to depths of 1000m (3280ft)
Size:	Up to 10cm (4in), depending on species
Reproduction:	Egg-laying
Life span:	Unknown
Typical diet:	Small crustaceans, fish and plankton

European Starfish

The European starfish is one of the ocean's most curious creatures. Its body is composed of five tapered arms, which radiate out from a flat, central area. It is here that the starfish's mouth and anus are located. Contrary to expectations, its mouth is on the bottom, so that it can to suck up food from below, and its anus is on the top. At the end of each of its arms are sucker-like feet, which allow it to pull itself along the ocean bed at a sedate 5cm (2in) per hour. They also give it an extremely powerful grip, which it uses to prise open the shells of oysters and clams – its preferred food. Each of these amazing arms contains both reproductive and digestive organs. As a result, even if the starfish loses three of its arms to a predator, it can still re-grow most of its 'lost' body.

Asterias rubens

Where in the world:	Northeast Atlantic; Northern Mediterranean; Black Sea; Baltic
Habitat:	Around cool coastal waters
Size:	50cm (20in) in diameter; arms up to 25cm (10in) long
Reproduction:	Sexually mature at 1 year; lays up to 2 million eggs per spawning
Life span:	Up to 4 years
Typical diet:	Mussels, oysters, fish eggs and carrion

Alligator Gar

There are seven species of gar, which are found mainly in freshwater rivers and lakes, although some species do venture out as far as the brackish waters around coastal estuaries.

These huge fish are members of an ancient family, which has changed little since their ancestors prowled the waters some 145 million years ago. As their common name implies, they have a distinctive long, alligator-style snout, which is lined with razor-sharp, elongated, canine teeth. Their bodies are streamlined for speed, and covered in large, overlapping, protective bony scales. Like all fish, the alligator gar has gills, but its swim bladder also functions as a primitive lung, enabling it to breathe air when water levels in the rivers fall during the summer. As another survival trait, its eggs are extremely poisonous to predators, which means that most of its young make it to adulthood.

Atractosteus spatula

Where in the world:	Primarily in the Mississippi Basin
Habitat:	Lakes and bayous
Size:	Up to 3m (9ft 10in) long; up to 135kg (298lb) in weight
Reproduction:	Lays large green eggs, which are poisonous to predators
Life span:	Up to 50 years
Typical diet:	Fish, crabs and young alligators

Triggerfish

The 40 or so species of this brightly coloured fish can be found around the shores and coastlines of the world's warmer oceans. With flattened bodies, long snouts and small, tooth-lined mouths, triggerfish are instantly identifiable, but it is one specific physical characteristic that has earned them their peculiar name. Their dorsal fin has three spines. When a triggerfish spots danger, it wedges itself into the nearest rock crevice. The first two spines on this fin can be locked upright and held in place by a smaller spine that clicks into a notch at the base of the fin. Once locked, not even the most determined predator is able to dislodge the triggerfish from its hiding place. The triggerfish's family name, Balistodae, means 'crossbow' in Latin, reflecting that fact that the fish's fin spines act in a similar way to the firing mechanism of a crossbow.

Family Balistodae

Where in the world:	Tropical and subtropical oceans
Habitat:	Reefs and rocky shores in warmer waters
Size:	Up to 60cm (24in), depending on species
Reproduction:	Lays demersal (deep-sea) eggs in specially dug hole
Life span:	Unknown
Typical diet:	Small crustaceans, molluscs and algae, depending on species

Viperfish

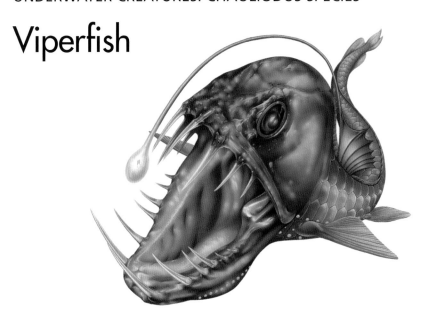

The viperfish is a truly nightmarish-looking creature. With a narrow, eel-like body, broad, distendable jaws, and massive fangs (which reach over its head), the viperfish is a fearsome sight. Yet few people have seen this aggressive predator close, as it is an inhabitant of the mesopelagic zone, which lies 200–1000m (656–3280ft) down in the ocean depths. As food is scarce in this region, the first ray of the viperfish's dorsal fin is elongated and tipped with a luminous lure, which is used to attract food. The viper's underbelly is also dotted with light-producing glands, called 'photophores', which emit a faint blue glow. The viper can adjust the amount of light given out to match the level of sunlight that is filtering down through the waters from the world above. This helps it to blend in with its surroundings and hunt virtually unseen.

Chauliodus species

Where in the world:	The world's oceans
Habitat:	Deep waters, to depths of 1000m (3280ft)
Size:	Up to 35cm (14in), depending on species
Reproduction:	Eggs float to the surface; adults return to the depths
Life span:	Unknown
Typical diet:	Fish and crustaceans

Box Jellyfish

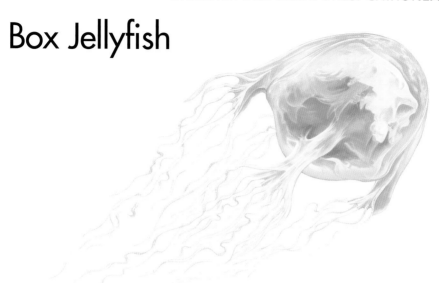

There are 16 species of box jellyfish worldwide, but the most infamous and deadly belong to the *Chironex* species, which travel through far northern Australian waters during the wet season – October to April. Box jellyfish are often known to 'swarm', especially after rains, when they head for estuaries in search of prey that has been washed down-river. The box jellyfish's body is square in shape, with around 15 tentacles on each corner. Each of these tentacles is armed with around 500,000 stinging cells, called 'nematocysts'. These inject a chemical cocktail into their victims, which is designed to paralyse and ultimately kill. This toxin is primarily used for defence, as any large creatures which get caught in the jellyfish's tentacles can cause serious damage if not dealt with quickly. Around 70 per cent of all humans stung by box jellyfish die – often within a matter of minutes.

Chironex species

Where in the world:	Worldwide; most dangerous species found in Australia
Habitat:	Shallow coastal waters
Size:	Body up to 20cm (8in) long; tentacles up to 3m (9ft 10in)
Reproduction:	Jellyfish grow from polyps by a process called 'budding'
Life span:	Unknown
Typical diet:	Small fish, crustaceans and molluscs

North American Sea Nettle

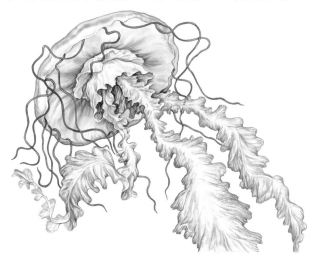

In the summer, the North American sea nettle swarms in vast numbers along the Atlantic coast of the USA. These bell-shaped jellyfish are unusual in that they prefer river estuaries to the salty waters of the open ocean. This presents serious problems to bathers, as the sea nettle, as with all members of the phylum Cnidaria, uses stinging cells to capture prey and defend themselves from attack. These cells inject coiled poisonous barbs into the victim's skin. These are usually toxic enough to paralyse fish, but are equally harmful to any human unlucky enough to wander past their trailing tendrils. Stings are not usually fatal, unless the toxin causes an allergic reaction, but they are extremely painful and require immediate medical attention. One of the few creatures to actively seek out sea nettles is the small cancer crab, which often hitches a ride inside the jelly's bell.

Chrysaora species

Where in the world:	Atlantic Ocean
Habitat:	Eastern coastline of USA, especially estuary waters
Size:	Up to 1m (40in) long bell, depending on species
Reproduction:	Jellyfish grow from polyps by a process called 'budding'
Life span:	Unknown
Typical diet:	Small fish, fish larvae and plankton

European Conger Eel

There are around 115 species of conger eel, many of which are so similar in appearance that identification is difficult. The European conger is a common sight around rocky coastlines, reefs and wrecks. This is a shy species and, when it is seen, divers will often spot just its large, powerful head jutting out from a favoured hiding spot. Adult congers are usually slate grey–blue in colour, with smooth, scale-less skin, and a long continuous fringelike fin that runs the length of their body. When congers are ready to spawn, they change appearance dramatically. They stop eating and lose their teeth and stomach. All body reserves are used to return to the Sargasso Sea, where the female lays up to eight million eggs before dying. The larvae can drift with the tides for up to two years before reaching the shallows, where the eggs begin to hatch.

Conger conger

Where in the world:	Eastern Atlantic Ocean
Habitat:	Lives in shallow waters; returns to the Atlantic depths to breed
Size:	3m (10ft) long; 110kg (243lb) weight. Female twice the size of male
Reproduction:	Sexually mature at 5–10 years; spawns once before dying
Life span:	Up to 15 years
Typical diet:	Fish, crabs, squid and carrion

217

Lion's Mane Jellyfish

The lion's mane is the world's largest jellyfish. Typically its thick, bell-shaped body reaches 30cm (12in) across, with tentacles more than 2m (6ft 6in) long. However, the record holder is an example that was washed up in Massachusetts in 1865, which had a bell measuring 23m (75ft 5in) wide, and tentacles more than 36m (118ft) long. It is these tentacles which give the lion's mane its common name. The transparent filaments are arranged in groups around the rim of the bell and form an extremely effective 'net' with which to catch prey. The lion's mane is well known for the potency of its venom. Each tentacle is armed with thousands of stinging cells, called 'nematocysts', which shoot out toxic threads that penetrate the skin. Large quantities can be fatal to humans, as Conan Doyle's (1859–1930) fictional detective, Sherlock Holmes, proved in *The Adventure of the Lion's Mane*.

Cyanea capillata

Where in the world:	Northern Atlantic and Pacific oceans
Habitat:	Coastal waters
Size:	Up to 2m (6ft 6in) wide bell; tentacles up to 35m (114ft 10in) long
Reproduction:	Jellyfish grow from polyps by a process called 'budding'
Life span:	Unknown
Typical diet:	Small fish and jellyfish

Porcupine Fish

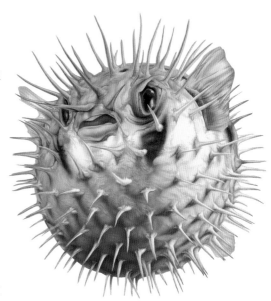

The porcupine fish – or globe fish, as it is sometimes called – makes its home primarily among the world's coral reef beds. This widespread member of the family Diodontidae is characterized by the long, sharp spines embedded in its skin and two, fused teeth, which create a beaklike mouth. These spherical fish are slow swimmers, as their fins are too small to generate any great speed. They do, however, enable the fish to make delicate and precise manoeuvres in and out of crevices in the coral. Like puffer fish, porcupines are able to 'inflate' their bodies to deter predators. The puffer does this by filling a special 'air sac' with gas; the porcupine has a simpler but just as effective method. It gulps down water until its stomach is distended. If this startling transformation does not scare away aggressors, each spine is loaded with toxins, which it releases into the water.

Family Diodontidae

Where in the world:	The world's oceans
Habitat:	Primarily warm waters near coral reefs
Size:	Up to 90cm (38in) long
Reproduction:	Large quantities of eggs laid annually
Life span:	Unknown
Typical diet:	Molluscs and coral

Sea Urchin

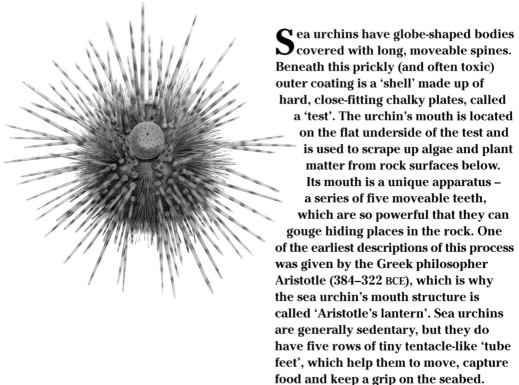

Sea urchins have globe-shaped bodies covered with long, moveable spines. Beneath this prickly (and often toxic) outer coating is a 'shell' made up of hard, close-fitting chalky plates, called a 'test'. The urchin's mouth is located on the flat underside of the test and is used to scrape up algae and plant matter from rock surfaces below. Its mouth is a unique apparatus – a series of five moveable teeth, which are so powerful that they can gouge hiding places in the rock. One of the earliest descriptions of this process was given by the Greek philosopher Aristotle (384–322 BCE), which is why the sea urchin's mouth structure is called 'Aristotle's lantern'. Sea urchins are generally sedentary, but they do have five rows of tiny tentacle-like 'tube feet', which help them to move, capture food and keep a grip on the seabed.

Class Echinoidea

Where in the world:	The world's oceans
Habitat:	Adaptable, found in shallows and deep oceans
Size:	Averages 8cm (3.2in) wide
Reproduction:	Sexually mature at 2–5 years; lays millions of tiny jelly-coated eggs
Life span:	Unknown
Typical diet:	Plants and organic matter

Electric Eel

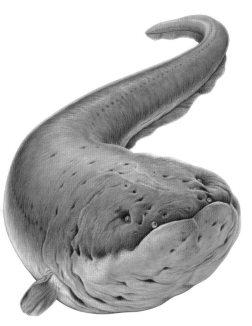

In among the slow-moving, muddy waters of the Amazon and Orinoco rivers lurks one of nature's most remarkable fish. All 'Gymnotoids', or knife fish, are able to generate weak electrical charges, but the electric eel is unique among this group. Along each flank of its body are rows of electricity-generating organs, which have evolved from muscle tissue. These enable the electric eel to unleash short but intense bursts of electricity, which are used to stun and kill prey, as well as for defence. These short, sharp shocks increase with intensity as the eel grows in size. Discharges of up to 550 volts have been recorded for an eel 2m (6ft 6in) long. Reports that electric eel discharges can be used to power household items such as TVs and light bulbs are, however, misleading. The eel's 'shocks' come as a series of short pulses that are too brief for this purpose.

Electrophorus electricus

Where in the world:	Tributaries of the Amazon and Orinoco rivers
Habitat:	Shallow river tributaries, stagnant pools and swamps
Size:	Up to 3m (9ft 10in) long; up to 40kg (88lb) in weight
Reproduction:	Gives birth to live young, which are cared for by both parents
Life span:	Unknown
Typical diet:	Small amphibians, fish and aquatic species

Deep Sea Gulper Eel

To survive in depths of up to 3000m (9842ft), gulper eels have had to make some amazing adaptations. There is little to eat in the deep oceans, so the gulper's body has been pared down to the bare essentials to save energy. Its scale-less body is narrow, with small fins and a slender tail. In fact, it is really little more than a mobile, extendable stomach, with a huge gaping maw at one end to sift the waters for food. This mouth comprises up to two-thirds of the gulper's body length, and is generally lined with pin-sharp teeth, although the umbrella gulper is tooth-less. At the other end, is a tapered tail, which contains a glowing, bioluminescent 'lure'. It is believed that this may be used to attract prey or even a mate, as finding a partner in the watery gloom must be a tricky process.

Eurypharynx & Saccopharynx species

Where in the world:	The world's oceans
Habitat:	Warmer waters, to depths of 3000m (9842ft)
Size:	Up to 60cm (24in) long
Reproduction:	Leptocephalus larvae found at shallower depths
Life span:	Unknown
Typical diet:	Small fish, crustaceans, plankton

Sea Horse

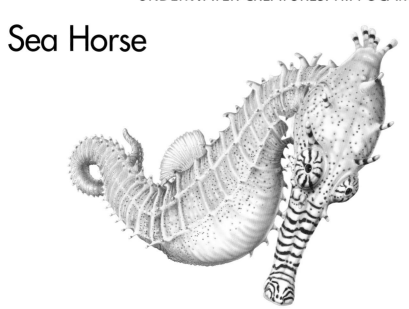

There are around 35 species of sea horse, ranging in size from the tiny pygmy, to the largest of the species, the Eastern Pacific sea horse. Most make their homes in eel grass and seaweed beds, often using their prehensile tails to anchor themselves to a piece of vegetation. Juveniles anchor themselves in a similar way, tail-to-tail with other sea horses for safety. When swimming, tiny pectoral fins on the side of the head, and a small dorsal fin on its back, help to keep the sea horse upright and stable. These attractive creatures are well camouflaged, and can move their eyes independently and without moving their head. This means that they are able to stay completely still while hunting. As it is toothless, the sea horse feeds primarily on small shrimp and plankton, which it can swallow whole, sucking food up through its long tubular snout.

Hippocampus species

Where in the world:	Tropical and temperate oceans
Habitat:	Coral reefs, among eel grasses, coral reefs and seaweed beds
Size:	1–35cm (0.4–14in), depending on species
Reproduction:	Male carries eggs in tail pouch until they hatch
Life span:	1–4 years, depending on species
Typical diet:	Small shrimp and plankton

Sea Cucumber

There are around one 1150 species of sea cucumbers, which make their homes throughout the world's oceans. These simple, nocturnal creatures feed on the decaying waste that falls to the seabed, often swallowing sand to extract the organic matter, and leaving a trail of digested mud behind them. When in danger, sea cucumbers are able to 'liquefy' their bodies so that they can hide in the smallest of rock crevices. They can also vomit up their own digestive system to distract predators. While the attacker nibbles on their discarded innards, the sea cucumber crawls away. It takes around three months to regrow the abandoned body parts. In Asia, the dried bodies of sea cucumbers (known as trepang) are considered a delicacy and, even now that some bans on commercial fishing are in place, many species numbers have not yet recovered.

Class Holothuroidea

Where in the world:	The world's oceans
Habitat:	Primarily ocean floors, to depths of 3km
Size:	2cm–2m (0.8in–6ft 6in) depending on species
Reproduction:	Eggs develop into free-floating larvae; some species brood their eggs
Life span:	5–10 years
Typical diet:	Decaying waste matter

Tigerfish

Tigerfish can be considered Africa's equivalent of the Latin American piranha. Although they belong to a different family, both groups have a fearsome reputation as voracious hunters. These aggressive predators are streamlined for speed, with a mouth bristling full of razor-sharp, wedge-shaped teeth. Tigerfish have a gas-filled sac in their body, which is used as a sound receiver. This transmits vibrations from the water, enabling them to detect any animals nearby, and respond accordingly. A shoal of juveniles will tackle a meal of almost any size, including any land animals unlucky enough to stray too close to the water's edge. Adults tend to travel in smaller groups of four or five, but even an individual will take on prey as large as itself. These muscular fish will also resort to cannibalism when food is scarce or the competition for food is too great.

Hydrocynus species

Where in the world:	Central, Southern and Western Africa
Habitat:	Lakes up to 600m (1968ft) above sea level
Size:	2m (6ft 6in) long; 50kg (110lb) in weight, varying with species
Reproduction:	Egg-laying
Life span:	Up to 8 years
Typical diet:	Fish and mammals

Coelacanth

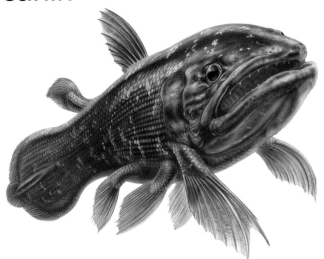

Until 1938, the coelacanth – an ancestor of the first vertebrates to crawl from the oceans, about 350 million years ago – was believed to be long extinct. Then an example was caught at the mouth of the Chalumna River, off the eastern coast of South Africa. In 1998, another species was spotted for sale in the food markets of Sulawesi. Unlike the South African coelacanth, which is a striking steel-blue colour, this was a dun, brownish fish, which was well known to locals, who called it the 'raja laut', or the king of the sea. The existence of not one but two species of a fish that was believed to have died out long before the dinosaurs walked the Earth startled scientists. Coelacanth live at great depths, and die when they are brought to the surface, but even the few examples which have been caught offer a unique insight into our past.

Latimeria chalumnae

Where in the world:	Comoro Islands; Madagascar and Mozambique
Habitat:	Possibly live in ocean caves, to depths of 200m (656ft)
Size:	Biggest specimen 1.8m (6ft) long; 95kg (209lb) in weight
Reproduction:	Gives birth to live young; little more is known
Life span:	At least 11 years
Typical diet:	Small fish

Goosefish

For many centuries, members of the *Lophius* genus, known as goosefish, were the only known species of 'anglerfish'. Anglerfish get their common name from their unusual method of catching prey. Attached on a bony spine between their eyes is a flexible 'rod', tipped with a fleshy lure, which they use to 'fish' for food. When prey attempts to eat this fake bait, the angler simply opens its mouth and sucks in its prey whole. Anglerfish are an extremely varied group, which can be divided into 18 families and more than 300 species. Most are identifiable by their flat-bodies, huge gaping mouths and fake lures. They can be found both in the deep oceans and along shallow coastal regions. Of the 25 species of *Lophius*, monkfish (*Lophius piscatorius*) is one of the most well known, and often makes a popular addition to the menu in British fish and chip shops.

Lophius species

Where in the world:	The world's oceans
Habitat:	Warm, temperate and tropical waters
Size:	3.5cm–1.8m (1.4in–6ft) long, depending on species
Reproduction:	At spawning, eggs swell into a free-floating raft
Life span:	Unknown
Typical diet:	Fish, crustaceans, seabirds

Hagfish

Hagfish belong to an ancient group that has remained virtually unchanged for more than 200 million years. These pale wormlike creatures have no eyes, no stomach and no jaw. This does not prevent them from being voracious eaters. Inside their round mouths is a long, rasping tongue, equipped with toothlike projections. Hagfish are blind, but using their excellent sense of smell and taste they can easily hunt out carrion on the seabed. Once a meal has been found, a hagfish will bury its head in the carcass and begin to tear at the meat. Occasionally, it will even tie itself in knots to get a better grip on the flesh. This unappealing fish is especially known for the huge quantities of mucus it secretes. This may be used as a protection from predators. If food is scarce, hagfish have such slow metabolisms that they can survive up to seven months without eating.

Family Mixinidae

Where in the world:	Asian, Indian and Pacific oceans
Habitat:	Cool waters, to depths of 600m (1968ft)
Size:	Up to 70cm (28in)
Reproduction:	Lays small number of large, tough eggs
Life span:	Unknown
Typical diet:	Mainly small invertebrates or carrion

Ocean Sunfish

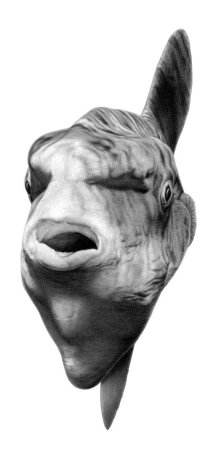

The ocean sunfish is one of the fish world's more odd-looking specimens. This huge, flat, disc-shaped fish is actually taller than it is wide, with skin so abrasive that it can take the paintwork off a ship's bow just by swimming past. The sunfish gets its common name from its habit of basking near the ocean's surface. This may be a method of controlling its body temperature, although it also benefits from frequent visits by seabirds, which eat the parasites that infest its tough, scale-less skin. The sunfish's preferred food are molluscs, jellyfish and starfish, which it eats by sucking them up into its narrow, puckered mouth. The sunfish has no teeth, but instead uses the fused bony plate around its mouth like a beak to crush food. This is then spat out, and sucked back up until the food is small enough to swallow.

Mola mola

Where in the world:	Tropical and temperate oceans
Habitat:	Found close to the water's surface
Size:	2.5–3m long (8ft 2in–9ft 10in); 3.5m (11ft 5in) tall
Reproduction:	Lays up to 300,000,000 eggs
Life span:	Unknown
Typical diet:	Algae, molluscs, jellyfish, starfish and plankton

Mudskipper

Lungfish are gobies, which is a large and diverse fish family that includes around 2000 individual species. Of these, there are around 35 species of mudskippers. These amphibian-like fish are a common sight on mud flats and in swamps throughout Africa, Asia and Australia, where they can often be seen crawling from their underground burrows at low tide to feed. These curious fish actually spend more time out of the water than in. They can do this by extracting oxygen from the air, using specially developed blood vessels in the skin. They also have strong pelvic fins and a powerful tail, which helps them to 'walk', in a series of slow, jerky motions, on the muddy surface. Once out of the water, mudskippers are highly territorial and use their dorsal fins in aggressive displays, and when competing for a mate during the breeding season.

Sub-Family Oxudercinae

Where in the world:	Tropical and subtropical Africa; Asia and Australia
Habitat:	Primarily mangrove swamps and mud flats
Size:	Up to 20cm (8in) long, depending on species
Reproduction:	Eggs laid in a burrow
Life span:	Up to 2 years in captivity
Typical diet:	Small crustaceans, insects and fish

Sea Lamprey

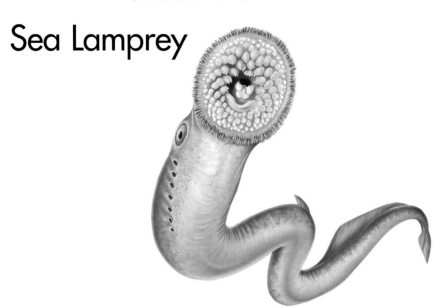

Fish can be divided into those with jaws and those without. Lampreys are jawless, which means that they belong to the superclass Agnatha, as do hagfish. This is an ancient group that dates back 500 million years to the Cambrian period. There are 38 known species of lamprey, but many are now threatened due to pollution. Although some lamprey live in freshwater habitats all their lives, most are anadromous – they migrate from the sea to fresh water to mate. It is in this environment that the larval young (called 'ammocoetes') spend the first three to six months, so pollution in these waters is particularly damaging. As a hunter, the lamprey's mouth is its main offensive weapon and can be attached, sucker-like, to prey. Inside is a disc of spiny teeth and a rasping tongue, which strip away scales and purée flesh, allowing the lamprey to suck down a liquid meal.

Petromyzon marinus

Where in the world:	North Atlantic; some species found in fresh water
Habitat:	Primarily in coastal waters and shallow streams
Size:	Up to 1m (40in) long; female generally larger
Reproduction:	Spawn then die; anadromous
Life span:	Unknown
Typical diet:	Mainly fish

Leafy Sea Dragon

Sea dragons are close relatives of sea horses, although they are slightly larger in size, with a characteristic 'leaf sprout' adornment covering their bodies. This spectacular natural camouflage enables them to pass virtually unnoticed in the beds of seaweed where they make their homes. Males of the species are well known for brooding their young. In the mating season, during an elaborate 'dance', the female deposits her eggs on the male's tail. In sea horses, there is a fully formed pouch to hold the eggs, but in dragons this has been replaced with a 'brood patch' of blood-rich tissue, which nourishes the young. At around five weeks, the male sea dragon 'gives birth' to around a 140 young per brood. These tiny dragons have voracious appetites and eat up to 300 times a day. Their preferred food is plankton, which they suck up through their long snouts.

Phycodurus eques

Where in the world:	Southern coast of Australia
Habitat:	Among the seaweed beds in shallow waters
Size:	Up to 43cm (17in) long
Reproduction:	Mates in spring; male carries eggs until they hatch
Life span:	Averages 5 years
Typical diet:	Small crustaceans and plankton

Portuguese Man-of-War

Once thought to be a jellyfish, the man-of-war is actually a member of the phylum Cnidaria, the group that includes sea anemones and sea firs. The man-of-war looks like one individual, but is really a colony of separate, interdependent life forms. The multicoloured canopy floating above the waves (called the 'pneumatophore') is the colony 'founder' and produces the other colony members. Hanging below this canopy are dozens of tentacles (the 'dactylozooids'), which continually scour the water for food. When prey approaches, cells within these tentacles discharge barbed stingers, which embed themselves in the flesh. They carry such a toxic poison that death follows in seconds. The tentacles then take the prey to the gastrozooids, the colony's feeding and reproductive 'organs'. As the colony grows, these organs produce polyps from which new men-of-war are 'born'.

Physalia species

Where in the world:	The world's oceans
Habitat:	Warmer waters
Size:	Up to 30cm (12in) body; tentacles up to 12m (39ft 4in)
Reproduction:	Asexual reproduction; new colonies bud from polyps
Life span:	Unknown
Typical diet:	Fish and crustaceans

Sawfish

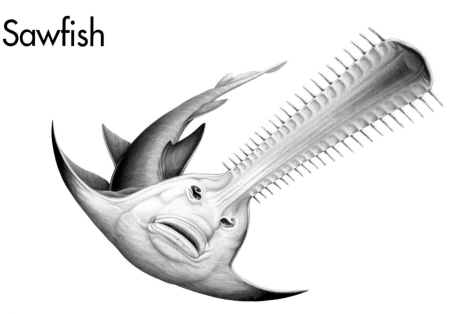

About one-third of this distinctive-looking fish's entire body length is made up of its characteristic 'saw' – an elongated snout studded with up to 30 peglike teeth. Surprisingly, this awesome weaponry is primarily used to dig for small crustaceans and molluscs, which make up a large part of its diet. Sawfish have also been seen to charge into shoals of fish, sweeping their saws from side-to-side, in an attempt to stun prey. The saw may also be used during battles with rivals for a mate. At birth, these saws are sheathed in a protective membrane so that the young do not injure their mother when they are born. Sawfish are common in tropical seas, but are also tolerant of freshwater environments, with species found in the Zambezi River in Africa. They are primarily bottom-dwellers, which spend much of their time rooting for food in the sand of sea or river beds.

Pristis species

Where in the world:	Tropical and subtropical oceans; freshwater rivers and streams
Habitat:	Primarily a bottom-dweller
Size:	Up to 7m (23ft) long; up to 1.8 tons (2 tonnes) in weight
Reproduction:	Gives birth to live young
Life span:	Unknown
Typical diet:	Fish, crustaceans and molluscs

African Lungfish

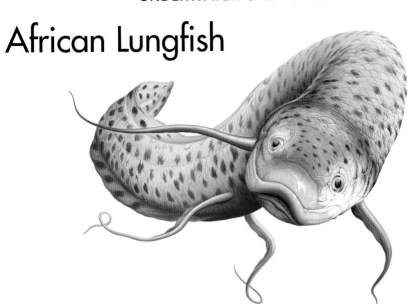

Africanlungfishes are relics of an ancient group of fish the ancestry of which can be traced back 380 million years. Their importance to science is that they form a visible link in the evolution of land-dwelling animals. As their name suggests, they are air-breathing fish, equipped with lungs as opposed to gills. (Australian lungfish have one lung; African and Latin American species have two.) They would drown if they did not come to the water's surface regularly to take gulps of air. This means that, even in droughts, lungfish are quite able to live in the shallowest of puddles. When the rivers dry out entirely, the lungfish buries itself in the mud, forms a cocoon around its body and waits in a dormant state for the rains to come. In water, lungfish move with an 'anguilliform', or eel-like, motion, but they are also able to crawl along the mud, using their fins like legs.

Protopterus species

Where in the world:	Central Africa
Habitat:	Principally shallow water
Size:	Up to 2m (6ft 5in) long, depending on species
Reproduction:	Lays egg in a purpose-built nest which both parents guard
Life span:	Unknown
Typical diet:	Small crustaceans, molluscs, amphibians, insect larvae

Lionfish

L ionfish are also commonly known as turkeyfish, dragonfish and firefish, due
to their rather ostentatious appearance. When young, lionfish are almost
transparent, but as they mature they develop their distinctive bold stripes and
feather-like fins. In some of the eight known species, these fins are tipped with 'eye
spots', similar to those found on a peacock's fan. There are two reasons for such
bold coloration. First, it provides this small fish with excellent camouflage, which
helps to keep it hidden from the large predators that present a constant threat to
inhabitants of coral reefs. Secondly, it is defensive. When threatened, the lionfish
will dip its head towards an attacker, displaying the spikes of its large dorsal fins
menacingly. If that does not work, the lionfish is more than just bluff: each of the
pointed tips of its fins are loaded with enough venom to paralyse and even kill.

Sub-Family Pteroinae

Where in the world:	Indian and Pacific oceans
Habitat:	Shallow waters and coral reefs, typically on sheltered ledges
Size:	40cm (16in) long; 2kg (4lb 8oz) in weight, varying with species
Reproduction:	Egg-laying
Life span:	Up to 15 years in captivity
Typical diet:	Small fish and crustaceans

Oarfish

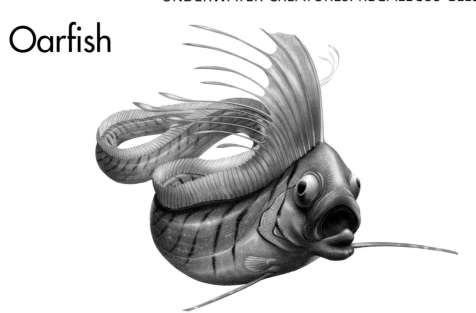

Little is known about this elusive giant of the sea. It is believed to be the largest bony fish in the world, but few people have ever seen an oarfish alive, although specimens are occasionally washed up, dead, after storms. One known example, found still living on a beach in New Zealand, was reported to give out powerful electric shocks when touched. This suggests that oarfish may hunt in a similar way to the electric eel, using bursts of current to stun and disable prey. This curious fish has been credited with creating many of the myths told about sea serpents, including that of the Loch Ness monster. With its elongated metallic silver body and an oar-shaped head, it certainly matches many of the descriptions of these legendary marine monsters. In Europe, the oarfish is known as 'the king of the herring' because it seems to follow herring shoals.

Regalecus glesne

Where in the world:	Temperate and tropical oceans
Habitat:	To depths of 20–200m (65–656ft)
Size:	Averages 5–8m (16ft 5in–26ft 2in); reported up to 17m (55ft 8in)
Reproduction:	Lays large red or gold-coloured eggs
Life span:	Unknown
Typical diet:	Fish and crustaceans

Scorpionfish

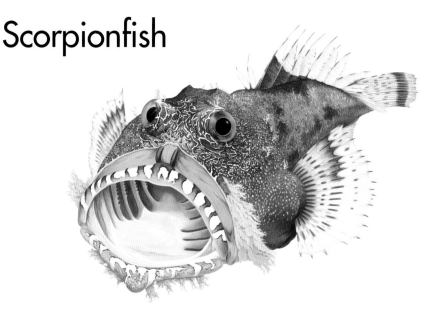

There are around 400 species within the family Scorpaenidae. These include stonefish, sea robins and scorpionfish. Lionfish belong to a distinct division within this group – the subfamily Pteroinae. All of these species share two similar characteristics. First, they have large, gaping mouths. When hunting, scorpionfish are able to open their mouths so quickly that they effectively create a vacuum, which can suck in prey, half their total body size, in 15 milliseconds. Secondly, they have spiny dorsal, pelvic and anal fins. These fins are tipped with venom, which is so toxic that it remains dangerous for days after the fish has been killed. Unlike many venomous animals, a scorpionfish's natural coloration is designed to blend in with the surroundings. They 'flash' their warning colours (by opening their mouths or turning their fins around) only when they are in danger.

Family Scorpaenidae

Where in the world:	The world's oceans
Habitat:	Varies greatly depending on species
Size:	35cm (14in) long; 1.5kg (3lb 5oz) in weight, varying with species
Reproduction:	Egg-laying
Life span:	Averages 5 years in captivity
Typical diet:	Small fish and crustaceans

Piranha

There are around 18 species of piranha found throughout the river systems of Latin America, especially in the tributaries of the mighty Amazon. Naturally, piranha are lone predators; it is when they gather together in huge shoals that their famous 'feeding frenzies' occur. A shoal of piranha is quite capable of reducing a fully grown, 45kg (99lb) pig to bone in under a minute. They are particularly aggressive during the breeding season, when any unusual movement in the water may trigger an attack. A piranha's teeth are relatively small, but very sharp and interlocking. When the piranha closes its overlapping jaws, it forces these flat, razor-sharp wedges together with such force that they slice off circular hunks of flesh. These bite marks are often seen on the fins and tails of Amazonian fish. Despite their reputation, not all piranha are carnivores. Some eat rotting fruit that falls into the river.

Serrasalmus species

Where in the world:	River systems of Latin America
Habitat:	Amazon region
Size:	15–60cm (6–24in) long; 2kg (4lb 8oz) in weight, varying with species
Reproduction:	Males guard eggs and young ('fry') until they are mature
Life span:	Averages 5 years
Typical diet:	Fish, small mammals, insects, fruit and carrion, depending on species

239

Stonefish

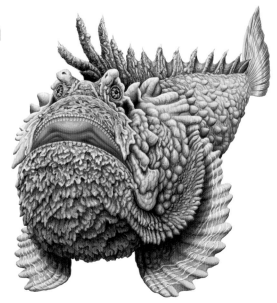

There are around 400 species of fish within the family Scorpaenidae. These include stonefish, sea robins and scorpionfish. Until 1973, estuary and reef stonefish were the only two known species of stonefish. Several more have now been identified, but these are confined to the Indo-Pacific region. In common with all members of the family Scorpaenidae, stonefish have large, gaping mouths. When hunting, they open them so quickly that they effectively create a vacuum, which sucks in prey. They also have stout spines on their dorsal fins, which are tipped with venom. Stonefish are one of the ocean's most toxic fish and a sting is capable of killing a human. The danger to divers is increased by the stonefish's incredible natural camouflage. On the seabed, these lumpy, grey-brown fish are easily mistaken for a piece of rock. Many even have algae growing on their skin.

Synanceia horrisa; Synanceia verrucosa

Where in the world:	Indo-Pacific oceans, including the Red Sea
Habitat:	Bottom-dwellers, to depths of 40m (131ft 3in)
Size:	20–40cm (8–16in), depending on species
Reproduction:	Egg-laying
Life span:	Unknown
Typical diet:	Small fish and crustaceans

Toadfish

With their broad, flat heads, cylindrical bodies and rows of barbels (bristles) around their mouths, toadfish are not an attractive species of fish. They are, however, devoted parents. These shy fish spend much of their time hiding in rock crevices, or in specially dug holes. During the breeding season, these holes are turned in to 'nests', which become the centre of an elaborate mating ritual. Toadfish are famed for their 'singing', and in the early summer males will try to entice females to mate by serenading them. They do this by creating vibrations in their gas-filled swim-bladder, which creates a similar effect to banging a drum. The Atlantic midshipman is a particularly tuneful species. Once the females release their eggs, the male fertilizes them and takes sole responsibility for their care until they are hatched and the young fry are able to fend for themselves.

Sub-Family Thassophryninae

Where in the world:	The world's oceans
Habitat:	Under rocks and in reefs in coastal waters
Size:	7–22cm (2.8–8.7in) long, depending on species
Reproduction:	Male builds 'nest' and vigilantly guards eggs and young (fry)
Life span:	Up to 3 years
Typical diet:	Small crustaceans and molluscs

Electric Ray

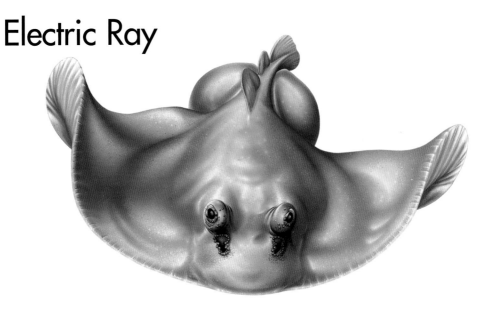

There are 69 species of electric rays, which are divided into two distinct families. The best known are members of the family Torpedinidae, or 'torpedoes'. These fish are closely related to sharks, but look very different, with their flat, round bodies and short, stubby tails. On either side of their tiny eyes are two bulges, which are the ray's electricity-generating organs. Electric rays are able to generate a powerful current (up to 200 volts), which they deliver in short bursts to stun prey. As many as 100 bursts may be used in quick succession to paralyse groups of fish. Rays are slow and sluggish, and spend much of their time hidden in the mud in shallow waters, waiting for a meal to pass by. Preferred food are small crustaceans and molluscs, which they crack open with their broad, platelike teeth. They are also opportunists and will eat carrion if available.

Family Torpedinidae

Where in the world:	Tropical and temperate seas
Habitat:	Adaptable bottom-dwellers found in shallows or deep oceans
Size:	2m (6ft 6in) long; 90kg (198lb) in weight, varying with species
Reproduction:	Gives birth to live young
Life span:	Unknown
Typical diet:	Mainly molluscs and crustaceans

Archer Fish

There are six species of archer fish belonging to the family Toxotidae. These small, attractive fish get their name from their ability to shoot jets of water out of their mouths at land-bound prey. This powerful, air-propelled missile knocks prey into the water, where the archer quickly gobbles it up. Thanks to forward-facing eyes and a pointed snout, which does not impair its vision, archers have excellent eyesight. They are able to 'shoot' accurately at targets up to 2m (6ft 6in) away. However, this is not an innate skill. They have to practise, and young archer fish can often be seen taking 'pot shots' at rocks and leaves on the river bed. They are also extremely athletic, and, if they cannot bring down a meal by shooting it, they have been known to leap up to 30cm (12in) out of the water to snatch insects from the air as they fly past.

Toxotes species

Where in the world:	Indo-Australian region
Habitat:	Mangrove swamps and brackish coastal waters
Size:	Up to 30cm (12in) long, depending on species
Reproduction:	Spawns around coral reefs; young head for fresh water once born
Life span:	Unknown
Typical diet:	Insects, invertebrates and small fish

Weeverfish

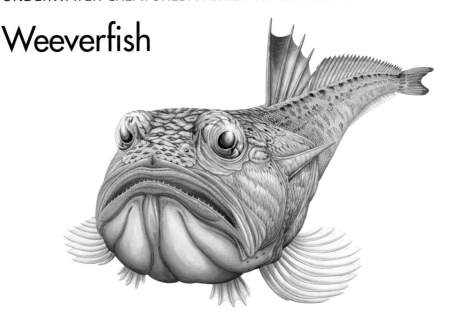

There are four known species of weeverfish, which can be found in shallow waters as far afield as Europe to West Africa. There may even be species in the Pacific Ocean, although this is still to be confirmed. Weevers are nocturnal hunters and spend much of the day hidden in the sand on the seabed, waiting for a meal to swim by. This is a stubby bodied but muscular fish with a spiny, venom-laden dorsal fin and toxic 'opercular' spines covering the gill slits. Unlike most fish, which have a gas-filled sac to help keep them afloat, the weever spends most of its time on the ocean floor, so it does not need a swim bladder. Despite their venom, weevers make a popular addition to menus in restaurants in Europe. However, as they can still sting when dead, care is needed in their preparation.

Family Trachinidae

Where in the world:	North East Atlantic Ocean; Mediterranean Sea
Habitat:	Coastal waters, to depths of 100m (328ft)
Size:	Up to 45cm (17.7in) long, depending on species
Reproduction:	Egg-laying
Life span:	Unknown
Typical diet:	Small fish, crustaceans and molluscs

Sea Robin

S ea robins – or gurnards, as they are also called – belong to a distinct subdivision within the family Scorpaenidae. This is a group that includes stonefish and scorpionfish. This bizarre bottom-dweller uses its two pectoral fins like legs to crawl along the seabed. At the tip of each fin are three 'rays', which are loose from the main fin membrane. These contain sensory organs that allow the fish to probe for food in the sand. Each fin can be moved independently, allowing the sea robin to make a wide 'sweep' of the area in search of a meal. These flat, scaly fish are famed for the loud noises which they make when distressed. They do this by vibrating their muscles against their swim bladder – the gas-filled organ which helps them to maintain buoyancy in water. The result is a sound similar to a drum being beaten.

Sub-Family Triglidae

Where in the world:	Tropical and temperate oceans
Habitat:	Bottom-dwellers, in cool coastal waters, to depths of 800m (2625ft)
Size:	Up to 90cm (36in) long
Reproduction:	Egg-laying
Life span:	Up to 7 years
Typical diet:	Small fish, crustaceans and molluscs, marine invertebrates

Stargazer

Stargazer is the name given to around 50 species of fish belonging to the family Uranoscopidae. These are a bottom-dwelling (or 'benthic') species, which spend much of their time buried in the mud of the seabed, lying in wait for prey. Their eyes, nostrils and mouth are set high on the head, enabling them to see while almost completely submerged. In some species, a small flap of skin on the bottom lip is used as a lure to attract a meal. Other species are able to stun prey by discharging a short electric pulse. Stargazers of the family Uranoscopidae are found mainly in the oceans of the Southern Hemisphere. Sand stargazers of the family Dactyloscopidae are very closely related and share many physical characteristics, as well as a benthic lifestyle. Dactyloscopidae stargazers, however, live primarily in the waters of the Northern Hemisphere.

Family Uranoscopidae

Where in the world:	Southern oceans
Habitat:	Bottom-dweller
Size:	Up to 70cm (28in) long; up to 9kg (19lb 13oz) in weight
Reproduction:	Mates in spring and summer; lays free-floating eggs
Life span:	Unknown
Typical diet:	Small fish and crustaceans

Marine Iguana

Unlike most islands, which were joined to a larger mainland at some point in their history, the Galapagos Islands were created by volcanic activity. The islands and the animals on them have developed in complete isolation. The effect of this is that there are numerous species on the Galapagos which can be found nowhere else on Earth – and one of the most interesting is the marine iguana. Many lizards are perfectly at home in the water, but the marine iguana is the only true aquatic lizard. Living on a diet of algae and seaweed, this remarkable reptile uses its powerful, rudder-like tail to power through the water. It also has specially adapted glands in its nose to excrete salt. As the waters of the Galapagos can be cool, marine iguanas spend much of their time basking on the rocks, in order to raise their body temperatures high enough to swim.

Amblyrhynchus cristatus

Where in the world:	Galapagos Islands
Habitat:	Coastal regions
Size:	Up to 1.4m (5ft) long; up to 12kg (26lb 5 oz) in weight
Reproduction:	Lays 2–3 eggs, which are buried in the sand
Life span:	20–40 years
Typical diet:	Marine algae and seaweed

Green Anole

There is only one species of anole to be found in the USA – but it is perhaps the most attractive of them all. The American green anole is a common sight on urban walls and fences, where its bright green body makes it extremely easy to spot. Often mistaken for a chameleon, the anole can, and does, change colour, but this vibrant coloration is what tells us that this little lizard is happy and healthy. The green anole's other major distinguishing features are its padded toes, which enable it to grip smooth surfaces in a similar way to the gecko, and the large flap of loose skin under its neck. This pink sack is called a 'dewlap' and it can be inflated during courtship displays or territorial standoffs to make the anole's slender body and head seem more imposing.

Anolis carolinesis

Where in the world:	Southeast USA
Habitat:	Sunny woodlands, scrub and gardens
Size:	12–20cm (4.7–8in) long
Reproduction:	Lays 1 egg
Life span:	5–10 years
Typical diet:	Insects and spiders

Basilisk Lizard

In classical mythology, the basilisk was a giant serpent, which could kill its victims simply by looking at them. Fortunately, the real life basilisk is a little less formidable. Of the nine species, most can be found in the forests of Central and Northern Latin America. These vary in appearance, but share many characteristics with the common basilisk, *Basiliscus basiliscus*. This has a distinctive sail-like crest on its back and a long, tapered tail, which it uses as a counterweight when running. Like their close relatives, the iguanas, basilisks are at home among the trees, where their long, powerful legs help to make them natural climbers. They are also excellent runners. Reaching speeds of up to 12km/h (7.5mph), they can even run – for brief periods – on water. It is an ability which has earned them the nickname 'Jesus lizards'.

Basiliscus species

Where in the world:	Southern Mexico to Venezuela
Habitat:	Primarily a forest dweller
Size:	Male 1m (40in) long; 60g (2.1oz) in weight, varying with species
Reproduction:	Up to 18 eggs may be laid, 8 times during the breeding season
Life span:	Around 7 years
Typical diet:	Insects, birds, fish, fruit and flowers

Ground Chameleon

Although not as showy or as colourful as many of their larger relatives, the 24 known species of tiny 'pygmy' chameleons are some of the most fascinating members of the lizard family. Clad in an array of spines and horny plates, with a brown, earthy coloration, these miniature reptiles are virtually invisible in their natural habitat. Pick up a handful of leaf litter from the rainforest floor, and you would still be hard-pressed to spot a ground chameleon. Only the occasional flash of pink from a sticky, telescopic tongue (which is common to all chameleons) may give the game away. In fact, they are so hard to spot that, in Madagascar, local people are terrified to venture out into the forest for fear of accidentally stepping on these tiny creatures. In legend, anyone who does so will be cursed for ever with bad luck and ill health.

Brookesia species

Where in the world:	Mainly Madagascar
Habitat:	Rainforests and mountains
Size:	3–10cm (1.2–4in) long, depending on species
Reproduction:	Mates in spring; lays 2–4 eggs, depending on species
Life span:	Unknown
Typical diet:	Small insects

Jackson's Chameleon

Chameleons are perhaps the most well known of all lizards, but their fame is based on a misconception. Their ability to alter their skin colour is a response to variations in the environment or the lizard's emotional state, not an attempt to blend in. Nor is it a unique ability; many other lizards do it. Distributed throughout humid forest areas, these fascinating members of the family Chamaeleonidae are fiercely territorial. Yet encounters between males rarely result in a physical battle. As is common in the animal kingdom, contests for land or a mate are often settled by bluff. The lizard which looks bigger and more aggressive will generally win! In fact, the characteristic triple horns on the head of Jackson's chameleon probably developed for this very reason. Females of the species may also have horns, although they are much smaller, and can be missing entirely in some sub-species.

Chamaeleo jacksonii

Where in the world:	Native to Africa; introduced into parts of the USA
Habitat:	Primarily a forest-dweller
Size:	Averaging 20–32cm (8–12.6in) long from nose to tail
Reproduction:	Sexually mature at 5 months; gives birth to 5–50 live young
Life span:	Up to 6 years in the wild; 10 in captivity
Typical diet:	Mainly insects

Frilled Lizard

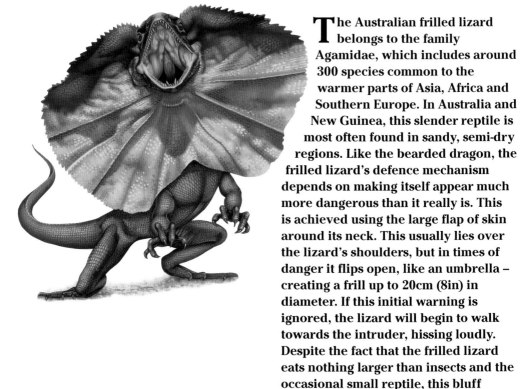

The Australian frilled lizard belongs to the family Agamidae, which includes around 300 species common to the warmer parts of Asia, Africa and Southern Europe. In Australia and New Guinea, this slender reptile is most often found in sandy, semi-dry regions. Like the bearded dragon, the frilled lizard's defence mechanism depends on making itself appear much more dangerous than it really is. This is achieved using the large flap of skin around its neck. This usually lies over the lizard's shoulders, but in times of danger it flips open, like an umbrella – creating a frill up to 20cm (8in) in diameter. If this initial warning is ignored, the lizard will begin to walk towards the intruder, hissing loudly. Despite the fact that the frilled lizard eats nothing larger than insects and the occasional small reptile, this bluff usually pays off.

Chlamydosaurus kingii

Where in the world:	Northern Australia and Southern New Guinea
Habitat:	Primarily a forest-dweller
Size:	60–75cm (24–30in) long; up to 700g (1lb 9oz) in weight
Reproduction:	Lays 10–15 eggs
Life span:	5 years in the wild; up to 10 in captivity
Typical diet:	Insects and small reptiles

Sungazer Lizard

The sungazer belongs to a family of stout, heavy lizards called Cordylidae. All of the 20 or so species from this family are thickly armoured, with large spines all over the body and tail. When attacked, a sungazer uses these spines defensively – lying flat out, with its arms and legs extended, to protect its soft underbelly. Although they have large claws and long, powerful legs, sungazers use these for digging burrows, rather climbing tress. A typical burrow can be 42cm (16.5in) deep and 1.8m (6ft) long. Each is occupied by a single lizard, although small family groups, especially mothers and young, may share for short periods. During the day, the sungazer likes nothing better than basking in the sun at the entrance to its burrow. An Afrikaans legend says that sungazers always face the sun – hence the rather evocative name.

Cordylus species

Where in the world:	Southern and Eastern Africa
Habitat:	Dry, rocky regions
Size:	15–40cm (6–16in) long, depending on species
Reproduction:	1–2 live young a year, depending on species
Life span:	Up to 25 years in captivity
Typical diet:	Reptiles, including snakes and small mammals

Flying Lizard

The tree-dwelling lizards, or 'dragons', of Southeast Asia have a remarkable ability. They can fly – or, at least, glide. This is made possible through a set of elongated 'ribs', which extend out from the body to support a thin membrane of skin. When the dragon wishes to 'fly', it leaps from the tree and stretches out the membrane to form a pair of static wings, a little like a hang-glider. It used to be believed that flying lizards could do little more than 'controlled falling', but studies have shown that they can direct their flight by slight movements of the membrane and their tail. On average, a flying lizard can cover about 60m (196ft), which is enough to put a safe distance between itself and any potential predator. In comparison, the flying gecko can manage around only 10m (32ft 10in).

Draco volans

Where in the world:	Southeast Asia
Habitat:	Primarily rainforest
Size:	15–22cm (6–8.5in) in length
Reproduction:	Lays 2–5 eggs
Life span:	Up to 10 years
Typical diet:	Mainly ants and termites

Panther Chameleon

Lizards are some of nature's most colourful creatures. None more so than the panther chameleon, which comes in an amazing array of hues and tones. In general, these colours vary depending on where the chameleon is found. On the island of Ambanja, for example, males have vibrant turquoise and green bodies, with striking flashes of red and gold radiating out from their eyes. In North Havea, they are equally appealing and come in a glorious green colour, which is broken with striking purple bands. Found in warm, damp regions of coastal Madagascar, Mauritius and Réunion, these beautiful lizards prefer to live off the ground, on trees and in bushes. In their native regions, they are currently in danger, due to the destruction of their habitats, but have long been an extremely popular species with lizard breeders and reptile enthusiasts.

Furcifer pardalis

Where in the world:	Mainly Madagascar
Habitat:	Humid, tropical rainforest and scrubland.
Size:	Male up to 50cm (20in) long; female up to 35cm (14in)
Reproduction:	Sexually mature at 1–2 years; lays 5–8 clutches of 12–30 eggs a year
Life span:	Around 3 years in the wild
Typical diet:	Insects, small birds and reptiles

Mexican Beaded Lizard

Famous as one of the world's few venomous lizards, the Mexican beaded lizard has a fearsome reputation. With its heavy, sturdy body, thick neck and mighty limbs, this large reptile has all the making of a powerful and formidable predator. Yet, while its bite can be fatal to humans, it rarely preys on anything bigger than rodents. When it does hunt, the black-and-yellow banding on its beadlike scales help it to blend in with the foliage of thorn scrub, which is common in its native habitat. Like a snake, the beaded lizard is also able to 'taste' its prey's scent using its 'bifid', or forked, tongue to pick up chemical signals from the air. Once bitten, its prey is quickly paralysed by poison, which is injected into the wound by the lizard chewing down on the wound.

Heloderma horridum

Where in the world:	Mexico and Guatemala
Habitat:	Primarily scrubland
Size:	Up to 1m (40in) long
Reproduction:	Mates in spring; lays 8–10 eggs
Life span:	Up to 20 years
Typical diet:	Rodents, birds and eggs

Green Iguana

There are more than 860 species of iguana, of which the common or green iguana is one of the largest and most distinctive-looking. When young, this spectacular lizard has bright green and blue markings. This natural coloration tends to become less dramatic with age, although many mature iguanas will develop orange marks on their front legs. The green iguana is primarily a tree-dweller, and is found throughout the tropical forests of Latin America, where its long hind legs are particularly useful in helping it to climb and grip bark. When in danger, it is equally at home in the water and swims well, using its powerful tail to propel it forwards. This tail can be shed if the iguana is captured – an ability known as 'autotomy' – which is especially useful in regions where its flesh is considered a local delicacy.

Iguana iguana

Where in the world:	Central Latin America; the Caribbean; introduced into USA
Habitat:	Primarily a forest-dweller
Size:	1.5–2m (5ft–6ft 6in) long; up to 12kg (26lb 8oz) in weight
Reproduction:	Sexual maturity at 2–3 years; lays 20–70 eggs per clutch
Life span:	Averages 10 years
Typical diet:	Leaves and insects

Thorny Devil

There are more than 350 members of the family Agamidae, and undoubtedly the most striking in appearance is the thorny devil, which bears the Latin name *Moloch horridus*, after the terrible Canaanite demon Moloch. This squat, short, flat-bodied lizard looks more like a cactus than a living creature, being covered from head to toe with horns and large thornlike spiny scales. The largest of these are positioned just above the eyes and in a collar around the neck. These undoubtedly have some defensive uses, but, surprisingly, their main purpose seems to be to help the moloch survive in the parched desert environment where it makes its home. Each spine is arranged so that any rainwater that falls is automatically channelled downwards towards the moloch's mouth – thereby giving this ugly little devil access to an invaluable additional supply of fresh water.

Moloch horridus

Where in the world:	Central and Western Australia
Habitat:	Primarily arid regions
Size:	15–18cm (6–7in) long; 35–90g (1.2–3.2oz) in weight
Reproduction:	Lays 3–10 eggs between September and December
Life span:	Up to 20 years
Typical diet:	Insects, especially ants

Regal Horned Lizard

T he flat, squat appearance of this spiny member of the family Iguanidae is responsible for the fact that it is also known by the name 'horned toad' (*Phrynosoma* means 'toad body'). Found mainly in sandy deserts of Southwest America and Mexico, this broad-bodied lizard is generally reddish-brown in colour, with a pale, yellowish underbelly. These colours may change depending on local temperature, humidity and the lizard's emotional state. One of the regal horned lizard's most striking features, however, is not immediately obvious. It occurs only when the lizard is under threat. By restricting the flow of blood from its head, it can cause small veins in its eyes to burst. The result is a jet of blood from its eyes, which can be propelled forwards up to 1m (40in). This feat usually distracts aggressors long enough for this regal reptile to make a swift getaway.

Phrynosoma solare

Where in the world:	Sonoran Desert region of Northwest Mexico and Arizona
Habitat:	Arid, desert regions
Size:	Up to 13cm (5.1in) long
Reproduction:	Sexually mature within 2 years; lays 10–30 eggs in May–August
Life span:	Unknown
Typical diet:	Mainly ants

Bearded Dragon

Central Australia is home to seven species of this stocky lizard – two of which are beardless. It spends much of the early morning basking in the sun to warm its body before becoming active for the day. Its name comes from its behaviour when threatened. If intimidated, mature males will open their mouths to inflate a collar of semi-rigid spines that lie around the lizard's blunt, triangular head. This 'beard' daunts potential attackers. Bearded Dragons can be aggressive, especially during the mating season, when rivals often fight. During such encounters, these squat males may also change colour, as pigments in the skin react to the lizards' changing emotional state. Such displays can make a spectacular spectacle.

Pogona species

Where in the world:	Australia
Habitat:	From coastal regions to desert environments, depending on species
Size:	30–50cm (12–20in) long, depending on species
Reproduction:	Sexually mature at 1–2 years; lays 11–16 eggs
Life span:	5 years in captivity
Typical diet:	Insects and vegetation, including fruit and flowers

Chuckwalla

Only one species of chuckwalla, the common chuckwalla, is native to the USA, and this is the country's second-largest lizard – just smaller than the great gila monster. They look like fierce predators, but chuckwallas are timid and shy creatures. If approached, they will often retreat to the nearest rock face and wedge themselves into a crevice. By inflating their lungs, they increase their body size, making it almost impossible for them to be removed from their hiding place by force. They are also strict herbivores and particularly enjoy yellow flowers of the type found on brittle bushes. In fact, they will often perform great acrobatics to get to these prized delicacies. In their native habitats – in the deserts of California and in Nevada, Utah and Arizona – chuckwallas are currently a 'Federal Concern Species', although they thrive in areas where there is little human activity.

Sauromalus species

Where in the world:	Mainly Mojave and Sonoran deserts
Habitat:	Arid, desert environments
Size:	28–40cm (11–16in) long; 2kg (4lb 8oz) in weight, varying with species
Reproduction:	Lays up to 20 eggs, depending on species
Life span:	Up to 25 years
Typical diet:	Mainly flowers and leaves

Sandfish Skink

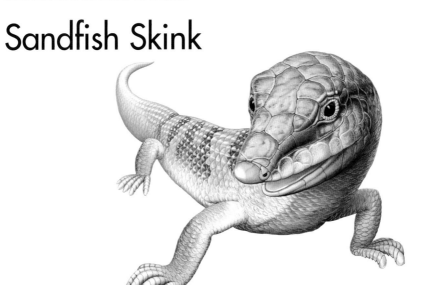

With their long, thin, almost limb-less bodies, most skinks look so similar to snakes that they are often mistaken for them. However, the eight species of sandfish skink belong to a unique group of lizards the bodies of whic h have adapted to a life spent burrowing through the desert sands. Unlike other members of the Scincidae family, sandfish skinks have powerful though small fully formed limbs, a smooth, sleek streamlined body and a tapered tail and head. These help them to 'swim' just below the surface of the sand with ease. When hunting using this technique, these small skinks are silent and efficient, homing in on insect vibrations to strike quickly and without warning. Sandfish skinks need abundant heat to thrive and so make their homes in some of the world's most arid and inhospitable regions – in the deserts of North Africa and Egypt.

Scincus species

Where in the world:	North Africa; Arabia; West Pakistan
Habitat:	Arid, desert regions
Size:	15–20cm (6–8in), depending on species
Reproduction:	Lays up to 10 eggs, depending on species
Life span:	Varies with species
Typical diet:	Mainly insects and small reptiles

Tuatara

The tuatara may look like a lizard, but it is not. This amazing creature is the last survivor of a group of reptiles called Sphenodontia, which roamed the Earth 200 million years ago. It is a genuine 'living fossil', the closest relatives of which died out 60 million years ago. Tuataras used to be found on the New Zealand 'mainland', but now survive on only 32 of the more isolated offshore islands. Of the two known species, the Cook Strait tuatara is the most common – around 50,000 live on Stephen's Island. There are believed to be fewer than 400 adult *Sphenodon guntheri* (Brother's Island tuataras), although the population is stable. The tuatara's most famous feature is a fascinating 'pineal' third eye. This looks like a tiny spot on the reptile's forehead, but is actually a light-sensitive region, which allows the young tuatara to extract vital vitamin D from the sun's rays.

Sphenodon punctatus

Where in the world:	New Zealand's North and South islands
Habitat:	Cool mountainous regions
Size:	Male up to 60cm (24in) long; 1kg (2lb 4 oz) in weight
Reproduction:	Sexually mature at 15–20 years; lays 10–20 eggs every 2–5 years
Life span:	Up to 100 years
Typical diet:	Insects, spiders, birds and eggs

Shingleback Skink

T here are more skinks than any other type of lizard. Yet this diverse and widespread family nevertheless shares many physical similarities. One of the most obvious is their short, stubby limbs, which makes them poor climbers – although they are surprisingly fast runners. Many also have large, thick, fleshy tongues. In the case of the shingleback, and many other Australian skinks, this comes in a vivid blue colour, which is extremely effective at startling would-be attackers. Most skinks are also able to shed their tails if caught by predators. This ability is called 'autotomy'. Usually the shed tail can be regrown within a few months, although occasionally this process goes wrong, resulting in two or even more tails. This is not a problem which the shingleback or bobtail skink is ever likely to have. In fact, its stubby remnant of a tail is often mistaken for its head.

Trachydosaurus rugosus

Where in the world:	Southern Australia
Habitat:	Prefers dry regions
Size:	Grows to 40cm (16in) long; up to 1kg (2lb 4oz) in weight
Reproduction:	Mates in spring; gives birth to 2–3 live young
Life span:	Up to 40 years
Typical diet:	Flowers, fruit and small insects

Leaf-tailed Gecko

The leaf-tailed gecko, which lives in the forests of Eastern Madagascar, was once believed to be the only member of the family Uroplatidae. Today, however, it is classified as a gecko, one of the 900 species making up the widespread family Gekkonidea. Geckos are easy to distinguish from other lizards because of the flattened bodies and adhesive pads on their hands and feet, which help them to walk with ease on vertical surfaces. As their names implies, leaf-tailed geckos also have a distinctive, flat, leaf-shaped tail, which forms part of their natural camouflage. Like many lizards, this species can change its skin colour, using hormones to lighten or darken its mottled brown coloration. This ability has also earned it the name 'bark gecko' because, when resting on the branch of a tree, it can be extremely hard to spot.

Uroplatus fimbriatus

Where in the world:	Madagascar
Habitat:	Dense forest
Size:	20–30cm (8–12in) long
Reproduction:	Lays 3 clutches of 2 eggs per breeding season
Life span:	Up to 10 years
Typical diet:	Mainly insects and spiders

Savannah Monitor

As its common name implies, the savannah monitor is found primarily on the grasslands, where its natural grey-brown coloration helps it to blend in perfectly with its surroundings. For this large, heavy lizard, life on the savannah is one of feast and famine. During the eight-month wet season, food is plentiful and this natural carnivore will eat birds, small mammals and even carrion. In one day, it is estimated that this ravenous reptile can consume up to a tenth of its own body weight. These reserves – which are mainly stored in its tail – are vital for survival in the dry season. If things get really tough, though, this resourceful lizard will simply become dormant until food is plentiful again. Such adaptability has made the savannah monitor abundant in its natural habitat – even in regions where its tough skin is popularly used for bags and shoes.

Varanus exanthematicus

Where in the world:	West and Central Africa
Habitat:	Primarily grasslands
Size:	Up to 1.5m (5ft) long; up to 5.5kg (12lb 2oz) in weight
Reproduction:	Lays 20–50 eggs
Life span:	10–25 years
Typical diet:	Birds, small mammals and carrion

Nile Monitor

Although they are a familiar sight on the Upper Nile River, the two sub-species of Nile monitor (*Varanus niloticus nilocticus* and *Varanus niloticus ornatusis*) are suited to life in many habitats. With their large, powerful legs, these big lizards are both good climbers and excellent burrowers. They are also proficient swimmers and can dive and lie submerged in the water for at least an hour. Growing to around 2m (6ft 6in) in length, the Nile monitor is able to feed on a wide range of prey. Other lizards, small mammals and birds form part of these giant reptiles' regular diet, but crocodile eggs are a favourite. Like all monitors, the Nile variety boasts a long, powerful tail, which is often used in preference to teeth for defence. They can also rear up on their huge hind legs when threatened – making an impressive and terrifying spectacle.

Varanus niloticus

Where in the world:	Africa
Habitat:	Primarily rivers, coastal regions and swamplands
Size:	Up to 2m (6ft 6in) long; 2kg (4lb 8oz) in weight
Reproduction:	Lays 20–60 very large (50g/1.8oz) eggs
Life span:	Up to 15 years in captivity
Typical diet:	Insects, eggs, birds, small mammals and reptiles

Salvador's Monitor

The Salvador's monitor is known in its native Papua New Guinea as the 'tree crocodile' due to its reported habit of dropping down from trees to carry away domestic animals and local hunting dogs. However, this reclusive reptile is actually very docile and can even be tamed and kept as a pet. The Salvador's monitor spends much of its time in the trees, where its massive, curved, black claws and incredibly long prehensile tail enable it to hang, almost upside-down, from branches. The Salvador's is officially the longest lizard in the world, and much of its length (around two-thirds) is comprised of tail. Once the lizard is on the ground, this is usually kept coiled; however, when the lizard is in danger, it can be used as an extremely effective weapon. Zoo keepers have even reported the Salvador's monitor using it, whiplike, to aim blows at keeper's eyes.

Varanus salvadori

Where in the world:	New Guinea and Northern Australia
Habitat:	Tropical forests and mangrove swamps
Size:	Up to 4.75m (15ft 6in) long; up to 14kg (30lb 13 oz) in weight
Reproduction:	Egg-laying
Life span:	Up to 12 years in the wild; 20 years in captivity
Typical diet:	Small mammals, reptiles and carrion

Death Adder

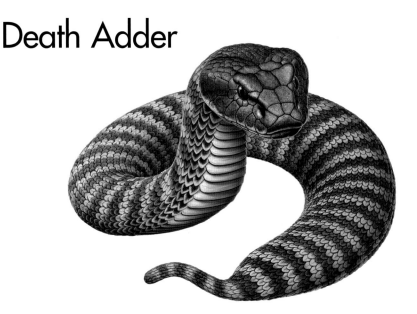

Australia was isolated from the rest of the world 200 million years ago, when the great continental landmass of Pangaea began to break apart. This meant that species in Australia were free to thrive and develop in their own way. Vipers never reached the great island continent, but snakes from the family Elapidae did. These include the adder, which has adapted over the millennia to fill the same niche as the viper. This is especially true of the death adder. Australia is home to at least three species of this secretive snake – the northern, southern and desert death adder – and all have the same stout bodies and broad, triangular head as vipers. Unlike vipers, death adders are all venomous and will often use their thin tails as bait to lure prey within striking distance.

Acanthophis species

Where in the world:	Australia and New Guinea
Habitat:	Varies with species
Size:	Up to 1m (40in) long, depending on species
Reproduction:	Gives birth to 2–8 live young, depending on species
Life span:	Unknown
Typical diet:	Small reptiles, mammals and birds

Cottonmouth Snake

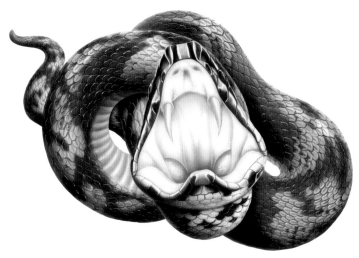

This poisonous and bad-tempered snake belongs to the genus *Agkistrodon*. This group includes the copperhead, which makes its home in the Eastern United States and Mexico. Its South Coast equivalent is the cottonmouth snake, also known as the water moccasin. When young, this large, heavy, water-loving snake has a distinctive orange–brown banding. This fades, leaving a grey or green-black colour, with the occasional indistinct stripe, along the body. The cottonmouth gets its rather strange name from the colour of the inside of its mouth, which it displays aggressively when threatened. One of the largest of America's venomous snakes, the cottonmouth often reaches 2m (6ft 6in) in length. Like its relative the copperhead, the cottonmouth gives birth to live young, which are born with a yellow tail-tip. This is used to lure prey, a little like an angler baiting the hook.

Agkistrodon piscivorus

Where in the world:	Southern USA
Habitat:	Bayous, swamps and wetlands
Size:	Up to 2m (6ft 6in) long
Reproduction:	Gives birth to 1–16 live young
Life span:	Unknown
Typical diet:	Small reptiles mammals, amphibians and fish

Long-nosed Tree Snake

The eight species of long-nosed tree Snake – or 'whip snakes', as they are sometimes called – are extremely slim-bodied snakes, with a remarkably narrow head and pointed snout. This snout is an adaptation designed to help hunting. Grooves running from the snake's eyes to the tip of the snout act as 'rifle sights', allowing the tree snake to zero-in on prey with incredible accuracy. In fact, the snake's snout is so narrow that not only does it have unpaired forward vision, but also the visual range of each eye overlaps. The result is that the tree snake can see in 3D. Unlike other snakes, which focus on prey by moving the entire eye lens in and out (like a camera lens), the tree snake's eyes have lenses that change shape to focus, like a human eye. This is faster and more efficient, giving the tree snake the ability to strike prey quickly and accurately.

Ahaetulla species

Where in the world:	Asia, from India to Southern China
Habitat:	Primarily arboreal
Size:	1–1.8m (3ft 3in–6ft) long, depending on species
Reproduction:	Gives birth to 3–24 live young
Life span:	Averages 6 years
Typical diet:	Small reptiles and birds

Bush Viper

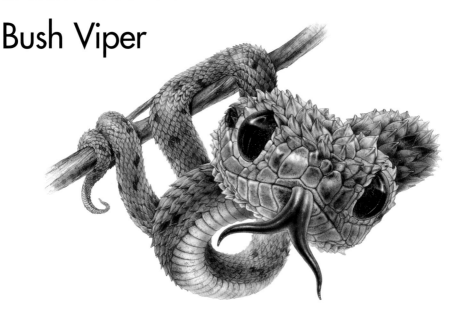

Bush vipers – or leaf vipers, as they are also known – are true tree-dwellers. Of the nine known species, only two (*Atheris supercillaris* and *Atheris hindii*) are terrestrial. The others make their homes among the tropical forests and swamps of Central Africa – and species are found from Guinea to Mozambique. Bush vipers are generally shy and little is known about them, except that their numbers are declining rapidly. Forest species are particularly at risk as loggers clear areas for agriculture or to build housing. As a result, bush vipers have moved into coffee plantations, where they are even more unwelcome. Like all arboreal species, bush vipers have long prehensile tails, which they use to hold onto branches when they leap forwards to catch prey. They also have superb natural camouflage, and come in a variety of colours from pale leafy greens to woody browns.

Atheris species

Where in the world:	Central Africa
Habitat:	Excepting *Atheris supercillaris* and *Atheris hindii*, all are tree-dwellers
Size:	Up to 75cm (30in) long, depending on species
Reproduction:	Gives birth to 20–50 live young
Life span:	20 years
Typical diet:	Small reptiles, rodents, birds and other snakes

Puff Adder

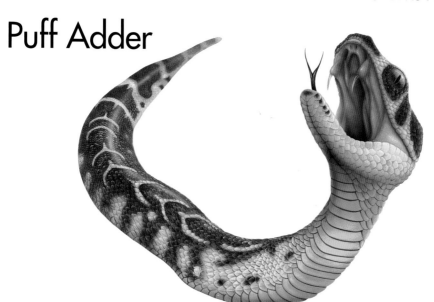

Good camouflage is an essential tool for any successful hunter. Being able to blend with your surroundings gives you an immediate advantage over other species – and in Africa's scorched deserts and savannah, puff adders are masters of the art. These heavy, stout snakes come in all shades of desert camouflage, from pale mottled browns to yellows and greys. These colours harmonize so well with the environment that, by lying completely still, puff adders become virtually invisible. This enables them to capture small animals such as frogs without need of venom. Larger animals are bitten, and the venom is injected into the wound. Once the poison has done its deadly work, the adder will follow the prey's scent and swallow it whole. Like all snakes, it can do this because its jaw is split from the skull at the chin, allowing it to flip open on strong elastic ligaments.

Bitis arietans

Where in the world:	Throughout Africa and parts of Arabia
Habitat:	Primarily savannah, though very adaptable
Size:	Up to 2m (6ft 6in) in length
Reproduction:	40–150 live young
Life span:	Averages 10 years
Typical diet:	Small reptiles and mammals

Gaboon Viper

Snakes of the genus *Bitis* tend to be heavy, with thickset bodies, a short tail and a wide, oversized head. This is especially apparent in the case of the Gaboon viper and its two sub-species, which have pale leaf-shaped heads and bulbous, beautifully geometrically patterned bodies. Such a large head is needed to house the viper's massive fangs. The Gaboon viper has the longest fangs of any snake, growing up to 5cm (2in) in length. At rest, these lie flat against the roof of the snake's mouth, protected by a fine membrane sheath. Once prey is in sight, the viper lunges forwards, opening its mouth fully to allow its fangs to swing forwards. Such large fangs can deliver massive quantities of venom very quickly, making the Gaboon viper an extremely efficient and deadly hunter.

Bitis gabonica

Where in the world:	Central and East Africa
Habitat:	Primarily arboreal
Size:	1.2–2m (4ft–6ft 6in) long; up to 15kg (33lb) in weight
Reproduction:	Gives birth to 16–60 live young
Life span:	Up to 8 years
Typical diet:	Small mammals

Rhinoceros-horned Viper

With its bold geometric body pattern and long hornlike bulges on its snout, the rhinoceros-horned viper is one of the most curious-looking members of the viper family. At rest, coiled up in the undergrowth, these bulky snakes can seem sleepy and unresponsive, but they can move with surprising speed if necessary. During an attack, a rhinoceros-horned viper can propel itself forward at around 3m (9ft 10in) per second. As it reaches its target, it opens its mouth wide to allow its long fangs, which lie flat at rest, to swing forwards. Once it has injected its venom, the snake withdraws quickly. With such long fangs, it has no need to bite down hard to inject its poison; in fact, it risks breaking its fangs by holding on too long. If a fang is broken, though, it has up to six replacements growing at any one time – just in case.

Bitis nasicornis

Where in the world:	Central and West Africa
Habitat:	Primarily tropical rainforest
Size:	Up to 1.5m (5ft)
Reproduction:	Gives birth to 6–40 live young
Life span:	Up to 15 years
Typical diet:	Small reptiles, mammals and amphibians

Mangrove Snake

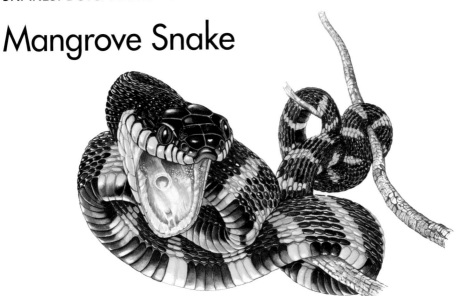

This spectacular yellow-and-black patterned snake is equally at home in both the trees and the rivers of its Asian forest homelands. It is an excellent climber and an accomplished swimmer, with a slightly flattened body, which enables it to slide between branches and foliage with ease. Although it is a nocturnal hunter, this large snake is often seen basking in the sun on trees and river banks, where it regularly encounters humans. While most snakes will avoid confrontation, the mangrove snake has a reputation as irritable and aggressive. It is poisonous, but will also often use the coils of its body, constrictor-like, to help subdue its prey. Despite their hostile nature, the attractive appearance of this boldly coloured snake makes them popular pets. They are also one of the many species used by snake charmers to entertain crowds throughout Asia.

Boiga dendrophila

Where in the world:	Southeast Asia
Habitat:	Mangrove swamps and rainforests
Size:	2–2.5m (6ft 6in–8ft 2in) long
Reproduction:	Lays 4–15 eggs.
Life span:	Unknown
Typical diet:	Small reptiles, mammals, birds and eggs

Eyelash Viper

There are two main groups of vipers: 'true vipers', such as the European viper or the bush viper; and 'pit vipers', which include the eyelash viper. Common in Central and Northern Latin America, this distinctive tree-dweller can be recognized by the raised scales around its eyes, which give it its common name. Like all pit vipers, the eyelash viper has a highly developed, heat-sensitive organ, which can be found in pits near the eyes. These enable the snake to locate food by sensing their prey's body heat. Vipers also have elongated fangs – often as long as their entire head. These fold back on a hinged bone when not in use, but can be quickly swung forwards and upwards when the snake strikes. This characteristic means that, unlike the short-fanged cobra, vipers do not need to hold on to their prey to inject it with poison.

Bothriechis schlegelii

Where in the world:	Central and Northern Latin America
Habitat:	Primarily arboreal
Size:	50–80cm (20–32in) long
Reproduction:	Gives birth to 11–24 live young
Life span:	Up to 10 years in the wild
Typical diet:	Small reptiles, mammals and amphibians

Jumping Viper

This chiefly nocturnal snake gets its common name from its alarming habit of throwing itself at prey with such force that it actually leaves the ground. This enables it to deliver a bite quickly with little danger of being injured by the started or struggling prey. Front-fanged snakes, like cobras, have short fangs, which deliver small amounts of venom. This tends to be highly toxic and will paralyse or kill prey instantly. Vipers have fangs which are so long that they sit at the back of the mouth and have to be folded back when the snake's mouth is closed. The viper's venom is 'hemotoxic'. It does not cause instant death, but slow bleeding and severe tissue damage. Often the prey will crawl away to die, leaving the viper to track its victim using its specially developed heat-sensitive 'pit' organs.

Bothrops nummifer

Where in the world:	Central Latin America
Habitat:	Primarily rainforest
Size:	Up to 60cm (24in) long
Reproduction:	Gives birth to 6–12 live young
Life span:	Unknown
Typical diet:	Small lizards, rodents and frogs

Fer De Lance

The fer de lance, or lancehead, gets its name from the snake's V-shaped head, which looks like an ancient knight's blunt lance tip. Well known throughout Latin America, it is also a familiar sight on plantations in the West Indies, where it is a genuine hazard to workers. This tree-loving reptile is nocturnal, but will attack humans if it feels threatened, even during the day. Like many members of the viper family, the fer de lance is highly poisonous, and attempts were made in the nineteenth century to control the threat it posed by introducing mongoose to the islands. This tenacious little predator is one of the snake's few natural enemies and was so successful in controlling its numbers that it eventually became a pest itself. Left unmolested, however, the fer de lance is shy and secretive, leaving its lair only in the dead of night to hunt for birds and small rodents.

Bothrops species

Where in the world:	Central and Northern Latin America; West Indies
Habitat:	From rainforest to savannah, depending on species
Size:	0.8–2.5m (32in–8ft 2in) long, depending on species
Reproduction:	Mates all year round; gives birth to 50–80 live young
Life span:	Up to 20 years
Typical diet:	Small mammals, rodents and birds

Krait

There are around 12 species of krait, which range in appearance from the white-striped, black common krait to the stump-tailed black-and-yellow banded krait. All are highly poisonous – around 15 times more deadly than cobras. In fact, the common krait is responsible for more deaths in its native Sri Lanka than any other snake. Of the terrestrial species, most are fairly inactive during the day, and often take refuge in animal burrows or termite mounds, or coil up in the undergrowth until nightfall. They also have tendency to crawl into open sleeping bags, boots or bags, where they pose a deadly threat to any human unlucky enough to discover them. Once darkness comes, these snakes are skilled and active hunters. Rats, small lizards and mammals are their main prey, but the banded krait includes common kraits on its menu.

Bungarus species

Where in the world:	India; China and much of Southeast Asia
Habitat:	Varies from forest to open grasslands
Size:	Up to 2.25m (7ft 4in) long, depending on species
Reproduction:	Lays up to 12 eggs, which females guard for 2 months until they hatch
Life span:	Unknown
Typical diet:	Small mammals and reptiles, including other snakes

Desert Horned Viper

This slim viper has 'keeled' scales, which have ridges down the centre, making them feel rough to the touch. Its broad head is triangular in shape, with distinctive thornlike horns over each eye, to protect them from injury. Like the saw-scaled snake, the horned viper is a desert-dweller with its own unique way of getting about in the shifting sands. By using its head and tail as supports, the desert horned viper is able to lift it body at an angle of 45 degrees to the direction of travel and cross the sand without sinking. This 'sidewinder' motion leaves behind a familiar S-shaped indentation in the sand. The desert horned viper is a nocturnal hunter and buries itself in the sand, with just its head showing, to wait for prey to pass by. When threatened, it will rasp its keeled scales together to make a 'sawing' alarm sound.

Cerastes cerastes

Where in the world:	North Africa
Habitat:	Arid, desert regions
Size:	60–85cm (24–34in) long
Reproduction:	Mates April–June; lays up to 20 eggs; 8-week incubation
Life span:	Up to 17 years in captivity
Typical diet:	Small reptiles, mammals and birds

Golden Tree Snake

As would be expected from an arboreal species, the golden tree snake is a skilled climber, with one particularly useful adaptation which sets it apart from other snakes that make their homes in the forests and gardens of Southern Asia: it can glide. Taking off from the top of branches, this slim tree-dweller spreads its ribs to create a rigid 'parachute', which helps it to travel from tree to tree, or tree to ground, with ease. In fact, it takes such huge leaps that it is often described as a 'flying snake'. A proficient hunter with excellent vision, the golden tree snake's favourite meal is gecko, and its gliding ability is used to best effect when chasing these fast little lizards. It also helps the snake to avoid larger, predatory species, such as the mangrove snake, which often makes a meal of juvenile tree snakes.

Chrysopelea ornata

Where in the world:	Southern Asia
Habitat:	Primarily arboreal
Size:	Up to 1.3m (4ft 3in) long
Reproduction:	Lays 6–12 eggs which hatch in around 10 weeks
Life span:	Unknown
Typical diet:	Small lizards such as geckos

Emerald Tree Boa

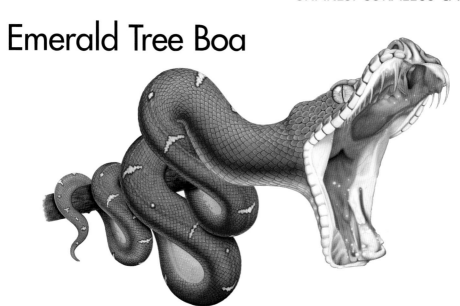

As juveniles, these striking emerald-green snakes come in shades of orange and red – often a mix of each colour will occur in just one litter. The emerald tree boa only adopts its full adult coloration at between three to twelve months. This powerful snake's Latin name, *Corallus canina*, refers to the white, coral-shaped patterns that occasionally occur on the bodies of the mature snake. '*Canina*' means 'doglike' and is a reference to the snake's large, bulbous head and its doglike teeth. Emerald tree boas are constrictors, but like pit vipers they have an adaptation which lets them track their prey by sensing its body heat. In the small scales around their lips and snout, they have heat-sensitive 'labia pits'. These are so accurate that they can detect changes in temperature of less than three-hundredths of one degree Celsius, giving them warning of any approaching animal.

Corallus canina

Where in the world:	North and Central Latin America
Habitat:	Primarily rainforests
Size:	1.5–2m (5ft–6ft 6in) long
Reproduction:	Gives birth to 7–14 live young
Life span:	Up to 17 years in captivity
Typical diet:	Small reptiles, mammals and birds

Western Diamondback Rattlesnake

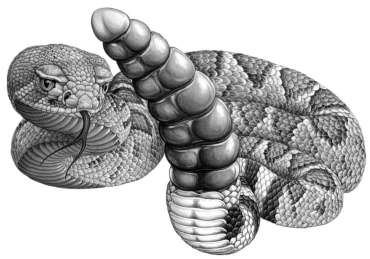

The western diamondback rattlesnake is highly poisonous, but its most distinctive feature – its rattle – is used for defence rather than offence. A rattle is a bonelike tip at the end of the snake's tail, which is made from hardened keratin. (The same substance forms hair and nails.) When alarmed, the rattlesnake will hiss loudly and shake its rattle to warn intruders to stay well away. The snake's rattle grows in size along with the snake, and extra segments are added every time the rattler sheds its skin. At around eight segments, the rattle will produce a warning sound that can be heard up to 1m (40in) away. When in 'stealth mode', though, the diamondback is a skilled hunter. Like all rattlers, it is a member of the pit viper family and uses its heat-sensitive 'pits' to detect a prey's body heat.

Crotalus atrox

Where in the world:	From California to the Gulf of Mexico
Habitat:	Dry wooded regions
Size:	Up to 2m (6ft 6in) long; up to 5kg (11lb) in weight
Reproduction:	Gives birth to 4–25 live young
Life span:	Up to 30 years in captivity; 15–20 in the wild
Typical diet:	Small reptiles, mammals and birds

African Egg-eating Snake

The best known of all egg-eating snakes are the African and East African varieties (*Dasypeltis scabra* and *Dasypeltis medici*), which are also known as 'rhombic egg-eaters' because of the distinctive patterns on their scales. Although they look similar to small vipers, this is an example of Batesian mimicry – a relatively harmless species copying the physical attributes of a more dangerous one to protect itself from aggressors. The egg-eater is entirely harmless, and has neither poison nor teeth. The process of eating an egg would seem to be quite tricky, as an average meal is around three times the width of the snake's own head. By unhinging its jaw, it is able to swallow it quite easily. The whole egg reaches the throat, where sharp projections, which form part of the snake's backbone, pierce the shell, enabling the egg-eater to swallow the contents and eject the rest.

Dasypeltis species

Where in the world:	Southern, Eastern and Western Africa
Habitat:	Forests and scrubland
Size:	0.8–1m (32–40in) long, depending on species
Reproduction:	Lays 6–18 eggs, depending on species
Life span:	Unknown
Typical diet:	Eggs

Black Mamba

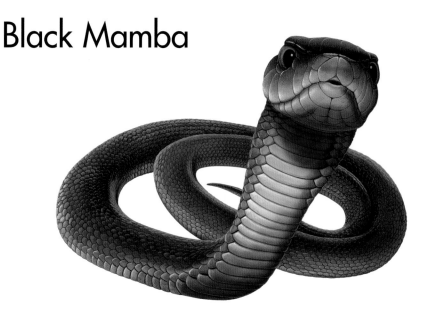

Surprisingly, black mambas are not black. As juveniles, they are bright green. This colour changes to a dark, gun-metal grey or muddy brown as they reach maturity. The only black is inside the snake's mouth, which becomes visible when it adopts a defensive pose – rearing up, cobra-like, and opening its mouth as wide as possible. Of the four species of mamba, the black is the most terrestrial, and more likely to come into contract with humans. Black mambas are not only Africa's most venomous snake, but also the fastest. With its thin, slender body and dark coloration, it is easy to confuse the mamba with many of Africa's other dark-skinned snake species, and a common problem in treating their bites is that they move so quickly that identification is difficult. The fastest mamba was recorded reaching 11km/h (6.8 mph).

Dendroaspis polylepis

Where in the world:	Eastern and Southern Africa
Habitat:	Primarily savannah
Size:	2.2–3.5m (7ft 2in–11ft 6in) long
Reproduction:	Lays 6–17 eggs
Life span:	Unknown
Typical diet:	Small mammals and birds

Green Mamba

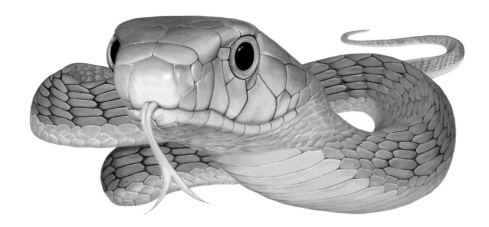

Like all tree-dwelling snakes, the green mamba has a long, slender body and a tapered prehensile tail, which enables it to move with ease through the tree tops. On its underbelly are rows of large, flat scales, which help it to climb and grip bark, while its bright green colour provides it with excellent camouflage when hunting for small birds and reptiles among the forest foliage. Both sub-species of green mamba (the East and West African) are highly poisonous; however, in their natural forest habitat, they generally do not encounter humans. Most attacks on humans occur among plantation workers, who may inadvertently disturb the snake during harvest. The green mamba is one of the few snakes to be uniformly green in colour, although as juveniles they are blue-green. Most other snakes, even arboreal species, have some variation in colour.

Dendroaspis angusticeps

Where in the world:	Sub-Saharan Africa, from Kenya to South Africa
Habitat:	Primarily rainforests
Size:	1.5–2.5m (5ft–8ft 2in) long
Reproduction:	Lays 10–17 eggs
Life span:	Up to 15 years in captivity
Typical diet:	Small reptiles, rodents and birds

Boomslang

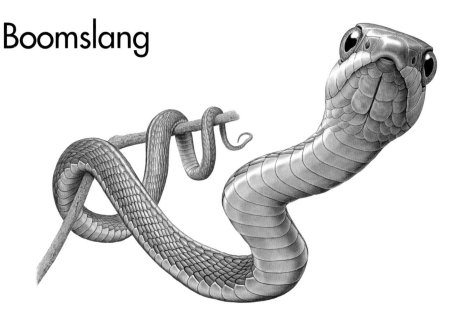

In the Afrikaans language, the word '*boom*' means 'tree' and '*slang*' means 'snake'. So, the boomslang is a South African tree snake. In fact, even without a translation of its South African name, one look at the boomslang is enough to tell you that it is a tree-dweller. It varies greatly in colour. Juveniles tend to be grey or brown, females are usually a pale olive-brown, while males are a vibrant green – but all of these shades are designed to help the boomslang blend in with its arboreal surroundings. It is also an extremely long and slim snake, with a short, blunt head. This is an ideal shape if you spend your days lying in the tree tops imitating branches. When disturbed, the boomslang can inflate its head, and even its entire body, to make itself look more threatening.

Dispholidus typus

Where in the world:	Africa, South of Sahara
Habitat:	Open woodland and savannah
Size:	Up to 2m (6ft 6in) long
Reproduction:	Lays clutches of 10–15 eggs
Life span:	Unknown
Typical diet:	Small reptiles and birds

Saw-scaled Viper

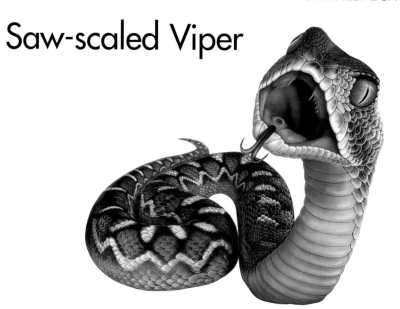

The saw-scaled viper is a common sight in desert regions, mountains and scrublands, from as far afield as India to Israel. Its common name comes from the rows of slightly raised diagonal scales along the side of its body, which produce a rasping, sawlike sound when the snake's agitated. This beautifully patterned snake is also called a carpet viper because of its attractive mottled grey and brown camouflage. As a desert-dweller, the saw-scaled viper has had to devise its own unique way of moving in the shifting sands. By using its head and tail as supports, the viper is able to lift it body at an angle of 45 degrees to the direction of travel and cross the sand without sinking. This 'sidewinder' motion leaves behind a familiar S-shaped indentation in the sand. Once on solid ground, the viper reverts to the usual snake method of movement, called 'lateral undulation'.

Echis carinatus

Where in the world:	North Africa and Southern Asia
Habitat:	Prefers drier regions, often found in rural areas
Size:	Up to 90cm (38in) long
Reproduction:	Gives birth to 4–16 live young
Life span:	Up to 2 years
Typical diet:	Small reptiles and mammals

Rainbow Boa

Rainbow boas are so called because of the spectacular, iridescent sheen of their brightly coloured scales. There are nine known sub-species of rainbow boa in the wild, and reports of several more, which have been bred in captivity. These sub-species vary greatly in appearance from region to region, but possibly the most striking are those which make their home in the Brazilian rainforest. These have vibrant orange and brick-red oval markings set against a dark, almost black, background. Brazilian rainbow boas are also the largest of the sub-species, growing up to 2m (6ft 6in) in length. In common with the emerald tree boa, all rainbow boas have heat-sensitive 'labia pits', which are located in the small scales around their lips and snout. As a primarily nocturnal hunter, these pits help them to locate prey in the dark and among the gloom of the rainforest canopy.

Epicrates cenchria

Where in the world:	Central and Southern Latin America
Habitat:	Primarily arboreal
Size:	1.5–2m (5ft–6ft 6in) long; up to 4.5kg (10lb) in weight
Reproduction:	Sexually mature at 2–3 years; gives birth to 10–30 live young
Life span:	Up to 20 years in captivity
Typical diet:	Small mammals and birds

Anaconda

Anacondas are often called 'water boas' because they spend most of their lives in or close to the water. While sluggish on land, both species (green and yellow) are proficient swimmers and can hold their breath for up to 10 minutes. When hunting, these huge constrictors lie patiently in wait in shallow waters, ready to grab any passing animal. Once prey is near, they strike with surprising speed, wrapping their powerful coils around their victim to slowly suffocate or drown it. Fish, caiman, deer, jaguars and capybara are all regularly on the menu. Anacondas are naturally solitary, apart from during the breeding season, when up to 12 males may form a 'breeding ball' with the female. Once this mammoth four-week mating marathon is over, the males return to their bachelor lifestyles. At birth, the young are able to swim, hunt and feed themselves within minutes.

Eunectes species

Where in the world:	Central Latin America; Trinidad
Habitat:	Rainforests; swamps; yellow anacondas often inhabit flooded grasslands
Size:	6–10m (19–33ft) long; 250kg (551lb) weight, varying with species
Reproduction:	4–80 live young, depending on species
Life span:	Up to 30 years in captivity
Typical diet:	Reptiles, mammals, fish and rodents, depending on species

Ringhals

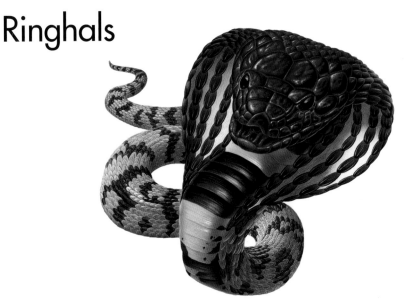

The name ringhals (or rinkhals) comes from an Afrikaans word for 'ring-necked', which refers to the distinctive pale bands around the snake's neck and throat. This stout, muscular species has a small head and pointed snout, which it uses a little like a rifle sight, to get a better aim on its prey when hunting. The ringhals is often described as a spitting cobra because, when alarmed, it will flare open the flaps of skin around its neck to create a cobra-style hood, and will also spit venom at its attacker's eyes. The ringhals also copies another common cobra tactic for avoiding danger – it plays dead by rolling onto its back and lying with its mouth open. This works because most predators prefer a fresh kill to potentially rancid meat, which could make them ill. Although it is similar in appearance to the *Naja* species, the ringhals is not a true cobra.

Hemachatus haemachatus

Where in the world:	Eastern parts of Southern Africa
Habitat:	Varies from swamps to grassy mountains
Size:	1–1.5m (3ft 2in–5ft) long
Reproduction:	Gives birth to 20–60 live young
Life span:	Unknown
Typical diet:	Small mammals and birds; toads are a favourite

Bushmaster

I n Latin, the South American bushmaster's name means 'silent fate' – a tribute to this large, brightly patterned snake's hunting prowess. Unlike many vipers, which give birth to live young, the bushmaster is 'oviparous', which means that the females lay eggs. Bushmaster mothers are particularly testy and will aggressively guard their nests from predators for the full two-month incubation period. They do this by lying coiled on top of their clutch of eggs, alert for any intruders. Bushmaster poison is very toxic and, should an unwary farmer be unlucky enough to stumble across a nesting female, a bite may prove fatal, unless an antitoxin is administered quickly. In less heightened circumstances, the bushmaster is fairly timid, and may warn intruders to stay away by beating the undergrowth with its tail; the sound is similar to a rattlesnake's alarm.

Lachesis muta

Where in the world:	Central Latin America
Habitat:	Lowland rainforest
Size:	2–3.5m (6ft 6in–11ft 5in) long
Reproduction:	Lays 5–18 eggs, which the female guards
Life span:	Unknown
Typical diet:	Small mammals and birds

Sea Krait

The sea krait is a species of semi-terrestrial sea snake, which inhabits coastal regions as far afield as India to Australia. With broad ventral scales on the underside of its belly, the sea krait is able to move easily on land, but it also has some special adaptations that fit it for a life at sea. Its nostrils can be closed when submerged, and it has a flattened tail to help propel it through the water. However, unlike true sea snakes of the family Hydrophidae, sea kraits are ovoviviparous. This means that they lay eggs. During the winter breeding season, kraits head for sandy beaches to mate. It is there that the female lays her small clutch of eggs. These incubate and hatch on land. By comparison, sea snakes give birth to live young, which are born at sea.

Laticauda species

Where in the world:	Oceans of Southeast Asia, southwestern Pacific islands and northern Australia
Habitat:	Coastal waters
Size:	Up to 1.4m (4ft 7in) long; female can be twice the size of male
Reproduction:	Lays up to 20 eggs on land
Life span:	Averages 10 years
Typical diet:	Fish, especially eels

Coral Snake

There are around 60 species of coral snake, characterized by their bands of red, black and yellow, which make the species one of the most visually striking of all. Bold colours are often used in the animal world as a form of defence, and the coral snake's vivid skin tones have very little to do with camouflage. They are designed to warn predators to stay well away. The coral snake's relatively narrow mouth means that it can eat only small prey animals, but this does not stop it from inflicting a potentially lethal bite on anything which disturbs it. In the USA, several nontoxic snakes have adopted the coral snake's distinctive markings. This can make identification difficult, but generally those that are dangerous have red and yellow bands next to each other. The harmless snakes have red and black bands – hence the saying, 'Red touching yellow, dangerous fellow.'

Micrurus species

Where in the world:	From Southern USA to Argentina
Habitat:	Varies, depending on species
Size:	Up to 1.5m (5ft), depending on species
Reproduction:	Lays 1–13 eggs in summer
Life span:	Up to 7 years
Typical diet:	Reptiles, including other snakes

Green Tree Python

When they are born, green tree pythons are more likely to be red, yellow, brown or orange than green. It is only as the snake grows and matures that it begins to change colour. This transition may happen within a week, but it can take up to three months. The change is a slow and subtle process, as the centre of each scale gradually turns green. Even once the snake is fully mature, it might not be green. Yellow and blue green tree pythons are also possible – and very popular with snake breeders. While still young, the tip of the python's tail tends to have prominent white markings, which it uses to attract small prey, a little like an angler using a worm as bait. These white flecks gradually fade as the python becomes large and powerful enough to hunt larger animals.

Morelia viridis

Where in the world:	Cape York, Australia; New Guinea
Habitat:	Dense tropical forests
Size:	1–1.5m (3ft 4in–5ft) long
Reproduction:	Lays 6–30 eggs
Lifespan:	Unknown
Typical diet:	Small mammals, birds and bats

Asian Cobra

The Asian cobra is also known as the Indian spectacled cobra, due to the distinctive round mark on the back of its neck. There are seven sub-species of this well-known Asian snake, the colours of which vary from the plain brown variety, found in Sri Lanka, to the dark grey or black spectacled cobras of Nepal. According to legend, the cobra got its 'spectacle' mark as a gift from Buddha after it used its hood to shield the meditating prince from the harsh rays of the midday sun. For this reason, the cobra is revered by Buddhists. In India, though, it has a reputation as a man-killer, which has resulted in harsh treatment over the centuries. It is poisonous and will react aggressively if disturbed, but is fairly docile if left unmolested. In the wild, the Asian cobra is now on the endangered list, and it is now protected in India.

Naja naja

Where in the world:	South and Southeast Asia
Habitat:	Varies, but often found near human habitation
Size:	Up to 2m (6ft 6in) long
Reproduction:	Lays 10–30 eggs
Life span:	10–20 years
Typical diet:	Small reptiles, mammals, amphibians, birds and eggs

Black-necked Spitting Cobra

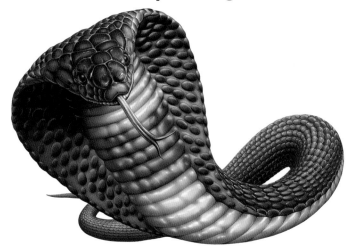

There are three sub-species of black-necked spitting cobra: the black-necked, the black spitting cobra (*Naja nigricollis woodi*) and the western barred spitting cobra (*Naja nigricollis nigrincta*). All three are heavy built, long snakes, which vary in colour depending on their habitat, although the *Naja nigricollis* is probably the most attractive. It is believed that all spitting snakes take visual aim, peering down their long snouts to get a good 'fix' on their victim. A spitting cobra's fangs curve up, and, by flexing the muscles around their poison glands, they are able to propel their venom forwards up to 2m (6ft 6in). On the skin, this venom is relatively harmless; however, if it enters the eyes, it can momentarily blind and confuse an enemy, allowing the cobra to make a quick getaway. Juvenile black-necked cobras take around two weeks to perfect their spitting technique.

Naja nigricollis species

Where in the world:	Throughout Africa
Habitat:	From woodland to semi-desert
Size:	Up to 2.8m (9ft 2in) long
Reproduction:	Mates February; 10–24 eggs hatch after 60–70 days
Life span:	Up to 22 years in captivity
Typical diet:	Small reptiles and mammals

Tiger Snake

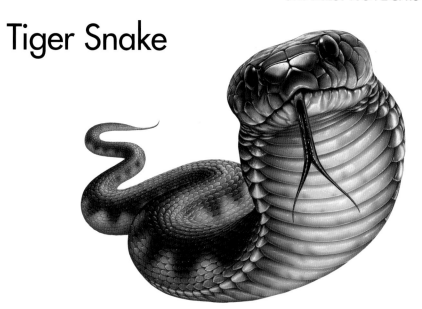

Despite their name, tiger snakes come with a variety of markings and may have no 'tiger stripes' at all. Typically, though, the body of this highly venomous snake is banded with 40 to 50 pale yellow or cream stripes, set against a green or brown background. The tiger snake is an adaptable species and naturally makes its home in both wetlands and dry mountainous regions. The males are especially prone to wandering, and will often follow prey into built-up areas, where they present a serious threat to the safety of homeowners. The venom of the tiger snake is one of the most potent known, and as little as 3 milligrams may be enough to kill a human. Tiger snakes have small fangs and need to chew down on their victims to inject venom, but in just one bite they can pump around 35 milligrams into a wound.

Notechis scutatus

Where in the world:	Southern Australia
Habitat:	From wetlands to dry, mountainous regions
Size:	1.2–2.1m (4ft–6ft 8in) long
Reproduction:	Mates late January; gives birth to 10–100 live young
Life span:	Up to 17 years in captivity
Typical diet:	Small lizards, birds and carrion

King Cobra

King cobras are 'ophiophagus' – their favourite food is other snakes. They do occasionally attack and kill larger animals, but only when they are threatened, not for food. Female cobras are especially volatile when defending their eggs, which they guard from a hidden burrow built close to the nest site. King cobras are the world's largest venomous snake, and can inject enough poison to kill 20 people in just one bite. In India, a third of all human fatalities from snake bites are caused by cobras – often because someone strayed too close to an expectant mother. Compared to the puff adder, a King cobra's fangs are quite small, so it has to chew down on its prey to force poison into the wound. Some snake venom affects the victim's skin and muscle tissue, but a cobra's acts directly on the nervous system to cause paralysis.

Ophiophagus hannah

Where in the world:	South and Southeast Asia
Habitat:	Primarily tropical forests
Size:	Up to 5.5m (18ft) long; up to 6kg (13lb 3oz) in weight
Reproduction:	Lays 20–50 eggs in specially built nests, which the female guards
Life span:	Up to 20 years
Typical diet:	Other snakes

Vine Snake

The vine snake is perfectly adapted for a life spent among the tree-tops. At first glance, this extremely long, slender snake (with a body no thicker than a pencil) could easily be mistaken for a climbing plant or vine. This amazing example of natural camouflage allows it to blend in perfectly with its surroundings and has helped to make the vine snake an extremely successful and widespread species. Most commonly found in the rainforests of Brazil, species have spread throughout Latin America and into the Southern USA. These lightweight snakes have specially strengthened backbones, which enable them to bridge wide gaps between branches in the pursuit of prey, as well to as reach out to capture birds passing overhead. Their poison is lethal to the small lizards and birds that make up the bulk of its diet, but is rarely fatal to humans.

Oxybelis species

Where in the world:	Southern USA through to Peru
Habitat:	Primarily arboreal
Size:	Up to 2m (6ft 6in) long, depending on species
Reproduction:	Lays a single clutch of 3–6 eggs
Life span:	Unknown
Typical diet:	Mainly birds and arboreal reptiles

301

Fierce Snake

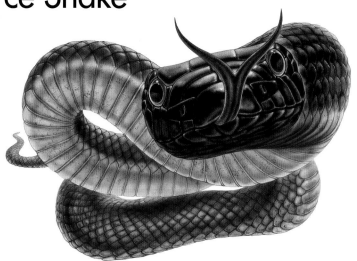

The fierce snake is also known as the inland taipan, or the small-scaled snake. This infamous reptile is the most toxic snake in world. Just one bite from a fully grown adult is enough to kill 250,000 mice – its preferred food. Fortunately, this deadly creature prefers to live in the arid desert regions of Australia and rarely comes into contact with humans. In fact, although it was first discovered in the nineteenth century, it was not seen again until the mid-twentieth century. A slender snake, with olive-brown markings, the fierce snake blends in well with its surroundings in the 'ashy downs', an area of dry cracked soil surrounding Australia's interior desert. It is naturally shy, and often retreats into deep cracks in the dried-out river beds for safety. However, it will bite repeatedly if it ever feels threatened.

Oxyuranus microlepidotus

Where in the world:	Central Australia
Habitat:	Mainly found on the outskirts of Australia's interior desert
Size:	2–2.5m (6ft 6in–8ft 2in) long
Reproduction:	Lays 12–20 eggs
Life span:	Unknown
Typical diet:	Small marsupials and rodents

Mulga

The mulga, or king brown snake, is a creature that prefers to ambush its prey rather than give chase. This is apparent from its stout body and broad head. Snakes that actively hunt down their prey tend to be much slimmer and have narrower heads because they need slender bodies to be able to move through the undergrowth quickly. Mulgas are adaptable, and make their homes throughout Australia, from rainforest to desert environments. Compared to snakes such as the coral, which warn others how dangerous they are with vibrant colours, this mid- to reddish-brown snake may seem fairly harmless. Yet it has the distinction of being Australia's second most venomous snake – just behind the taipan in the infamy stakes. Strangely, though, its venom is less toxic than that produced by many of Australia's venomous snakes; it simply injects vast quantities into its victim.

Pseudechis australis

Where in the world:	Australia and New Guinea
Habitat:	From desert to tropical rainforest
Size:	Up to 3m (9ft 10in) long
Reproduction:	Gives birth to up to 20 live young
Life span:	5–10 years
Typical diet:	Small reptiles, mammals and birds

Red-bellied Black Snake

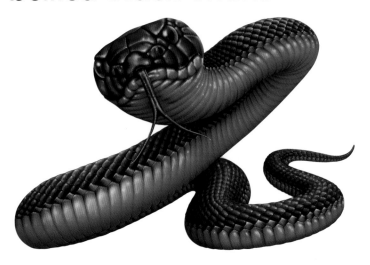

The Red-bellied black snake is one of Eastern Australia's larger venomous snakes. As its common name implies, this is a predominantly black snake with red ventral (underside) scales. It has a small rounded head, with the occasional splash of brown visible on its snout, close to its large eyes. In recent years, numbers of this water-loving species have fallen dramatically, thanks to the introduction of a Latin American marine toad (the cane toad). This toad was introduced to control pests on sugarcane plantations, but numbers have increased so quickly that they are wiping out many native frogs, which are the red-bellied's preferred food. This glossy-looking snake is perfectly at home in the water, and when in danger will often submerge itself entirely. It can stay this way for up to an hour before it needs to come up again for air.

Pseudechis porphyiacus

Where in the world:	Eastern and Southern Australia
Habitat:	Damp regions such as swamps and river banks
Size:	2–2.7m (6ft 6in–8ft 10in) long
Reproduction:	Gives birth to 8–40 live young
Life span:	Up to 20 years
Typical diet:	Mainly frogs and small reptiles

Brown Snake

Of Australia's estimated 120 venomous snake species, its seven brown snakes are among some of the deadliest. The eastern brown (*Pseudonaja textilis*) is especially aggressive and responsible for most of the continent's human deaths from snake bites. When alarmed, most brown snakes rear up, opening their mouths in a typically threatening pose, to display their small but effective fangs. They also flare out the skin around their neck to create a small, cobra-style 'hood', which is the reason for their species name – '*pseudonaja*', meaning 'false cobra'. Coloration varies from species to species; however, as their name suggests, most adult *Pseudonaja* are brown or black, with long, slender bodies, a tapering tail, small head and rounded snout. This round snout means that there is little to obstruct the snake's forward vision, which makes it a very effective hunter.

Pseudonaja species

Where in the world:	Australia and New Guinea
Habitat:	Varies with species; highly adaptable
Size:	Up to 2.5m (8ft 2in) long, depending on species
Reproduction:	Egg-laying
Life span:	Up to 15 years, depending on species
Typical diet:	Small reptiles, mammals and birds

Asian Python

The Asian python – or Indian rock python, as it is also known – is easily identifiable from its characteristic pattern of pale brown geometric shapes against a dark, almost black background. A powerful constrictor, this huge snake has been known to eat deer, large cats and even the occasional human, although its main diet tends to be small mammals. It is a skilled hunter, but its constricting ability is not just used to kill. Female pythons also use it to keep their eggs warm. Reptiles are 'cold-blooded' and cannot generate their own internal heat. So, by coiling herself around the nest and continually flexing her muscles, the mother python is able to raise her body temperature by an average of 8 degrees Celsius. This is enough heat to effectively 'incubate' her eggs. She does this for around two months until the eggs begin to hatch – a remarkable feat for a cold-blooded animal.

Python molurus

Where in the world:	Southern Asia
Habitat:	Tropical lowlands; forest regions; swamps and savannah
Size:	Up to 7m (23ft) long; up to 100kg (220lb) in weight
Reproduction:	Lays 20–50 eggs, which the female incubates
Life span:	Up to 40 years
Typical diet:	Mainly small mammals

Massassauga

Like all rattlesnakes, the massassauga uses its rattle to warn predators to stay well away. However, this dark-skinned pygmy is so small that it produces more of a warning buzz than a full-blooded rattle. Luckily, should you fail to hear its 'stay away' alarm, although its poison is highly toxic, it is produced in such small doses that it is unlikely to kill a human. Of the three known sub-species of this tiny rattlesnake, the eastern variety, which is also known as the 'swamp rattler', is the rarest. It used to be a common sight in the swamps and marshes of the USA and Canada before they were drained for agriculture. The western and desert massassaugas, which prefer drier, more arid regions, are faring much better then their eastern cousin, but agriculture, especially cattle ranching, is starting to encroach on their traditional territories, too.

Sistrurus catenatus

Where in the world:	From the Great Lakes to Mexico
Habitat:	Swampland and prairies
Size:	50–80cm (20–32in) long; 1–1.5kg (2lb 4oz–3lb 5 oz) in weight
Reproduction:	Sexually mature at 3–4 years; mates in spring; 2–20 live young
Life span:	Up to 20 years
Typical diet:	Small reptiles, mammals, amphibians and eggs

African Twig Snake

With extremely long, slender bodies, elongated, pointed heads and horizontal, keyhole-shaped pupils, twig snakes are so distinctive in appearance that they are unlikely to ever be mistaken for anything else. Which is just as well. Africa has no shortage of dangerous snake species, but, whether you are on grasslands or in dense woods, *Thelorornis kirtlandi* (the forest twig snake) and *Thelorornis capensis* (the savannah twig snake) are two of the deadliest snakes that you are likely to encounter. Poison from a twig snake may not be as fast-acting as that of the black mamba, but there is no known antidote. Its venom causes internal bleeding and a slow and painful death. They are not actively aggressive towards humans, but even experts, such as the famous herpetologist Dr Robert Mertens, have been killed after being bitten when handling them.

Thelorornis kirtlandii

Where in the world:	Throughout Africa, south of Sahara
Habitat:	Primarily savannah
Size:	Over 1m (40in) long
Reproduction:	Mates in midsummer; lays 4–18 eggs per clutch
Life span:	Unknown
Typical diet:	Small lizards and birds

Asian Pit Viper

Asian pit vipers belong to the same family as the western diamondback rattlesnake, the cottonmouth and the fer de lance. Within this grouping, pit vipers of the genus *Trimeresurus* are common throughout Asia, with around 12 species in India alone. Vipers can be either stocky or slender in build, depending on their habitat. The lighter and slimmer the snake, the more likely it is to be a tree-dweller. Asian pit vipers fall into both categories, but all are extremely dangerous and produce a highly damaging 'necrotic' venom, which destroys both blood and body tissue. Like all pit vipers, the 25 or so Asian species hunt using heat-sensitive pits, just below their eyes, to track animal's body heat. They also have acute vision, with eyes towards the front of the head, which allows them to judge distances more accurately when striking prey.

Trimeresurus species

Where in the world:	Asia, from India through to China and Borneo
Habitat:	Primarily arboreal
Size:	45cm–2m (18in–6ft 6in) long, depending on species
Reproduction:	Gives birth to around 15 live young
Life span:	Up to 20 years
Typical diet:	Small mammals, reptiles and birds

Asp Viper

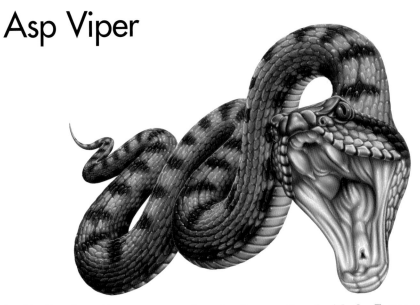

The Southern European asp viper is often confused with the European adder (*Vipera berus*). It is similar in appearance, but has a wider head, a slightly upturned snout and paler longitudinal (or 'keeled') scales. The fact that this is a poisonous species is emphasized by the two distinct bulges on either side of this snake's wedge-shaped head, which are its venom glands. Ranging across Switzerland, France, Italy and Spain, this is a sun-loving snake that spends much of its time basking lazily in the undergrowth, waiting for prey to approach. In the autumn, it retires to underground burrows, or finds a secure rock face or tree trunk in which to hibernate until late the spring. Typically hostile to intruders, the asp viper will not hesitate to bite anyone who strays into its territory, especially during the mating season.

Vipera aspis

Where in the world:	Mainland Europe
Habitat:	Warm, dry grasslands
Size:	50–75cm (20–30in) long
Reproduction:	Mates in March; 10–12 live young hatch end of summer
Life span:	Up to 20 years
Typical diet:	Small reptiles and mammals

European Adder

The European adder has the distinction of being the only venomous snake in the British Isles. In fact, it has the greatest northern range of any snake, and is the only species found within the Arctic Circle. This shy species can often be seen basking in the sun in open grasslands, but will generally slither away if disturbed. Although it is poisonous, its bite is rarely fatal to humans. Only 13 people have died as a result of an adder bite in the United Kingdom since 1900. This widespread and adaptable species makes its home in a variety of habitats, from forests to wetlands, from scrublands to sand dunes. It can be easily recognized by the dark zigzag patterning on its body and the clear 'v' mark on its neck. This pattern gives the snake its other common name – the northern cross adder. Female European adders are occasionally entirely black.

Vipera berus

Where in the world:	Throughout Europe, excluding Ireland
Habitat:	Open woodland, meadows and grassland
Size:	65–90cm (26–36in) long
Reproduction:	Gives birth to 4–20 live young
Life span:	Up to 20 years
Typical diet:	Rodents, small reptiles and birds

Glossary

Abdomen: Rear part of the body of an arachnid, bug or insect.

Amphibian: **Anal fin**: Located between a fish's **pelvic** fin and tail.

Antennae: Long, move-able feelers on the heads of crustaceans, bugs and insects. Often used for detecting prey.

Arachnid: Class of eight-legged insects with no **antennae** (feelers) or wings.

Arthropod: Any animal with segmented body, jointed limbs and hard external shell (exo-skeleton).

Bask: Lie in the warmth of the Sun.

Beetle: The largest order of insects. Beetles share the usual insect characteristics (three pairs of legs and antennae) but in addition, their fore wings have **evolved** into hard, protective wing cases.

Bugs: True bugs have no chewing or biting mouth parts, but suck their food through elongated 'snouts'.

Camouflage: Natural adaptations of colour, shape or size that enable animals to blend with their surroundings.

Cephalothorax: Combined head and middle body segment (**thorax**) of an **arachnid**

Constrictor: Snakes who kill by suffocation.

Crustaceans: An **arthropod** with a toughened outer shell covering their body and, typically, jaws and gills. Most are aquatic.

Diurnal: Active during the day.

Dormant: Inactive, sleep-like state.

Dorsal fin: One of a fish's major fins; used to control speed and direction. The dorsal fin is located on its back.

Evolution: A change in the physical characteristics of animals which is believed to happen over time.

Family: In the system of animal classification (taxonomy) animals are split into groups based on biological similarities. For every animal there are seven distinct groupings: Kingdom, Phylum, Class, Order, Family, Genus and Species.

Gastropod: Any **mollusc** with a large, singular muscular foot, like a snail.

Genus: See **Family**.

Habitat: Natural home.

Head: See **abdomen**.

Herbivore: Plant-eaters.

Invertebrate: Animals without backbones.

Lateral undulation: Method of movement used by snakes, where the action of flexing muscles creates a wave of motion, from head to tail.

Leptocephalus: Slender, transparent larvae of eels.

Lizard: A reptile, typically with an elongated body, four legs and long tail.

Metamorphosis: Some insects go through a complete metamorphosis (change) — from egg, to larvae, to **pupa** to adult. Larvae may take the form of a grub, caterpillar or maggot. Others have an incomplete metamorphosis — from egg, to nymph. Nymphs look very like adults, except they usually don't have wings.

Mollusc: Any invertebrate with a soft, un-segmented body in a tough outer shell.

Moult: When animals with a hard outer shell (exo-skeleton) shed their skin in order to grow.

Myriapod: Ground-dwelling **arthropods** with long, segmented bodies and many legs, such as centipedes.

Nocturnal: Active during the night.

Parasite: An animal that gets its nourishment by living off, or in, the body of another animal. This is usually harmful to the 'host'.

Pectoral fin: Generally smaller side fins on a fish.

Pedipali: Segmented appendages on either side of a spider's jaw which look like small legs, used to shred food. The last segment of each pedipali contains the male's sexual organs.

Pelvic fin: Also called the **ventral** fin, located on a fish's underbelly.

Phylum: See **Family**.

Prehensile: Adapted for grasping.

Pupate: When immature insects undergo a complete **metamorphosis** to become a fully formed adults. Pupas don't feed and are generally immobile.

Reptile: Class of cold-blooded, air breathing animals. Reptiles usually have strong, scaly outer skin and lay eggs.

Sac: A silk package holding a spider's eggs.

Sub-Family: See **Family**.

Swim bladder: An air-filled sac that regulates buoyancy in aquatic animals.

Territorial: In the animal kingdom, groups or individuals will often fight to defend their territory from intruders.

Thorax: See **Cephalothorax**.

Vertebrate: Animals with backbones.

Index